Leveling the Playing Field

Leveling the Playing Field

Justice, Politics, and College Admissions

Robert K. Fullinwider and
Judith Lichtenberg

ROWMAN & LITTLEFIELD PUBLISHERS, INC.
Lanham • Boulder • New York • Toronto • Oxford

ROWMAN & LITTLEFIELD PUBLISHERS, INC.

Published in the United States of America
by Rowman & Littlefield Publishers, Inc.
A wholly owned subsidary of The Rowman & Littlefield Publishing Group, Inc.
4501 Forbes Boulevard, Suite 200, Lanham, Maryland 20706
www.rowmanlittlefield.com

PO Box 317
Oxford
OX2 9RU, UK

British Library Cataloguing in Publication Information Available

Library of Congress Cataloging-in-Publication Data

Fullinwider, Robert K., 1942–
    Leveling the playing field : justice, politics, and college admissions / Robert K.
Fullinwider and Judith Lichtenberg.
        p.   cm.
    Includes bibliographical references and index.
    ISBN 0-7425-1410-2 (cloth : alk. paper)—ISBN 0-7425-1411-0 (pbk. : alk.
paper)
    1. Universities and colleges—United States—Admission.   2. Educational
equalization—United States.   I. Lichtenberg, Judith.   II. Title.
    LB2351.2.F85   2004
    378.1′61′0973—dc22   2003021995

Printed in the United States of America

∞ ™ The paper used in this publication meets the minimum requirements of
American National Standard for Information Sciences—Permanence of Paper for
Printed Library Materials, ANSI/NISO Z39.48-1992.

To my loving parents, Billy and Geraldine

R.K.F.

To the memory of my parents,
Al Lichtenberg and Friedel Rothschild Lichtenberg

J.L.

Contents

Acknowledgments

Many people have helped us, in a variety of ways, as we researched and wrote this book. We may well have forgotten some of them, since the popularity of our subject and its relevance to so many prompted interesting and useful conversations with all kinds of people in unexpected places—at dinner parties and doctors' offices, at PTA meetings and softball games. But we hope not to have forgotten most of those who have contributed to improving our work. Our colleagues at the Institute for Philosophy and Public Policy and in the Department of Philosophy at the University of Maryland—David Crocker, Arthur Evenchik, Bill Galston, Verna Gehring, Peter Levine, Xiaorong Li, Mark Sagoff, Jerome Segal, Robert Wachbroit, David Wasserman, Sam Kerstein, Christopher Morris, and Corey Washington—have contributed ideas both positive and critical, not to mention moral support. Judith Lichtenberg has for several years read student files for the Banneker/Key Scholarships at the University of Maryland; for this opportunity to participate in a selective admissions process we thank those involved in admissions and in the honors program at Maryland, especially Linda Clement, James Christensen, Barbara Gill, and Jenny Scott. Others who have shared information, ideas, and expertise include Peter Balint, Barbara Bergman, John Bois, Steven Cahn, Lenny Cassuto, Daniel Fallon, Heidi Li Feldman, Miriam Galston, Donald Horrigan, Roy Levy, Jerry Lewis, Frank Lichtenberg, Michelle Lichtenberg, Pat McDermott, Flavio Menasce, Bob Nelson, Gwen Pearl, Martha Phillips-Patrick, Jay Rosner, Kendra Sagoff, and Leroy Tompkins.

Steve Aylward provided research assistance at an early stage of the project. Bill Galston, Verna Gehring, Laura Hussey, and two anonymous reviewers read and commented on earlier versions of the entire manuscript. Celia Wolf-Devine commented on chapters 9 and 10. Jillien Dubé helped check sources at the end. Carroll Linkins and Barbara Cronin have kept the office afloat for years. Bill Galston deserves special thanks for helping us sort out some thorny issues at a crucial juncture and keeping us on track.

We thank our children, Daniel Luban, Rachel Luban, and Robbie Booska, for listening. Daniel and Rachel were in high school and beginning college during the writing of the book and, along with their friends and classmates, were a pipeline to the actual world of college admissions, providing many reality checks along the way.

Judith Lichtenberg's greatest debt is to David Luban, with whom she has engaged in countless conversations over the years talking through just about all the issues covered in this book. David coauthored "The Merits of Merit," which appeared in the *Report from the Institute for Philosophy and Public Policy* 17 (1997); a descendant of this essay forms part of chapter 2. We have discussed the issues as thinkers and writers, but also as parents of Daniel and Rachel as we all navigated the college admissions process while trying to keep a measure of perspective. To say that David's contributions to the development of my ideas are substantial would be an understatement. More fundamental still is the emotional sustenance he has given for more than twenty years.

1

Introduction: April Is the Cruellest Month

Every April, hundreds of thousands of college-bound high school seniors await letters notifying them whether they have been admitted to the colleges of their choice. The wait is mostly an anxious one, climaxing a yearlong—or these days often longer—series of stressful and pressure-filled events as these students set their sights on particular schools, take the SAT or ACT, visit campuses, polish their credentials, seek letters of recommendation, assemble their applications, and dream of getting into their favorite college. The dream is often punctured by rejection letters, which sometimes set off angry reactions by applicants—or by their parents, who have shared the long slog through the college admissions gauntlet.

This ordeal of hopes and dreams—dreams disappointed and dreams fulfilled—takes place across America not only in the privacy of students' homes, but in a broader, public context as well. In school and at home, in chat rooms and in coffee shops, students talk constantly about where to apply, whether to apply early, what schools are "hot," acceptance rates, who got in where and who didn't. The mass media return to the college admissions story again and again. With what sometimes seems like a touch of sadistic glee, they remind students and their parents of the increasingly difficult struggle to penetrate the mysteries surrounding admissions to selective colleges. Periodicals and books that rank and rate colleges fly off the shelves. Entire industries have emerged around admissions test-taking, including the firms that produce such instruments as the SAT and the ACT and the flourishing "test prep" companies that promise to boost test-takers' scores. Independent guidance counselors—filling an occupational niche that didn't exist two decades ago—proliferate to meet the burgeoning demand of parents and students for individualized, and expensive, assistance in choosing and applying to college.[1] Lawsuits challenging admissions procedures make headlines. Everyone is looking for an edge.[2]

Bright, hard-working, and ambitious students find themselves in an increasingly competitive college admissions climate. Consider: Princeton turns away two-thirds of the valedictorians who apply and 75 percent of applicants who score above the 95th percentile on the math SAT. To get the highest admissions ranking at Stanford, which sorts applicants into five categories, a student not only needs all As in a top-flight high school and SAT scores above the 90th percentile, but also extracurricular accomplishments that earn national or international recognition, such as winning an Olympic medal, a top place in a national science fair, or a prize in a nationwide piano competition.[3] The competition remains tough even when applicants drop down from the tier of the Yales and Browns and Amhersts to seek out places in still highly selective institutions such as William and Mary or Washington University. And the competition creates ripple effects, spreading to what were once quite unchoosy schools. Floods of applications put pressure on state universities. While Berkeley, Michigan, and Virginia have always been highly selective, less prestigious institutions are now harder to enter as well. Solid B students who would have been admitted to Virginia Tech in 1999 found themselves denied a place in 2000, as more than 18,000 applicants competed for 4,200 openings.[4] The University of Texas was so oversubscribed it cancelled spring admissions in 2000 and 2001.[5] High school graduates who a decade ago would have been sure admits to the University of Maryland at College Park now must settle for lesser institutions.[6] The same story can be told about a growing number and range of colleges and universities. And each year it gets tougher.

ANOTHER SIDE OF THE STORY

Yet for many high school graduates, April is only one month out of twelve. Many graduates don't plan to attend college at all and aren't caught up in the admissions scramble. Some look to the local community college as their starting point in higher education. For them, the busy month is August, when applications must be finished and financial support secured.

The students who don't go on to college are a varied lot. Some are simply tired of school and prefer to work. Some seek out a tour of military duty, perhaps as a prelude to higher education. Some have never aspired to college at all. Some performed so badly in high school they aren't college material. Even these low performers could find a second-chance opportunity at the local community college, but many don't seek it.

Many of these students attend low-performing high schools where going to a four-year college is the exception rather than the rule. Their parents are not likely to possess college degrees, and—for want of time, money, experience, or information—can't help them with the tricks of the college admissions trade. If these students think of college at all, it may be well into high school, when most of the important decisions have already been made. Although abstractly they may want to go to college, they don't really know what it takes to turn desire into reality. They haven't taken the math courses needed to meet the requirements of four-year colleges. They haven't acquired the reading habit, so the verbal SAT strikes fear in their hearts. They must rely for help mainly on college counselors and teachers who, even when dedicated, are overburdened with too many students to advise.

In 1989–1990, only 15 percent of students who entered postsecondary institutions were from the lowest quartile in terms of socioeconomic status (SES); 40 percent were from the top quartile. These numbers include community colleges and vocational schools. At four-year institutions the figures are more striking: entering students from the highest SES quartile outnumbered those in the lowest by more than 10 to 1 (57.5 percent versus 5.6 percent).[7] At the most selective colleges, "only 11 percent of students are from the lower end of the economic spectrum."[8]

We explore some explanations for these disparities in later chapters. Most important is that more affluent students generally go to better schools and tend to grow up in environments more conducive to academic success. So on the whole they finish high school with better skills than lower SES students. Thus, just about half of those in the highest SES quartile are in the top quartile in reading preparedness for college, while less than a fifth of those in the bottom SES quartile are; the gap is even wider in mathematics preparedness.[9] High school grades and SAT scores are also correlated with socioeconomic status.

But low-income students—as well as more middle-class students who, although better off, are not particularly privileged—also suffer from disadvantages less relevant to their genuine qualifications. They have less money to pay for college. Their college counseling resources are far inferior to those of more affluent students. And they are rarely in a position to benefit from policies such as legacy preference (admissions advantages for the children of alumni) and early decision, which (for reasons explained in chapter 5) give students a leg up in admissions to selective colleges.

Black, Hispanic, and Native American students are overrepresented among those with lower incomes, and therefore underrepresented in four-year institutions, especially selective ones. Even controlling for socioeconomic status, however, the academic attainments of black, Hispanic, and Native American students on average fall significantly short of those of white and Asian students.[10] The average SAT scores for black students are close to 200 points lower than for whites; for Mexican American and Puerto Rican students—the two least advantaged Hispanic groups—the differential is about 150 points. High school graduation rates and grade point averages are also lower. Although blacks comprise about 12 percent of the U.S. population, they receive only 7.5 percent of bachelor's degrees; 10 percent of the population is Hispanic but only 4.7 percent of bachelor's degrees are awarded to Hispanics.[11] These facts account for the persistent desire of many colleges and universities to employ affirmative action; university administrators fear that without it, the numbers of minority students they could enroll would decline precipitously and their institutions could come to resemble the segregated places they once were.

Even in a racially homogeneous society, or one without a history of racial discrimination, many people would find the inequities in education associated with socioeconomic inequality distressing. Education, after all, is widely regarded in our society as the key to mobility, self-fulfillment, and the good life. The special history of race and racial discrimination in the United States only deepens and complicates the problems of educational inequality. When members of minority groups are also economically disadvantaged—as they disproportionately are—they struggle against two obstacles; even when they come from more affluent backgrounds, their lesser prospects of academic success threaten the ideal of an integrated society.

This book is about justice and injustice in university admissions policies. We are especially interested in how these policies affect the prospects of lower-income and minority students and what alternative approaches might be put in their place. The book treats a variety of topics relevant to these questions: the meaning of merit, the missions of contemporary institutions of higher education, affirmative action after the Supreme Court's landmark decisions of 2003,[12] the role and significance of standardized tests like the SAT, and how "lower" education prepares students, or fails to, for higher education. We also examine legacy preference, early admissions policies, financial aid, college counseling, and athletics to see how they affect the distribution of higher education in the United States. These issues and policies bear on the prospects not only of lower-income and minority students, of course, but also on those of other college-bound students. Questions of justice affect students all across the board.

To lay the groundwork for our inquiry, it's important to get a clearer picture of the current college admissions landscape. We begin by offering some explanations for the increasingly competitive scene in which today's high school students find themselves.

THE FLUX OF SUPPLY AND DEMAND

Why are the better colleges and universities increasingly selective? Why does demand for places in selective colleges so outstrip supply? Several factors explain the trend.

For one thing, the baby boom that began after World War II begat a baby boomlet starting in the late seventies. Thus, after bottoming out in the early nineties, the number of nineteen-year-olds grew and will continue to grow for the rest of the decade.[13] In addition, a larger proportion of high school graduates go to college than ever before, and a far greater number take the academic subjects necessary to qualify them for better institutions. These upward trends are likely to continue.[14]

Another reason for the increasingly competitive environment surrounding college admissions has to do with well-known facts about the material advantages of higher education. According to a recent Census Bureau report, in 1997–1999, the average 25- to 64-year-old college graduate earned $52,000 a year while the average high school graduate earned $30,400. As of 1999, the college graduate's lifetime earnings, on average, were 1.8 times higher ($2.1 million) than the high school graduate's ($1.2 million)—up from one-and-a-half times higher in 1975. Those with doctorates enjoy lifetime earnings of around $3.4 million, holders of professional degrees about $4.4 million. High school dropouts earn about $1 million in their lifetimes.[15]

Also contributing to rising selectivity is the huge increase over the last few decades in the number of women attending college. Women now outnumber men as college students and are, on the whole, better qualified than men. In 2002, women received 57 percent of the bachelor's degrees awarded nation-wide. Among Hispanics, 60 percent of the degrees went to women; among blacks it was two-thirds. By contrast, in 1870 men received 85 percent of bachelor's degrees; even in 1950 they received 76 percent.[16] And when prestigious, formerly all-male schools such as Yale, Princeton, and Williams became coeducational three decades ago, the pool of possible applicants immediately doubled. No comparable increases in the number of slots have appeared to compensate for the larger numbers.[17] At many selective colleges, women's better qualifications work against them because they outnumber qualified men and because many colleges are committed to maintaining a balance between men and women. (Their reasons may be partly or wholly based on a fear that "too many" women will drive away prospective applicants, whether male or female.) So women are often at a competitive disadvantage, especially at small, liberal arts colleges.

Another likely reason for the increasingly competitive environment surrounding college admissions is the belief, widely held in upper middle class and professional circles, that going to a highly selective, "brand-name" college makes a big difference in one's life prospects. Many people—particularly those who consider shelling out thousands and thousands of dollars to send their kids to elite schools, and those who wish they could—would like to know whether this proposition is true. It's a question whose answer turns out to be difficult to ascertain. In chapters 2 and 3 we offer some reasons and evidence for thinking that where one goes to college makes a difference to one's later prospects. One reason is that because life is short, employers and graduate schools find it useful to take a student's alma mater as a proxy for her abilities, so they are likely to take an application from a Columbia graduate more seriously than one from an alumna of Oklahoma State, even if the students' credentials look the same. The preponderance of empirical studies on the subject confirms the proposition that the selectivity of a student's undergraduate institution has a positive effect on earnings— although the effect is probably not nearly as great as the intense competition for admission to such colleges would suggest.[18]

SELECTIVITY

It's important to put the scramble for college into perspective (something those in the thick of it find difficult to do). Higher education in the United States comprises a vast range of institutions. Forty-five hundred schools offer a postsecondary degree of some kind—an associate's, bachelor's, master's, or doctorate. Students can choose among public institutions—1,200 junior and 500 senior colleges—or they can select one of the nearly 200 private junior or 1,700 private senior colleges located throughout the country. They can also seek a degree from one of the many for-profit institutions now doing business.[19]

Most institutions of higher education are not selective: they accept almost any high school graduate who applies. Indeed, the public community college system in this country exists, at least nominally, to give every graduate, however mediocre his high school performance, an inexpensive opportunity to start down the path toward a bachelor's degree. Even among four-year institutions, the College Board reports that in 1995, only 38 percent admitted fewer than three quarters of their applicants; only 8 percent admitted fewer than half.[20] A quick search of the most recent *U.S. News & World Report* college issue shows well under a hundred colleges and universities nationwide accepting fewer than 50 percent of applicants.

Although private colleges and universities outnumber public ones by a considerable number, student enrollment overall inclines heavily toward the public sector. For example, although half the institutions of higher education in Tennessee are private, 47 percent of the state's college students are enrolled in public universities, another 32 percent in public junior colleges. While the junior college enrollees enter "open admissions" institutions, the 47 percent in Tennessee's four-year public facilities face varying degrees of selectivity.[21] Nearly all the state's colleges and universities reject 20 percent or more of their applicants.[22] Tennessee is typical of most states.

Selectivity, it's clear, is a relative thing. Most students in the United States are not competing for a place at Stanford or Harvard (which accept well under 15 percent of applicants), Williams or Georgetown (in the 20s), Oberlin or Northwestern (in the 30s). Still, most of those applying to four-year public institutions and many private ones encounter some degree of selectivity. At one end are such campuses as the University of California at Berkeley (whose admission rates are in the 20s) and the University of Virginia (30s); at the other are regional state schools such as the University of Nebraska at Omaha (80s), Southern Arkansas University (90s), and Northwestern Missouri State University (80s). In the middle lie many liberal arts colleges, as well as a broad range of state flagship and urban campuses: Occidental College (40s); Denison University (60s); the University of Massachusetts at Amherst (50s); the University of Illinois at Chicago (60s); the University of Maryland at College Park (40s).[23]

Although many rejected students get accepted by institutions comparable to those that turn them down, others must settle for schools a distinct cut below their first choice. The college admissions process leaves many thousands of students—and their parents, siblings, teachers, and friends—unhappy, frustrated, and wondering why their favored school did not appreciate their merits. The mass media return repeatedly to the college admissions story for a reason. The story taps into intense interest—and intensified feelings—among the broad middle classes in the United States.

THE PERSPECTIVE OF THE COLLEGES

April's anxieties are not confined to applicants. Admissions officers may also experience some sleepless nights. There are several reasons why. First, not all colleges and universities enjoy an excess of applicants. For some institutions—especially small private colleges of declining reputation—enrolling enough students to pay the bills is a life-and-death struggle, one they don't always succeed in winning. Roughly fifteen such institutions close their doors every year, 150 every decade.[24] Others scrape by, often by lowering admissions standards, targeting new sources of students (for example, foreign students or older, working adults), and marketing themselves aggressively (and sometimes deceptively).[25]

Public institutions can also find themselves facing enrollment fall-offs. Many community colleges have suffered flat or declining enrollments in recent years and have turned to professional enrollment consultants to help them increase applications.[26] Public institutions seldom risk going out of business if enrollment suffers, but an insufficient number of tuition-paying students can result in faculty lay-offs or financially starved programs. Indeed, not even colleges and universities in high demand are worry-free. An unexpected drop in enrollments can throw big budgets out of balance, and enrollments can drop even when applications far exceed open seats to fill.

How can this happen? High school students increasingly apply to many colleges, and many receive multiple acceptances. Obviously, then, a popular university that gets 20,000 applications for a class of 4,000 can't simply send out 4,000 acceptances and expect to fill its class. Its traditional "yield"—the proportion of admitted applicants that actually enrolls—may be only one in three, in which case it would have to admit not 4,000 but 12,000 applicants, hoping to attract the cream of this cohort to maintain its academic standards.[27] Even admissions officers at the best institutions can find themselves scrambling for good students, revising or renegotiating aid packages if necessary to pluck attractive applicants away from the competition. Such efforts can also hit unanticipated turbulence. For example, Princeton's decision in 2001 to replace student loans with scholarships for every student receiving financial assistance caught its peer institutions off-guard and forced them to rethink their own financial aid policies.[28] And if the yield formula used by the admissions office imperfectly forecasts outcomes in a given year, the university can find itself seriously under- or over-subscribed. In the former case, the university will turn to a waitlist to fill up the class, although that may not always suffice. In the latter case, the college can find itself scrambling for temporary housing, classrooms, and teachers.

The agonies of applicants and admissions officers are not unrelated. High school students feel increasingly compelled to apply to many colleges because getting accepted by any particular school, even among the very well-qualified, has become less predictable than it once was. In the mid-sixties, Al Gore, who ranked in the middle of his class at an elite Washington private school, applied only to Harvard, the alma mater of his father, a U.S. senator. Even alumni children better qualified than Gore would be unlikely to take that chance today. However, multiple applications make the job of the admissions officers that much harder. The more schools a student applies to, the less predictable any given college's yield. These dilemmas help to explain the rising popularity of early decision, where students submit an early application to one college on the promise that they will enroll if accepted. Early decision makes a college's task of crafting a class more manageable—but, as we shall argue, it raises its own problems.

Increased attention over the last decade to a university's standing in *U.S. News & World Report*'s annual rankings of colleges and universities, and similar guides, adds further complexities that can distort the admissions process. Students watch the rankings closely, and application rates at colleges rise and fall depending on their standing. So college administrators also feel compelled to monitor the rankings and do what they can to influence the numbers. Two closely watched measures of popularity in the *U.S. News* rankings have been *acceptance rate* (the lower the better, from the college's perspective) and *yield* (the higher the better). Because colleges relish high rankings, they have an incentive to encourage students to apply even if they are unlikely to be admitted. And to improve their yield, institutions have reason to admit students in binding early decision, whether or not that is beneficial to students, the institution, or the system of higher education as a whole. (In July 2003, *U.S. News* dropped yield as a factor in its rankings. It cited concerns about distorting effects and encouragement of early admissions as reasons.[29])

HIGHER EDUCATION AND THE
ENHANCEMENT OF OPPORTUNITY

College admissions clearly confronts us with a problem of supply and demand. Increasingly, a bachelor's degree from a good college or university is a scarce resource: there are fewer places than people who want them. But a bachelor's degree isn't just any resource, because—unlike caviar or a Caribbean cruise, say—higher education provides benefits that are especially important to an individual's well-being.

Developing one's mind, talents, skills, and knowledge enriches people's lives immeasurably. Indeed, at least since John Stuart Mill's famous argument that it is better to be Socrates dissatisfied than a fool satisfied, better to be a human being dissatisfied that a pig satisfied, liberal thought has taken self-realization and self-development to be fundamental human goods.[30] Despite slogans such as "Ignorance is bliss" and "What you don't know won't hurt you," few people would trade their later, more developed selves for earlier, more ignorant ones. Even if higher education is not in every case an essential precondition to such self-development, for most people it provides a vital source of growth and satisfaction.

If the intrinsic rewards of higher education weren't motivation enough, we know that it also improves people's material circumstances measurably. As we have seen, college graduates earn substantially more than high school graduates, those with advanced degrees more than college graduates—and the differential is increasing. In the United States today, for all but a few members of the rising generations (the occasional basketball player, rock star, and technology whiz kid), attaining basic middle class comfort and status requires a college education. In an information economy, those without advanced schooling find themselves relegated to low-paying, unskilled jobs.

The benefits of higher education are by no means limited to those educated. At least as important are the resources it provides to society as a whole. Universities teach and train doctors, lawyers, architects, accountants, engineers, journalists, teachers, and others who perform crucial jobs without which our society and the economy would come to a halt. Our point here, however, is to emphasize that higher education is a basic good for those who would be educated, and not just for others who would benefit from their education.

Because higher education is such a central good—one that deeply affects a person's life prospects and quality of life—how it gets allocated matters greatly. It is natural, then, to ask how the basic good of higher education *ought* to be allocated or distributed, and that is an ethical question and more particularly a question about justice. University policies, then, raise questions of distributive justice.

But what does justice require? To many people it will seem that we can make no progress in answering this question, at least not if we hope to gain widespread agreement. So, for example, one common answer is framed in terms of *equality of opportunity*, an idea that for many years has permeated discussions in the United States; one writer has called it American education's "Holy Grail."[31] Yet simple appeal to this idea is not helpful, because people possess very different and conflicting views of what equality of opportunity implies.

To some egalitarians, equality of opportunity is too conservative: it fits all too comfortably with the status quo, and simply reproduces the inequality of the prevailing order. The British social theorist R. H. Tawney, for example, writes that the consolation equality of opportunity "offers for social evils consists in the statement that exceptional individuals can succeed in evading them."[32] Others have followed Tawney in seeking to unmask equality of opportunity as "profoundly undemocratic" and a "cruel debasement of a genuinely democratic understanding of equality";[33] as a device for manipulating the powerless and maintaining the dominant order;[34] and as a means of keeping oppression invisible.[35] Equality of opportunity, on this view, may prohibit actual discrimination against individuals but demands no positive efforts to level the playing field. (In keeping with this conception, the American Heritage Dictionary defines "equal opportunity" as "absence of discrimination.") Nothing need be done to ameliorate serious economic inequalities, even if they result from previous legal barriers and even if they produce large differentials in individuals' abilities to excel.

At the opposite extreme, some scholars have taken equality of opportunity as anything but weak. For example, the noted political economist Friedrich von Hayek argues that to achieve equality of opportunity, "government would have to control the whole physical and human environment of all persons, and have to endeavor to provide at least equivalent chances for each. . . . This would have to go on until government literally controlled every circumstance which could affect any person's well-being."[36] This interpretation derives partly from the absolute, mathematical, and unyielding connotations of the word "equality," which suggests to some that, for equality of opportunity to be realized, "the interests and abilities of parents" would have to "be equalized among families."[37]

That different thinkers understand equal opportunity in such different ways shows the notion to be radically ambiguous. Even if we could cut through the ambiguity by defining distinct conceptions, each with a legitimate claim to the name "equality of opportunity," we would still be left to endorse one of these conceptions over the others. We believe the effort would not be fruitful, for we would find ourselves embroiled in the same tired ideological disputes that have plagued discussions in the past. Consequently, we forego both analysis and defense of equality of opportunity here and stipulate a different norm that guides our discussion. That norm holds that educational opportunities ought to be *enhanced* or *enlarged* for those who traditionally have been shortchanged. We believe this norm commands widespread support in our society. The roots of its appeal are various. Some would point to the waste in allowing so much human potential to lie fallow. Some focus on the deleterious consequences of a society deeply divided into haves and have-nots. Some object that it is fundamentally unfair that some people have opportunities to develop their talents while others, through no fault of their own, do not. Whatever the reason, the idea of enlarging the opportunities of those who have had fewer fits with the popular idea that America is the land of opportunity where privilege is suspect and talent and effort matter most.

In what follows, then, we assume the principle that *other things being equal, it is desirable to enhance educational opportunities for those whose opportunities have been significantly limited.* The difficult questions are about those "other things." We agree.

One such "other thing" is the apparent conflict between enhancing the opportunities of those who have been deprived of them and the institutional autonomy of colleges and universities. No one wants government to tell colleges how to choose their student bodies. Although in rare cases the state might be justified in prohibiting, or mandating, certain kinds of policies or conduct—typically when fundamental rights are at stake—any contemplated governmental prohibitions or requirements would have to be scrutinized with the greatest of care.

Yet the principle of enhancing opportunity is one that many colleges and universities, both public and private, have embraced as integral to the missions they have defined for themselves. Ironically, then, the aim to expand opportunity will more often mean defending universities' policies than interfering with them by forcing them to do what they don't wish to do.

Besides institutional autonomy, other values and principles also compete against the norm of enhancing opportunity. Some means of enlarging the opportunities of those who have fewer might violate individual's rights or otherwise threaten moral principles to which we are or ought to be committed. Although we do not offer an overarching moral theory or an account of individual rights, we rely on certain basic assumptions. So, for example, forcibly removing children from their natural parents in order to equalize opportunities (by moving the intellectually less well-endowed to more affluent families where they might have better educational choices) would, we assume, violate fundamental and widely held moral principles.

Even apart from basic rights, a multiplicity of legitimate values drives the decisions of institutions of higher education. For example, universities have long been committed to enrolling a geographically diverse student body. Yet promoting geographic diversity would not always lead to the same admissions choices as enhancing opportunity would.

We could—and in succeeding chapters we will—give many other examples of apparently legitimate institutional goals that compete with the aim of enhancing the opportunities of those who have been shortchanged. Clearly, the principle of opportunity enhancement does not wear its implications on its face. What other values and principles conflict with it? What are the legitimate goals of educational institutions? How do the practical constraints under which colleges operate enter in? The devil is in the details, and we confront them in the chapters that follow. We believe that this is the only way to make real progress in answering questions about the requirements of justice for our system of higher education.

JUSTICE FOR WHOM?

The principle of opportunity enhancement we have outlined emphasizes the interests of those at the lower end of the socioeconomic ladder, contrasting their circumstances with those of individuals and families higher up. How far down the ladder should the principle operate? In 2001, the Census Bureau set the poverty line at $18,104 for a four-person household; 11.7 percent of Americans, and 16.3 percent of children under 18 fell below this line.[38] One year at a selective private university costs twice the household income of a family at the poverty line; even more affordable public institutions may be out of reach for students from such families. For these students, attending selective institutions is almost always out of the question. The reason is not, however, simply economic. Most selective colleges would be eager to offer full scholarships to impoverished applicants possessing the academic qualifications for admission. But, as the data we cited earlier show, such applicants rarely possess these qualifications.

Many Americans above the poverty line also face limited educational opportunities. In 2001 the median household income in the U.S. was $42,228.[39] For many families with annual household incomes far above the official poverty line, the cost of college, whether public or private, can still be daunting. Scholarship and aid opportunities become more limited as income rises from the poverty line, yet one year even at a public college, whose full price today might approach $10,000 (not to mention the foregone income a would-be student might otherwise earn) can challenge the financial abilities of many American families, even those earning more than the median income. For these reasons, the principle of opportunity enhancement applies to far more people than the 11 or 12 percent of those below the poverty line.

Yet wherever we draw the line (and we do not draw it sharply here), it's clear that questions of justice do not concern only the interests of the least advantaged members of society. For example, competition for admission to the most selective colleges and universities, where policies such as legacy preference and early admissions reign, typically preoccupies students from the most affluent families and schools—perhaps the top 20 percent. Although college admissions frenzy at the top rarely directly affects low-income students, whose sights are likely to be set on different institutions, it may very well affect middle-income students directly. Among those most likely to be adversely affected by policies such as early decision and legacy preference are students who have stellar academic credentials but cannot afford to lock themselves into early admission policies that reduce their ability to negotiate financial aid packages, and whose parents don't have Ivy League backgrounds. These students are not poor, but they're not privileged (by American standards) either. The policies that hurt them conflict with the belief, widespread in our society, that unearned privilege is suspect and that the rich shouldn't receive added perks on top of the ones they already have. In assessing these and other educational policies, we assume a second principle that might seem to go hand in hand with the principle of enhancement of opportunity. According to this second principle, *individuals should be neither helped nor hindered in their efforts at educational advancement by factors irrelevant to the legitimate goals of educational institutions.*

Like the opportunity enhancement principle, this one too does not wear its implications on its face. It relies on an understanding of the legitimate goals of educational institutions, the other values and principles at stake in designing and executing educational policies, and the practical constraints under which institutions of higher education operate. These are crucial issues, best understood and treated not abstractly, but as they arise in context. We explore them in detail in subsequent chapters.

OUTLINE OF THE BOOK

How can the educational opportunities of lower-income and minority students be enhanced? How can the demands of justice be harmonized with other pressing goals of higher education and the practical constraints universities face? Chapters 2 and 3 set out the conceptual framework we employ to answer these questions. A common view is that educational places should be awarded purely on the basis of *merit*. In chapter 2 we analyze the concept of merit and attempt to clarify the confusion that has surrounded this provocative idea. A central point is that the concept of merit cannot be understood except in terms of an institution's missions. In chapter 3 we examine the multiple and diverse missions of contemporary colleges and universities, including vocational instruction, research, and liberal education—each of which is itself complex. Together they support a broader conception of merit than those who typically invoke the concept suppose. We also describe legitimate considerations apart from individual merit that are relevant to an institution's admissions decisions.

Chapters 4 and 5 examine two aspects of the controversies surrounding educational opportunity. In chapter 4 we recount the City University of New York's experiment with open admissions, and we examine the role of community colleges in providing access to higher education for minorities and low-income students. Chapter 5 describes advantages affluent students possess that do not reflect on their qualifications but that nevertheless give them a leg up in admissions. Among these advantages are money (not surprisingly) and the structure of financial aid policies, legacy preference, early admission policies, disparities in the use of testing accommodations for students diagnosed with disabilities, and superior college counseling opportunities.

Chapters 6, 7, and 8 are devoted to a detailed examination of standardized tests, particularly the SAT, and their role in college admissions. For thirty years, but especially in the last decade, such tests have been the focus of extensive public controversy and debate. Chapters 6 and 7 consider the charges that the SAT is culturally biased, that it distorts learning, that it fails to do what it claims to do, and that what it does is irrelevant or unimportant. We look at how the SAT works and explain how some representative schools use it, and we examine some alternatives that have recently been suggested for replacing it. We also evaluate the controversy about SAT coaching and test prep, which seem to challenge the integrity of the test. Chapter 8 describes some major legal battles that have been fought over the SAT and other standardized tests. Our general conclusion is that although tests such as the SAT are open to valid criticism on a variety of grounds, it's clear that from an equity point of view—one that aims to close the achievement gap between white and affluent students on the one hand and minority and low-income students on the other—every credible alternative to the SAT reproduces the same disparities.

Chapters 9 and 10 examine affirmative action. Chapter 9, centering on the 1978 *Bakke* case, describes the legal history of affirmative action. Chapter 10 explores affirmative action's legal and moral prospects in light of the landmark Supreme Court decisions of 2003, *Gratz v. Bollinger* and *Grutter v.*

Bollinger. We examine the concept of diversity, which has come to play the central role in defending affirmative action. In their attempt to defend affirmative action within the prevailing legal and constitutional framework, universities, we argue, have relied on a fatal equivocation in their use of the term "diversity." We justify affirmative action instead with an argument that—unlike most of the defenses that have been offered over the last two decades—appears capable of meeting the rigorous strictures American courts have imposed. The argument takes racial integration as a morally compelling end and shows that in American society today racial preferences are necessary to reach that end.

But affirmative action can play only a very limited role if our aim is to educate and integrate minorities into colleges and universities in anything like their proportions in the general population. Alternative strategies are essential. We examine some of these in chapter 11. We begin by describing some policies and proposed policies that have been developed as alternatives to race-based affirmative action: the "X percent solutions" now in place in Texas, Florida, and California, and "socioeconomic" affirmative action. We go on to examine strategies for expanding the educational opportunities and improving the academic qualifications of low-income and minority students well before they get to college, and we explore some of the explanations that have been offered for the minority-white achievement gap. Chapter 12 provides a summary of the book's conclusions and recommendations.

2

Demystifying Merit

How should places in colleges and universities be allocated? A common answer is that they should be awarded on the basis of merit. Former California Governor Pete Wilson articulated this view a few years ago when he enunciated a "fundamental principle" of American society: "individuals should be rewarded on the basis of merit."[1] This is a principle endorsed by jurists and political theorists as well as ordinary people.[2] Its antecedents extend back to the early modern period when feudal assignments to social positions by birth and connections were dissolved by "careers open to talents," the idea that occupations and public offices ought to be open to all who can perform the required tasks and duties. Hence, a society that rewards merit elicits effort from individuals and encourages them to take responsibility for their lives.

It is no wonder, then, that "merit" enters into debates about university admissions policies. Opponents of affirmative action protest that a person's race or ethnicity is not a merit factor because no one can take credit for these traits, and neither is related to academic talent. Thus, for example, Shelby Steele, a staunch opponent of affirmative action, writes "We Shall Overcome—But Only Through Merit,"[3] and Ernest Lefever decries Bill Gates's scholarship program for minority students as threatening to "subvert the cherished virtue of reward by merit."[4] So too, on the other side of the ideological divide, opponents of admissions tests such as the SAT insist that they fail to measure true merit and instead reward a narrow test-taking adroitness.

Yet the merit principle—the principle voiced by Governor Wilson and implicit in these critiques—is vague and its implications less than clear. One problem with the principle is that without further qualification, it seems to conceive the major social institutions of society to be in the business of handing out rewards. In fact, they have other principal functions and rewarding merit is at best a happy by-product of their carrying out those functions.

More important, the merit principle as it is typically invoked suggests that there is such a thing as merit full stop. But, as we shall argue, that is a mistake: merit is always relative to a particular end. This point is important because, as we demonstrate in the next chapter, colleges and universities have multiple ends, and qualities that might contribute to some of those missions will not be crucial or even relevant to others. The concept of merit, then, cannot be properly understood except by reference to an institution's missions. This is not to say that merit is "socially constructed," at least if this assertion means to deny real differences in abilities. No one really believes the latter. People genuinely differ in their skills and talents, but merit, although founded on skills and talents, must always be understood contextually.

We begin this chapter by raising some questions about the procedures commonly used to find or detect merit, leaving unquestioned what merit is. These procedures, we argue, can lead to distortions in how educational slots and jobs are allocated. We then take up the idea of merit itself, beginning with an examination of admissions criteria at two contemporary universities. The analysis gives rise to a discussion of the appropriate limits of merit in admissions decisions, and the common confusions that emerge between considerations of merit, other relevant admissions criteria, and moral reward. Finally, we conclude the chapter with a case study of the role of athletics in college admissions. Whether and to what extent athletic talent is an element of merit that universities should consider is controversial; the discussion highlights some of the ambiguities and fallacies common in the current debates.

DETECTING MERIT

Suppose we grant for the moment the assumption that jobs and admissions slots at selective colleges and universities ought to be distributed purely on the basis of merit. Let's suppose also that agreement exists on what constitutes merit for these desirable places. The criteria of merit might be relatively simple or very complex, and of course they will vary from job to job and at different institutions of higher education, depending both on their missions and their degree of selectivity. Engineering schools, however selective, might focus largely on mathematical and scientific ability and ignore traits that a small liberal arts college would covet.

The critique of meritocracy—an idealized place where all positions are awarded on the basis of merit—often begins with the observation that we don't in fact live in one. Coveted positions are often won not by the most meritorious, but by those whose good connections have brought them to the attention of those with positions to fill. High school students get prestigious internships at research hospitals because their parents have friends who run them. Students whose parents went to Princeton have a much better chance of getting in than those without such connections, because Princeton, like most selective colleges, employs a policy of legacy preference, favoring the children of alumni. Not only do good connections help students win places in selective colleges, but the scramble for such places itself derives in great part from the belief that a degree from a prestigious university opens doors that would otherwise remain shut or would have to be pushed much harder without a fancy degree.

These practices can be perfectly innocent, in the sense that it's natural, and even in many ways praiseworthy, to help those we know and like take advantage of attractive opportunities. We would be discouraging traits that are human in the best sense and whose effects are in many ways beneficial if we attempted to stamp out such tendencies. Moreover, social institutions couldn't operate smoothly without personal contacts greasing the wheels.

Nevertheless, connections and old-boy networks surely violate the merit principle. That was the original point of careers open to talents. One way to view preferences for minorities and disadvantaged applicants is as an antidote or counterweight to the power of old-boy connections, serving to counterbalance traditional "preferences" with ones that benefit the less privileged.

At least as important as old-boy networks and personal connections are the more official procedures employers and others use to identify meritorious candidates. Consider this example. Ninety-one percent of the undergraduates at Harvard, the most selective university in the country, receive their degrees with honors. More than half the grades awarded are As and A-minuses.[5] Despite this lack of differentiation, Harvard students have no difficulty getting good jobs. Why?

There's no mystery from the point of view of employers. They know that Harvard accepts only about 10 percent of its applicants. They are happy to take Harvard's word for it that these students are loaded with talent. (According to some, there are three kinds of colleges: Harvard, it's not Harvard, and Harvard it ain't.) The students' college applications were read by a team of expert admissions officers; for the employers to conduct a similar evaluation would cost tens of thousands of dollars. So employers are willing to free ride on the prior search done by Harvard and other similarly selective institutions.

We might describe the method used by employers in identifying attractive workers as a *rational search procedure*. It's not the search procedure that provides the most detailed and accurate information about the talents and skills of all possible candidates. But it provides very good information about them at low cost, and its cost-effectiveness makes it rational.

The important point is this: a rational (that is, cost-effective) search procedure will regularly select some candidates with less ability than others it passes over. For the procedure will less closely scrutinize candidates from lesser institutions, some of whom are more proficient than those from top-ranked schools. This outcome is even more likely when employers look at applications from students who are not at the very top of their class— whether at Harvard, the University of Illinois, or Texas Tech. For while the view that state universities produce some graduates who are second to none is (for good reason) widely accepted, students below the top rank will remain more vulnerable to the name brand value of their schools.

That such a search procedure misses some better prospects doesn't mean it is irrational, however. From the employer's point of view, the slight gain in accuracy from a more inclusive search isn't worth the added cost.

In their book *The Winner-Take-All Society*, Robert Frank and Philip Cook offer a similar reason for the rationality of selecting applicants from elite schools:

> Consider the CEO of a floundering Fortune 500 company faced with the task of hiring a management consulting firm. He interviews the consulting teams from two firms and finds that they are indistinguishable in terms of their ability to respond to his concerns and formulate initial strategic plans. One team, however, consists of graduates of Stanford, Harvard, and Chicago, while the other is made up of graduates of less distinguished institutions. With nothing more to go on, the CEO will have a compelling interest in choosing the former team. He wants, after all, to tell his board that he got the best advice available, and because the quality of advice is inherently difficult to evaluate, educational credentials can sharply increase the likelihood of a favorable assessment.[6]

Still, such entirely rational procedures may have serious *social* costs. They create one more obstacle for students who may already suffer competitive disadvantages as a result of their socioeconomic or minority status.

Such flaws in procedures designed to reveal merit need not reflect ill will or personal prejudice toward those with credentials from less lustrous places. Of course, some obstacles to evaluating a person's merit objectively *can* be located in people's attitudes, whether conscious or not, rather than in procedures and institutions. For example, surveys of male managers, business students, and college professors show that they rank the same resume significantly lower if they believe the applicant is a woman rather than a man, and that both men and women rate artwork and scholarly articles lower when they think a woman rather than a man is the artist or author.[7]

In another set of studies, the Urban Institute assembled pairs of "testers" to apply for low-skill, entry-level jobs. Each pair consisted of two men (actually college students posing as recent high school graduates), who were matched to be as similar as possible in every respect, except that one was black and one was white. Employers offered jobs to the white applicants 8

percent of the time and to the black applicants 4 percent of the time. In studies matching fluent English-speaking Hispanics with Anglos—the former
differed only in having slight accents, being somewhat darker-skinned, and
having Hispanic names—employers offered jobs to the Anglos 22 percent of
the time and to the Hispanics 8 percent of the time.[8]

These obstacles to detecting merit lie within the realm of those searching
for it—admissions officers, employers, and the like. But those whose merit
is under scrutiny can also take steps to manage the impressions others form.
One example is students who pad their college applications with inflated (or
on occasion invented) credentials to make themselves look more desirable.
Perhaps more important are the steps colleges and universities take to
improve their relative position in *U.S. News & World Report*, *Business Week*,
and other publications that rate colleges, graduate programs, and medical,
law, and business schools. The rankings industry, and its effects on colleges
and universities vying to improve or maintain their relative position, is
important for a variety of reasons, and we shall return to the issue at several
points in this book. Here we note only that because students are partly
judged by the schools they attend, institutions' attempts to game the rankings can compound the obstacles to detecting a student's merit.

HOW THE REWARDS OF MERIT RAMIFY

Even if we agreed about what constitutes merit, we have seen that various
kinds of barriers stand in the way of detecting it, and that these tend to
enrich the rich and depress the prospects of those lacking social advantages.
A further problem is that small differences in merit can lead to large differences in reward. Robert Frank and Philip Cook have described the increasing
dispersal of rewards across a variety of employment sectors in what they call
our "winner-take-all" society.[9] Fears of this sort of snowballing or piggy-
backing effect partly account for college admissions frenzy.

Consider a high school senior (let's call him Gold) who barely squeaks
into an Ivy League college. Perhaps he is a shade more talented than his closest competitor (let's call him Bronze), or maybe his father is an alumnus.
Whatever the reason, on graduating from college Gold has a much better
chance of being admitted to a top-flight law school. And this credential, in
turn, bolsters his chances of obtaining a prestigious internship, and then a
federal clerkship, and ultimately a successful legal career. Associated with
these positions is a range of attractions, including salary, pleasant working
conditions, security, fringe benefits, enhanced future opportunities, and
social status. Meanwhile, the less fortunate Bronze finds himself at a disadvantage at each of these thresholds, with reduced opportunities both for the
positions (places in law or graduate school, internships, and jobs thereafter)

and the rewards associated with them. We see in this tale the cumulative effect of one rational search procedure after another, which amplifies a small difference—or even no difference—in ability into enormous differences in positions and the rewards associated with them. A reward at each stage becomes a credential for the next.

It is of course possible that the difference in merit between Gold and Bronze genuinely *increases* over time. Gold, after all, may have benefited from a superior education, more stimulating fellow students, teachers at the cutting edge of research, and a more intense intellectual environment, so that even if Gold and Bronze began college with virtually indistinguishable qualifications, they are no longer so similar.

If this is true, however, the tale of Gold and Bronze speaks to the enormous advantages conferred by prestigious and high-powered academic surroundings that are capable of enhancing merit. A person's merit is not fixed; how it develops (or stagnates) depends partly on the academic environment in which a student finds herself. Given the opportunity to attend a selective institution, the less advantaged can also develop their talents and hone their skills, and may become well-matched to their excellent positions even on the most exacting use of the merit principle.

Those who care about merit ought to care about the disproportion between merit and reward. Indeed, the most plausible interpretation of the merit principle says that a person should be rewarded *in accordance with* or *in proportion to* her merit. But when small differences in merit lead to large differences in reward, we have merit run amok. That ought to disturb anyone who genuinely cares about the merit principle. And to the extent that more selective colleges *create* merit as much as they *reward* it, there is strong reason to think that broadening the opportunities to attend is a goal worth pursuing.

MERIT AND OTHER SELECTION CRITERIA

It's time now to look more closely at the idea of merit itself. It's useful to begin by seeing how it fits with the admissions criteria articulated by two large universities, one public and one private.

Consider first the following twenty-four factors listed recently in the Updated Admission Criteria of the University of Maryland at College Park, Maryland's flagship campus:[10]

High school grades
Grades in academic subjects
SAT/ACT scores
Quality of coursework

Progression of performance
Class rank
Essay (on college application)
Recommendations
Residency (i.e., in- or out-of-state)
Extracurricular activities
Extenuating circumstances
Ethnic diversity
First generation in college
Special talents/skills
Community involvement/community service
Geographic diversity
Demonstrated leadership
Academic endeavors outside the classroom
Breadth of experience
Children/siblings of alumni
Children of faculty/staff
Work experience
Language spoken at home
Demonstrated interest in the university

A footnote to the document adds that "these criteria are listed in random order," but the actual order surely reflects some priorities. We can assume, for example, that high school record counts for more than language spoken at home. Presumably the order reflects some prioritizing but is not a strict ranking: for example, "geographic diversity" is not necessarily more important than "demonstrated leadership"; "language spoken at home" does not necessarily count more heavily than "demonstrated interest in the university."

Not every college and university would include all these factors in its admissions decisions, and some may consider criteria not listed here. Some institutions, as we shall see in the next chapter, have quite specialized missions, with criteria reflecting their particular aims. Yet the list is quite typical in the sorts of considerations taken into account by a large number of institutions both public and private.

Compare, for example, the criteria used by one of the most selective universities in the country, described by a former director of admissions. At Stanford University,

> The primary criterion for admission is academic excellence. . . . A secondary criterion is personal achievement outside the classroom. . . . Persistence and marked effectiveness in one or more distinct areas of personal achievement count for more than scattered involvement but initiative, curiosity, and vigor

are significant. . . . A few categories of applicants receive special consideration provided they meet the basic requirements of academic excellence and personal achievement. Stanford University is committed to a substantial representation of Blacks, Mexican Americans, and Native American Indians in the undergraduate student body. Children of Stanford graduates receive preference in choices among applications of approximately equal qualifications. Children of eligible Stanford faculty and staff receive favorable consideration, once again provided they meet basic requirements. The Department of Athletics may designate outstanding athletes for special attention. . . . [W]e take note both of extenuating circumstances and a variety of cultural and economic situations including ethnic backgrounds, recent immigration to the U.S., and students who are the first in their families to attend college or are from economically disadvantaged backgrounds.[11]

Several things about these documents are worth noting. First, the lists of criteria are long and varied. They reflect a fact obvious to anyone directly involved with college admissions: there is no single, simple quality that colleges seek. Second, only the first six criteria or so (depending on how we count) on the University of Maryland's list constitute what we might call purely academic considerations—although these are probably in most cases the most important factors. The "merit" sought by colleges is complex, and it includes nonacademic factors, such as extracurricular involvement, demonstration of leadership, and the like.

How do institutions go about weighing and comparing these factors? This brings us to the third point. Although some use formulas to admit or deny especially strong and especially weak students automatically, many others do not.[12] Even those that do not may employ categories such as "presumptive admit" and "presumptive reject" for students at the top and bottom end of their applicant pools. Still, college admissions offices—perhaps especially at private universities—inevitably employ a large amount of judgment and discretion in weighing and comparing the various criteria they take to be relevant.

Fourth, several of the criteria Maryland and Stanford mention have nothing to do with merit in the most plausible sense of the term, namely personal skills or talents (whether academic or not). Critics of affirmative action like to remind us that being a member of a particular racial or ethnic group isn't a skill or talent. They conclude that characteristics such as race and ethnicity are therefore irrelevant and out of bounds. But growing up in Idaho (and thereby contributing to geographic diversity), or having parents who graduated from the university, are also not skills or talents. Should these criteria also be purged from the list?

Two possible answers are available. One is that merit is all that counts; geographic diversity and being the child of an alumni or an employee should not be admissions considerations because they are not part of merit. The other is that considerations apart from merit are sometimes legitimate, and so these criteria may be acceptable. (A third option would be to use "merit" in a broader sense to include any sort of relevant admissions criterion. For reasons discussed further below, we believe this option would obfuscate rather than clarify the matters at hand.) Each answer poses a challenge to the traditional defense of the merit principle. Those who give the first must repudiate legacy preference as well as geographic diversity, a widely accepted and uncontroversial factor in the admissions policies of many colleges. Those who give the second must explain why some factors apart from merit are acceptable criteria for admission but racial and ethnic considerations are not. We return to this point shortly.

THE LIMITS OF MERIT

Making sense of the points we have enumerated requires a deepened analysis of merit. Two points are crucial. First, merit is always a functional and relational notion. We can't decide what merit is—for a place in the freshman class, a faculty appointment, or a job in the private sector—without knowing the purposes to be served by the position in question. And that in turn requires an account of the goals and roles, or—in the jargon of higher education—the missions, of the institution seeking candidates. The idea is commonsensical. Universities have certain aims and purposes, and it is in light of these that they fill their places, seeking students who, they believe, will best help them to further their missions. Although the idea that merit is relational in this way may seem obvious, defenders of the merit principle rarely mention the institutional purposes that give it concrete and particular meaning.

Appreciating this point undermines some common but pernicious assumptions in debates about college admissions. For example, many people assume that high-achieving students are automatically more deserving of admission than students with lesser accomplishments. The assumption presupposes that educating the academically gifted is more important than educating the academically average student. Perhaps so, but such a view of the university's mission stands in need of defense. It might turn out that educating very bright students is of paramount importance for some purposes and constituencies of the university—professors, for example, generally prefer to teach such students—but not for others. We return to this point in the next chapter.

Second, if we understand merit in anything like its commonsense meaning—personal skills and talents—it is sometimes perfectly appropriate, and indeed indispensable, for institutions to consider criteria other than merit when making admissions decisions. For example, geographic diversity may advance a university's mission of creating a cosmopolitan community of scholars, but it would be odd to say that coming from Idaho or Indonesia reflects on a student's merit. The relevant question, then, is *which* of such non-merit-based criteria are appropriate.

In the next chapter we examine the notion of institutional mission more carefully. Although we find enormous variety among the thousands of institutions of higher education in the United States, and although some colleges have very specialized missions, we argue that the preponderance of four-year colleges and universities American students attend have multiple missions comprising several important goals, and that no clear priorities among them exist. Often uppermost in the minds of students is the university's vocational purpose: to prepare students for the world of work and sometimes for particular careers. Faculty are frequently inclined to emphasize the research mission of the university—in the words of the nineteenth-century writer James Morgan Hart, "to extend the boundaries of knowledge."[13] As important as each of these is the provision of liberal education, which comprises social, political, aesthetic, emotional, and moral dimensions in addition to the more obvious intellectual ones. Liberal education enhances the lives of those educated, and it also advances larger civic aims, such as making for a more engaged citizenry, and perhaps even a more just society. Developing future leaders, an important mission of selective public and private universities, encompasses all three strands—the vocational and research missions as well as the goal of liberal education. The missions of typical universities also involve social goals—purposes to be achieved for society at large—and not simply benefits to the institutions or to the students they admit.

The crucial point is that once we recognize how diverse and wide-ranging the missions of the typical modern university are, it becomes clear that they require something other than the simple view of merit—academic excellence as measured primarily by grades and test scores—that meritocrats typically assume. Which applicants are the most suitable? It depends on what an institution aims to accomplish. Most are trying to achieve a variety of purposes, for which a complex and multifaceted conception of merit is required, and for which other criteria that serve the institution's mission—apart from individual merit—are also relevant.

This is not to deny that traditional academic criteria are central. Facility with words and numbers matters for many things universities care about (and should care about). But universities also value other things for which sheer brainpower is not the relevant criterion. To the extent that colleges are engaged in liberal education to produce a more informed and engaged citizenry, for example, they have no particular reason to focus only on the most academically talented students. If universities aim to cultivate and develop leaders—and selective institutions do—they have strong reason to pay attention to other qualities that make for leadership. (And of course there are leaders in many different walks of life, requiring different virtues.) The diversity of admissions criteria we have examined supports the reality of multiple missions for multiple purposes. Universities, especially public ones, will seek students who can lead and represent the wide variety of groups found in American society.

Admissions criteria are relational in another way as well. What makes a student attractive depends not only on an institution's mission, but also on the mix of students already on site or in the applicant pool, and the effects of these on what are often quite specific needs of the institution. The marching band has a surfeit of saxophone players, but tuba players have proven harder to come by. The varsity softball team needs a shortstop. The campus's community service programs have suffered weak student leadership in recent years. When the college rejects a saxophonist and accepts a tuba player with otherwise comparable credentials, no one thinks it does wrong. The saxophonist may experience disappointment and may even take his rejection personally, thinking either that he wasn't good enough to get in, or that he was unjustly passed over. But anyone with insight into the behind-the-scenes deliberations of admissions offices knows that the decision need not reflect in any way on the saxophonist's personal qualities—his merit, in the usual sense—but depends rather on how these qualities mesh with the needs of the institution in pursuing its mission, and with the vagaries of its current crop of students and its applicant pool. Next year, the band might need a saxophonist, not a tuba player.

If we use "merit" in its usual, restricted sense—limiting it, roughly speaking, to a person's skills and talents, both academic and nonacademic—then it is clear that considerations other than merit are relevant in making admissions decisions, and that colleges and universities routinely do, and must, employ such considerations when deciding whom to admit. There is good reason to use "merit" in this restricted way, rather than more broadly to mean *all* the considerations potentially relevant to admissions decisions. For one thing, the more restricted usage conforms more closely to the way we ordinarily talk. For another, to use "merit" in the broad sense would deprive us of a way of distinguishing among different sorts of admissions criteria. We would find ourselves scrambling to invent a new term to distinguish "individual skills and talents" (what used to be called "merit") from other criteria a college might consider. Among the non-merit-based criteria sometimes taken as relevant are geographic origin; race, ethnicity, and socioeconomic status; and being the child of an alumnus, a university employee, or a celebrity. Which of these are in fact relevant remains to be seen.

But now it becomes clear that, even among the non-merit-based criteria that a college might legitimately employ, important distinctions must be made. Some of these criteria are directly connected to an institution's mission and others are not. We can make the point more clearly in terms of *reasons* for admitting a student. Admitting an applicant because her Idaho

origins will contribute to a diverse campus environment is directly connected to the college's mission of exposing its students to a wide variety of
human experiences. Admitting a student whose parent is an alumnus on the
assumption that legacy preference benefits the institution financially, on the
other hand, is not directly connected to the missions of any (nonprofit) colleges or universities we know of.[14] Of course, every college and university
must be concerned with its economic survival and flourishing. Unless it sur-
vives, it can't *fulfill* its missions. But making money is not part of its mission,
and criteria that serve such purposes, practically important as they are, have
a less weighty claim than those that are mission-related.

Since the term "merit" has been the source of so much controversy and
confusion, it is worth summarizing our conclusions so far.

First, in the context of admissions, merit should be understood to include
the collection of a person's skills and talents relevant to furthering a college
or university's missions. These are attributes we would normally say a person can take credit for: academic, artistic, athletic, moral, interpersonal, and
any number of other virtues individuals may possess.

Second, other criteria that do not reflect on an applicant's merit may be
relevant to an institution's missions. The least controversial example is geographic origin; more controversial ones include race, ethnicity, and low
socioeconomic status (or a proxy such as "first generation").[15]

Finally, practical considerations may enter into a college's decisions about
which students to admit—considerations neither merit-based nor otherwise
rooted in an institution's missions. To the extent that legacy and athletic
preferences rest on claims about their economic benefits to the college, they
fall into this category. So do decisions to admit paying students over otherwise comparable (or even superior) applicants who would require financial
aid. Such considerations may be legitimate—institutions of higher education,
like individuals, exist in the real world and must make compromises—but
we should recognize that they *are* compromises. They represent a departure
from the ideals colleges and universities describe in high-minded terms as
their missions—which constitute their true raison d'être. They also represent
a departure from pure meritocracy.

When we clarify the confusions and ambiguities surrounding the term
"merit," it becomes apparent that few people sincerely defend pure meritocracy, particularly in the narrow sense that identifies merit with academic
excellence measured by grades and test scores. But this fact, and merit's
ambiguities, has implications for the sorts of criticisms that can be brought
against universities' admissions decisions.

We suggest that there are four basic ways admissions decisions might be
challenged or criticized:

1. *Are the institution's missions appropriate and legitimate?* One might
question one or more of the goals and purposes that form an institution's

mission. A college that aimed to promote Nazi values would rightly be subject to denunciation. But few if any institutions do articulate missions that are inherently objectionable. More plausible as an object of criticism is the emphasis placed on a particular goal—for example, the role of research in a small liberal arts college. (In truth, few outside university administrations think much about the missions of universities—which is why we felt impelled to write the next chapter—and certainly not their connection with merit and admissions.)

2. *Are the university's means appropriate to achieving its ends?* We can question whether a particular criterion that has been articulated (such as those described in the Maryland and Stanford documents) actually advances the institution's mission. Although some criteria may be disputed as such—affirmative action and legacy preference are obvious examples—often the question is again more about emphasis and weight: how much should a given factor count? We look at a prominent example, the enormous admissions advantage athletes enjoy at selective colleges, in the last section of this chapter. (Legacy preference is discussed in chapter 5; affirmative action in chapters 9 and 10.)

3. *Is the institution playing by the rules laid down (by it or others)?* A third mode of criticism is that an institution's explicit criteria do not match those it really employs. For example, colleges rarely acknowledge publicly that the children of celebrities and potential big donors enjoy admissions advantages, but few would deny that such factors play a role.

4. *Are applicants playing by the rules laid down?* We may criticize applicants for gaming the system by taking unfair advantage of opportunities or following the letter rather than the spirit of admissions guidelines. Examples include students who suddenly discover exotic racial or ethnic roots they never knew they had, and those who exaggerate disabilities to earn extra time taking tests. And we may criticize institutions that ignore such gaming or even collude in it—for example, by accepting at face value implausible student claims to minority status so that they can inflate their enrollments of minority students.

MERIT AND DESERT

In most people's minds merit is closely related to desert, and the two concepts suffer from much of the same ambiguity. Assertions about desert often closely track those concerning merit. We say that one's race has nothing to do with merit; similarly a person doesn't deserve to get into college because of her race. But it is equally true that she doesn't deserve to get in because she grew up in Idaho. Of course, race or geography are never the sole grounds for admission anyway. Still, neither a person's race nor her geographic home have any bearing on her desert. But when we recognize that legitimate admissions criteria inevitably include factors other than individual skills and talents, it becomes clear that if desert tracks merit, then it is at best only part of the story: people rarely get admitted solely on the basis of what they deserve.

There is, of course, a line of thinking that leads to the conclusion that a person can't take credit even for her skills and talents, so that the notions of merit and desert are fictions, or at least mean nothing like what we ordinarily take them to mean. Some are led to this view abstractly, by the compelling logic of determinism. Others arrive at it by observing how much what people seemingly can take credit for depends on what they can't—because academic, athletic, and artistic talent often run in families, whether due to environmental or genetic influences or both; and because qualities of temperament and character are not necessarily within people's control. But in the real world (as opposed to the classroom or the study) we cannot afford even to entertain this deterministic conclusion. The assumption that there are some things people can take credit for is not just useful, it's indispensable. As Kant explained, the assumption is one we must make if moral judgment is to be possible at all.[16] But puzzles remain.[17]

A central puzzle is this: if the important thing is what people can take credit for, shouldn't we reward them not for what they have actually achieved, but for their effort? Shouldn't we subtract their initial endowments (natural and environmental) from their performance to discover their true merit?[18] Of course it would be unrealistic to suppose we can do this with any precision. But the idea seems to provide a basis for the view that in determining what people deserve, we should take into account their initial endowments, or lack of them, and the hardships they have had to overcome.

When universities consider students who are the first in their family to go to college ("first generation") or who have "overcome adversity," they implicitly or explicitly appeal to a principle of effort. But here again it is easy to conflate desert and merit in the usual sense—what a person can take credit for—with the broader conception admissions offices inevitably employ. Colleges are primarily interested in finding students who advance their missions and fill their needs.

Consider two students, Michael and James. Michael comes from a poor neighborhood and has gone to inferior schools. James attends a well-known New England prep school. James's credentials are better than Michael's in a variety of ways. Yet a college might judge that Michael's record, including his 1100 SAT scores, make him a better catch than James, with 1400 scores, for at least two reasons. First, James's stats may be artificially boosted by coaching courses and other benefits of a privileged background. Second, Michael's record provides evidence of determination and grit, traits that will serve him and the institution well in the future. Admitting Michael over James is often viewed as a reward for deservingness—for having tried harder.

It's a natural assumption, and an element in our thinking we can barely imagine expunging. But the better argument for admitting Michael over James is forward-looking—that the decision reflects values the institution holds and qualities it needs. The student who has overcome adversity has given the institution reason to think he's a good bet.

It should be clear from this discussion that our commonsense notions of merit and desert are enormously complex and not necessarily always consistent. Similarly with the language of "rewards" that pervades discussion of college admissions. Admission to a selective college is not a reward for past merit or desert in the way Heaven is supposed to be the reward for good behavior on Earth. One reason—but only one—is that, unlike God, we are generally in a poor position to say what a person deserves or can take credit for. More important is that admissions decisions are based on judgments about the benefits students will reap and how they will contribute to an institution's aims and purposes.

Sensitive admissions officers are themselves acutely aware of a hubris barely kept at arm's length as they do their jobs. On the one hand, *someone* has to choose which students to accept and which to reject; the college can't admit them all. And because at most institutions the choice isn't mechanical, admissions officers must exercise judgment, looking at the "whole person" as revealed in the admissions file. On the other hand, how easy it is for everyone—admissions officers, students, parents, casual observers—to see this process as passing judgment on the value of the human being, with all her deserts and entitlements. Rejection isn't merely refusal of a good; it's a moral indictment.

It's hard for students (and their parents) not to view admission to college as a reward for their efforts and for being who they are. Rewards are something you earn, we're led to believe, something you deserve when you've jumped over all the hurdles. How frustrating, then, infuriating even, to be told you don't get the reward of admission to a particular college because you aren't deserving and haven't earned it, although your grades and hard work match or exceed those of students who were admitted. When admissions officers declare proudly that all the admitted students have earned a place in the freshman class, they suggest, albeit unwittingly, that those rejected didn't deserve admission, and they thereby abet the widespread belief that admission is a reward for good behavior and accomplishment.

In fact, rejection implies nothing about desert. That should be the message college officials reinforce. Indeed, they know it in their reflective moments. When April's work is done, they pause to admire their handiwork. They look over the crop of wonderful students who will appear in the fall, and they feel pleased. The satisfaction can quickly turn bittersweet, however, when they remember the students they turned away.

SPORTS: A CASE STUDY

It's clear that when choosing students, colleges are justified in considering factors besides the academic criteria that spring first to mind. (In fact, the conventional wisdom has perhaps swung too far in the other direction, undervaluing mere academic excellence unadorned by impressive extracurricular activities or personal qualities.[19]) Colleges have multiple missions, as we argue in the next chapter, and the qualities revealed by nonacademic criteria are relevant to fulfilling them. The University of Maryland and Stanford, we saw earlier, enumerate a long list of admissions criteria, only some of which pertain to academic achievement.

Students focused on going to a selective college are supremely aware that "extracurricular activities" are important, and can make the difference between admission and rejection. It's especially helpful if, while still in high school, you establish an international relief organization, play cello at Carnegie Hall, or win a figure skating gold medal.[20] Most students have to settle for a little less. But the choices are nearly endless. Band, orchestra, chorus, theater, dance, the visual arts; church groups, Scouts, Amnesty International, the Gay/Straight Alliance, Free Tibet, Young Republicans, scores of community service organizations; the student newspaper, the literary magazine, the yearbook; debate, It's Academic, the chess team. The list goes on.

And then there are sports: football, basketball, ice hockey, soccer, lacrosse, baseball, softball, track, cross-country, golf, tennis, volleyball, crew, field hockey, wrestling, swimming, gymnastics—plus the occasional fencing, squash, badminton, or water-polo team.

But sports differ from other extracurricular activities. That is to say, colleges *treat* them differently from other extracurricular activities. Reflecting the importance our society attaches to athletes and athletic achievement, sports play a huge role in the campus life of many colleges and universities, and colleges give athletes a big leg up in the admissions process. Many people are aware of this phenomenon at the big state schools and a handful of other athletic powerhouses. They know about the student-athlete-stars on athletic scholarships, many of whom are aiming for the NBA and the NFL. Less well-known is that highly selective private colleges and universities such as Amherst and Williams and the Ivy League schools also give athletes big admissions advantages. These schools do not offer athletic scholarships, and it would be natural to infer that sports play a smaller role than at schools that do. Precisely because the athletes are not funded, however, the non-scholarship schools are under pressure to recruit more students than they are likely to need to field their teams. But we are getting ahead of the story.

In their groundbreaking 2001 book, *The Game of Life: College Sports and Educational Values*, James Shulman and William Bowen examine the role of sports in college admissions, its effect on campus climate, and what happens to athletes in college and after. Their empirical findings are based on a study of 90,000 students at thirty selective colleges and universities who entered college over three decades, in the years 1951, 1976, and 1989. There are also some data for students entering in 1999. The schools in the "College and Beyond" (C&B) database include, among others, the University of Michigan, Penn State, Miami University of Ohio, Yale, Columbia, Duke, Northwestern, Notre Dame, Williams, Swarthmore, Oberlin, Denison, Bryn Mawr, and Wellesley.[21]

Since Shulman and Bowen's research focuses on thirty selective colleges, their findings can't be generalized to the whole gamut of institutions of higher education with sports teams. But what they show certainly applies to other schools besides those in their database. For example, Williams and Swarthmore are included but Amherst and Haverford are not; Yale and Columbia are included but Cornell and Harvard are not. Even if their findings applied only to 60 or 70 colleges and universities, these are among the most selective and sought-after in the country. That said, *The Game of Life* provides powerful empirical support for the suspicion, long held by many, that athletics exert a profound influence on college admissions at an important set of institutions, and on the climate of many campuses. Here we describe the most relevant findings.

First, athletes enjoy a very significant statistical advantage in admissions at the C&B institutions, and it has grown substantially over the years. In 1976, at a representative school that does not offer athletic scholarships,[22] recruited male athletes were 23 percent more likely to be admitted than students at large, after controlling for SAT scores. That year the admissions advantage for legacies was 20 percent, for minorities 49 percent. By 1999, the weights were almost exactly reversed: the advantage for recruited male athletes was 48 percent, for legacies 25 percent, and for minorities 18 percent. Since 1976, in other words, the admissions trend has been upward for athletes and downward for minorities.[23] As Philip Smith, former dean of admissions at Williams College, put it in 2001, "Athletic recruiting is the biggest form of affirmative action in American higher education, even at schools such as ours."[24] At the time Smith made this remark, Amherst reserved 75 out of the 450 places in its freshman class for recruited athletes; Williams designated 71 slots for athletes in a freshman class of 550.[25]

Not only do recruited athletes enjoy an advantage in admissions, but they get admitted to college with lesser academic credentials than their classmates. Shulman and Bowen divide college sports teams into two categories: High Profile sports—football, basketball, and ice hockey—and Lower Profile sports, which includes all the others. Using SAT scores as a proxy for academic standing, their data show that in the High Profile sports the gap is very large, particularly in the C&B schools with "big-time" programs; it is largest in the Division I-A private universities (like Stanford, Duke, and

Notre Dame), where the combined SAT scores of recruited athletes are on average 284 points lower than their classmates'. In the Lower Profile sports the gap is smaller but still significant: from 100 to 120 points in Division I-A and from 25 to 40 points in Division III and the Ivy League. And the gap has grown over time, especially in the High Profile sports.[26]

It is widely believed that the enormous admissions advantage athletes enjoy makes highly selective schools much more racially and socioeconomically diverse. The High Profile sports have increased socioeconomic diversity somewhat; students playing those sports, especially at Division I-A schools, are much less likely to have fathers who graduated from college than the average student.[27] But this is not so for the Lower Profile sports—not surprising when we realize that this group, including crew, lacrosse, and golf, consists largely of sports that lower-income students rarely play. Overall, the effect of athletic recruitment on socioeconomic status is "less than one might have expected," both because those who play Lower Profile sports generally come from high socioeconomic backgrounds, and because there are relatively few High Profile athletes, especially in the large, Division I-A schools.[28]

Essentially the same is true of racial diversity. Minorities are not highly represented among the Lower Profile sports, which account for two-thirds of the athletes in the sampled colleges, so that the effect of athletics on minority enrollments is modest. And at the C&B Ivy League and the coed liberal arts colleges, minorities constitute a much smaller proportion even of the High Profile teams than they do at the Division I-A schools.[29] In the 1989 cohort, "If the athletic contribution to racial diversity had been eliminated," the percentage of black men in these colleges would have dropped 1 percent (from 6 percent to 5 percent)—assuming that other black students did not take those slots.[30] The athletic advantage, then, contributes very little to racial or socioeconomic diversity; what it does contribute depends on the premise that alternative admissions strategies would have no effect on these factors.

What other arguments can be made in favor of large admissions advantages for athletes? Shulman and Bowen focus on two. One is that on the whole athletes possess attractive characteristics off the playing field that promote universities' missions either on campus or in society at large, or both. The other is that the emphasis on athletics and the presence of good sports teams are a financial boon to universities that cannot practically be ignored.

Let us begin with the second argument, which has several aspects. One is the idea that athletes donate to their alma maters at higher rates than other students. Although there is some truth to this claim, athletes' comparative generosity at the C&B schools is declining over time, as college sports become more professionalized and athletes identify less with their schools.[31] In addition, not only athletes but "high academic achievers" and those very involved in extracurricular activities also give at higher than average rates—suggesting that what makes the difference may be the degree of involvement and enjoyment a student associates with her college years, and her success thereafter, rather than any factor specific to sports.[32]

The other strands of the financial argument play a more prominent role, certainly in public discussion. These include the ideas that a successful athletic program encourages alumni giving and, more broadly, that it makes money for the institution. Shulman and Bowen find that generally, surveyed alumni from all types of C&B institutions (except former athletes) want less emphasis on intercollegiate sports, not more.[33] In the Ivy League and at the Division I-A level, surprisingly, winning teams slightly depress alumni giving rather than increase it.[34] Winning does seem to have a modest positive relationship to giving at the Division III coed liberal arts colleges, which is probably explained by the high proportion of students who play intercollegiate sports.[35]

Finally, concerning the more general proposition that athletic programs make money for the institution, Shulman and Bowen conclude that

> Revenues from athletics, including gate receipts and television and bowl revenues, can offset most, and sometimes all, of the costs of big-time programs if (and only if) teams are consistently successful; even in these settings, most schools lose money, and it is unlikely that any school comes close to covering its full costs if proper allowances are made for the capital-intensive nature of athletics.[36]

Strong sports teams, then, are not the financial boon for C&B schools they are often believed to be. But, as Shulman and Bowen note, colleges contemplating reductions in their investment in sports and in the admissions advantage given to athletes face a collective action problem: although a general ratcheting down of the intensity and professionalization of college sports would leave no college worse off, schools who go it alone—particularly within their conference—could very well suffer.

Consider now the other argument for large admissions advantages: that the qualities athletes bring add value to college life and promote the missions of colleges and universities. Few would deny that athletes possess virtues that colleges may rightly deem relevant and valuable. They excel at something difficult that brings pleasure and fulfillment to many people; they possess discipline; they are (except for the lone golfers and a few others) team players. In addition, there is much to be said for the "sound mind in a sound body" idea. But the most crucial questions remain. What, if anything, do athletes' special traits signify about their lives and contributions beyond college sports, and what do these traits have to do with the aims and purposes of universities? Do athletes' virtues correlate with other, less desirable characteristics? And what about the foregone opportunities that come from admitting athletes over students who possess other attractive qualities?

We cannot offer exhaustive answers to these questions, but we can make some headway. As Shulman and Bowen's data show, in addition to their lower academic standing on entry to college, athletes at the C&B schools tend to bring with them a somewhat different set of interests and values than other students, and these also affect their lives after college. Male athletes are more focused on making money and on pursuing business careers than other students; they are less interested in "making original contributions to science or the arts."[37] These differences between athletes and other students, like a number of other differences, have become more pronounced over time as athletic recruiting has become more intense. Increasingly, athletes tend to cluster in a few majors, particularly economics and political science, which they appear to associate with business careers. In general, athletes identify with academics less than other students, which partly explains why they underperform in college even after controlling for their lower credentials upon entry; a disproportionate number wind up in the bottom third of their class, which was not true in the 1950s.[38]

Athletes' underperformance is not explained by the significant time commitment of playing a varsity sport; students involved in other time-consuming extracurricular activities tend to overperform relative to their SAT scores and other predictors. Shulman and Bowen conclude from these and other findings that "a distinct 'athletic culture' is appearing in essentially all sports and at all levels of play in the C&B schools, including the Division III co-ed liberal arts colleges. This culture tends to separate athletes from other students and exacerbates the problems of academic performance."[39]

In keeping with the interests and values they express in college, male athletes are more likely than their classmates to go into business and finance, and less likely to become scientists, engineers, doctors, lawyers, or academics, or to pursue careers in public affairs. Largely as a result of their choice of careers, as well as the utility of traits athletes tend to have for fields like financial services, male athletes make more money than their classmates.[40] But their earnings advantage is limited almost exclusively to the financial services industry.[41]

A common view is that athletes possess out-of-the-ordinary leadership traits, so that, to the extent that selective colleges are and ought to be developing future leaders, they have special reason to admit athletes. Athletes themselves come to college believing they have above-average capacities as leaders.[42] But the data from the C&B schools show that athletes stand out in terms of leadership only in two areas: alumni activities (where, in contrast to other alumni, they place a high priority on college sports), and youth groups, including team coaching. In other civic activities their performance tracks that of other graduates.[43] Athletes are no more likely (and perhaps slightly less likely) to go into public service than other graduates,[44] and, taking earnings as a proxy for leadership in the business world, they stand out only in the financial services sector.[45]

Athletes, then, appear not to possess notable leadership qualities. Academically their performance is subpar, and they tend not to identify with intellectual pursuits. On the C&B college campuses they increasingly form a subculture unto themselves, which tends to exacerbate their academic underperformance and their anti-intellectualism. They do not pursue careers in the sciences, engineering, medicine, public service, or higher education to the same extent that their classmates do. These facts—conjoined with the (at best) slight benefits of admissions preferences for athletes to racial and socioeconomic diversity and to the financial well-being of universities—give us strong reason to doubt that admissions preferences for athletes of the magnitude now prevalent are justified.

In at least one respect, the case for reducing these advantages—for recruiting fewer athletes—is especially strong at the nonscholarship schools: the Ivy League and the Division III colleges. As we suggested earlier, attention to the big state schools (and a few big private schools) with the most prominent teams is misleading. At those schools, a student forfeits her scholarship if she quits the sport for which she was recruited. At the nonscholarship schools, by contrast, a recruited athlete may suddenly decide she doesn't want to compete, and there is no financial incentive to change her mind. As a result, the nonscholarship schools must recruit more students than they are likely to need to ensure they can field their teams. Columbia, for example, generally enrolls 35 freshmen for the football team alone (the Ivy League limit) out of a total of 630 men in the freshman class. Six percent of the men in Columbia's freshman class, then, are football players.[46]

Recognizing the profound effects of choosing to recruit large numbers of athletes on the character of a class and a college—and the opportunities foregone—Swarthmore College decided in December 2000 to abolish its football team, as well as its wrestling and badminton teams.[47] The Athletics Review Committee, which made the recommendation, argued that in order to field a competitive football team (a mission that Swarthmore had not recently accomplished except, ironically, in 2000), "the College must recruit through reserved admissions spaces many, and often the majority, of the players who participate on those teams. These spaces give decisive weighting to athletic talent and interest and contrast with the nod given to other talents and interests such as music or political activism in the regular admissions process."[48] In order to field competitive teams in all 24 intercollegiate sports, university administrators argued, the college would have to recruit 30 percent of its class of 375 as athletes, admitting that many fewer students with a range of other talents. A Swarthmore vice president thought the college should aim to reduce athletic admissions to 10–15 percent.[49]

The dilemma faced by Swarthmore and other nonscholarship schools (but also, to a lesser extent, by some colleges in Division I-A) points to the most compelling reason to rethink the growing admissions preferences athletes have enjoyed over the last decades. Places in selective colleges have become scarcer and scarcer, competition is becoming fiercer and fiercer. Do athletes possess greater merit, do they contribute more to the missions of higher education than physicists, poets, painters, philosophers, polyglots, musicians, mathematicians, history buffs, tinkerers, debaters, computer jocks, and political organizers? Until we have some reason to think they do, such disproportionate admissions advantages for athletes deserve to be reexamined.

3

The Multiple Missions of Modern Universities

We saw in the last chapter that *merit*, often invoked as the simple answer to the question "On what basis should colleges admit students?," is anything but simple, and as an answer frequently incorrect. We offered several reasons why. First, a variety of elements—the most obvious being a student's academic record and her extracurricular involvements—enter into merit. Second, merit is clearly not, and could not be, the only relevant consideration in admissions for colleges and universities. Non-merit-based factors include geographic origin, race, ethnicity, and legacy status. Among these non-merit-based factors, some are related to the fundamental missions of the institution, while others speak instead to its pragmatic needs.

Moreover, the concept of merit is fundamentally a relational one in at least two senses. First and most important, merit cannot be understood—it has no clear meaning or implications—apart from its relationship to the basic *goals and roles* of the institution seeking students. By "goals," we mean the institution's own internally defined aims; by "roles," we refer to the part that colleges and universities play in enabling other social institutions to fulfill their goals. Both are important. Because colleges and universities do not exist in a social vacuum, their aims derive not only from their scholarly mission but also from the requirements of the larger society. A college that defined merit solely in terms of academic prowess without regard to whether its graduates were good workers or good citizens would fail at part of its mission; it would have defined merit too narrowly.

Second, from the institution's point of view, the attractiveness of a given student, whatever her objective qualities, depends in part on the attributes of other students already enrolled or in the applicant pool. Admissions officers are interested in "crafting a class,"[1] and so a student's desirability depends on how his qualities mesh with those of others to form a whole.

Colleges customarily use the term "mission" in speaking about their goals and roles; many have a public "mission statement" describing them. To understand how selective colleges and universities actually go about the difficult business of choosing students, then—and how they ought to—we must have a grasp of their missions. That is the subject of this chapter.

Yet if we accept the view that the appropriate admissions criteria for universities depend on their missions, several thoughts may immediately spring to mind that seem to hinder any effort to generalize about the missions of universities. Before continuing, we must address these questions.

LET A THOUSAND COLLEGES BLOOM!

First, recognizing the enormous number and variety of colleges and universities in the United States, one may doubt whether there is anything general to be said about the missions of universities. Different schools are different; they have, and ought to have, different criteria for admission. What more needs to be said?

Consider, for example, the following schools—all of which require students to have solid academic credentials—and how they describe their missions.

Calvin College in Grand Rapids, Michigan, is "a comprehensive liberal arts college in the Reformed tradition of historic Christianity" that aims to educate students to be "agents of renewal in the academy, church, and society." Thus, whatever else it wants in a class, Calvin College wants students who will offer their "hearts and lives to do God's work in God's world."[2]

The mission of Berea College in eastern Kentucky is to educate poor students from southern Appalachia who will take away a philosophy of life "characterized by plain living, pride in labor well done, zest for learning, high personal standards, and concern for the welfare of others." The college also hopes Berea graduates will remain in Appalachia and serve its needs. A rich student from Los Angeles who aims to acquire a law degree and practice with a top California firm need not apply.[3]

In contrast to Berea, the Juilliard School, at Lincoln Center in New York City, takes students from all over the United States and many foreign countries as well. Its aim is to "help talented students harness their dedication to become communicative artists, imbued with the passion and understanding to reach within themselves to affect and move audiences." The principal threshold its applicants must cross is a competitive performance audition in which they display their talent in dance, music, or theater.[4]

Morehouse College is a historically black men's liberal arts college in

Atlanta that was founded in 1867 as Augusta Institute. The alma mater of Martin Luther King, Jr. describes its mission this way: "Guided by a commitment to excellence, Morehouse . . . assumes a special responsibility for teaching students about the history and culture of black people."[5]

Prospective students at the U.S. Military Academy at West Point must be unmarried U.S. citizens in good health; if they are men, they must be able to do fifty-four push-ups in two minutes. These unusual requirements arise out of the academy's mission to train students to become officers in the U.S. Army, where physical as well as mental prowess will be demanded of them and where qualities of leadership are essential. Applicants to Calvin, Berea, Morehouse, or Juilliard need not show evidence of leadership but applicants to West Point do.[6]

In addition to these institutions with special religious, artistic, military, and social missions, among four-year institutions of higher education alone, there are, as we saw in chapter 1, a great variety of institutions, including state universities and colleges that vary in size, degree of selectivity, and curricular offerings; large private research universities; private universities focused primarily on teaching; and small liberal arts colleges. So it may seem impossible to give a general answer to the question: how should universities choose their students?

And of course it *is* impossible—or at least highly undesirable—if we take as our ideal a final list of "correct criteria," with precise weights attached to each, that should hold at each and every institution of higher education in the country. No sensible person would want to abolish or even reduce the diversity of educational institutions available in the United States, which reflect and serve a wide variety of values, interests, abilities, and styles of learning. Let a thousand flowers bloom! But in extolling this diversity, and the plethora of appropriate admissions standards that accompany it, we should not forget that institutions with such highly specialized missions are unusual. Most students in the United States attend colleges and universities of a few main types, and within each type the aims are more standard and less idiosyncratic.

In 1998, for example, of the 14.5 million students enrolled in degree-granting institutions in the United States, three quarters attended public institutions—with something over half (5.9 million) at four-year colleges and universities and the remainder at community or junior colleges. About 10 percent of the total—1.5 million—were enrolled in religiously affiliated schools; approximately the same number attended independent not-for-profit institutions. (About 365,000 attended for-profit schools.)[7] Among four-year institutions, almost two thirds of students were enrolled in public colleges and universities.

Of course, not all public colleges and universities have identical goals and purposes, and among the many private institutions we find variation as well.

These differences rest not only on institutions' particular religious or other ideals, but on variations in their degree of selectivity, the curricula they offer, and resulting differences in their constituencies. Schools that are not selective or only slightly selective generally serve students with different goals and purposes than do highly selective institutions; the missions of the institutions students attend reflect these differences. So, for example, selective schools—elite private schools and flagship campuses of state universities—focus more on cultivating future leaders and on producing scholars and scientists who will "extend the boundaries of knowledge" than other institutions.

But it doesn't follow that nothing general can be said about the missions of the dominant form of American colleges and universities—four-year general curriculum institutions, involved to some degree in research as well as teaching, in which courses and instruction are predominantly secular. In the remainder of this chapter we focus almost exclusively on institutions of this type. There is, we shall argue, a great deal of commonality and overlap in the missions of those colleges and universities, both private and public, that most students in the United States attend.

THE SOCIAL ROLES OF THE MODERN UNIVERSITY

There is another reason, in addition to the sheer diversity of institutions of higher education, why a general discussion of the missions of colleges and universities might be thought beside the point. On this view, universities define their own missions. Take a look—you can find a mission statement on the websites of most colleges. Putting the point cantankerously, someone might say that it's no one's business *but* the college's to decide its mission. We might describe this as the *libertarian* view of colleges' missions.

This claim is obviously false in the case of public institutions, where the majority of college students attend. Such schools serve the people of their state, and in theory at least are answerable to them or their representatives. As we argue in chapter 10, the representative character of public universities provides an important reason for admissions policies such as affirmative action that aim to produce a student body—and an educated citizenry—that demographically represents the state's population.

But the claim is false also of private institutions. Part of the reason is that most receive significant governmental benefits. But that's not the whole story. The missions of many private institutions, like those of public universities, are not mere inventions of bureaucrats or boards of trustees past or present. They have evolved slowly and subtly from a variety of sources, including the particular institution's histories and traditions, felt moral and social responsibilities, and the guiding hands of particular leaders. As we suggested in chapter 1, the missions of contemporary colleges and universities also derive from central roles they have come to play in our society, especially over the last half century, in distributing basic goods such as income, status, and rewarding work—not to mention the pleasures that come from developing one's mind and talents. From the point of view of students, parents, and many in the workforce, these are among the most fundamental missions of colleges and universities. By virtue of these roles—in addition to other related purposes that, as we shall see shortly, many universities take upon themselves—institutions of higher education have become public trusts. The reason is not simply that they distribute basic goods—for so do supermarkets and drugstores. The difference lies in the developed expectations members of the public have of institutions of higher education, both public and private, and the ways in which these institutions, through their conduct and through their words, reinforce those expectations. The public expects universities to go about the tasks of choosing and educating students fairly and with a seriousness of purpose suited to the goals at hand, and universities do everything they can to persuade the public that indeed they live up to these expectations. We expect supermarkets and drugstores not to gag us and not to gouge us, but we don't hold them to the same high standards.

While colleges and universities once served as finishing schools for society's elites, today they constitute nearly essential prerequisites for anyone hoping to achieve middle class comfort and respectability. As we saw in chapter 1, college graduates earn much more than high school graduates, who earn more than high school dropouts. Income increases significantly for those possessing doctorates and even more for those with professional degrees. And the gap has widened over the last twenty-five years. Furthermore, although minorities (except Asian Americans with advanced degrees) lag behind whites at every level, their gains from education are at least as great as those of whites.[8]

As noteworthy as the income differences themselves is the variable the Census Bureau figures emphasize: whether a person possesses a college degree (or advanced degree). Perhaps more successful students do better later in life, materially or otherwise, than those with lower grades. But simply having a college degree marks a crucial dividing line.

Not only does having a college degree make a difference; there is also evidence that *where* one gets one's degree matters. In their comprehensive survey of the literature, Ernest Pascarella and Patrick Terenzini conclude that the selectivity of an undergraduate institution has a small but statistically significant effect on earnings.[9] A 1990 *Fortune* survey of almost 1,500 current and former top CEOs found that more than 10 percent (166) had graduated from only seven universities—all elite private institutions (Yale, Princeton, Harvard, Northwestern, Cornell, Columbia, and Stanford).[10] And a neglected corollary of William Bowen and Derek Bok's *The Shape of the River*, well known for its data showing the benefits of affirmative action to black students at highly selective colleges and universities, is that a prestigious college degree makes a difference in earnings, at least for minorities.[11]

So higher education is a good closely linked to other basic goods: income, rewarding work, status, and even better health. As public trusts, universities are bound to act in accordance with the requirements of justice. Of course, people differ widely in their views of what justice requires, and we do not suggest that philosopher-kings or admissions-officer-kings should engineer their vision of the good society through the admissions process. We make only two assumptions about the demands of justice, which we described in chapter 1.

First, a concern with justice in American higher education today means a commitment to enhancing the opportunities for advancement and for improved well-being to individuals and groups that have traditionally been deprived of such opportunities. Second, individuals should be neither helped nor hindered in their attempts at advancement by factors irrelevant to the legitimate goals of educational institutions. Both halves of this second principle are important. Not only should individuals not be hindered in the admissions process by irrelevant factors, but those already favored should not receive further advantages.[12] We believe that these principles command widespread support in our society.

But this is the beginning of discussion, not the end. The most practically decisive questions remain. First, what does a concern with justice imply in terms of universities' admissions policies and procedures? Much of this book is taken up with this question. Second, how does the moral and social mission of universities—which derives from their central involvement, as public trusts, in distributing the good of higher education—relate to their other missions? Is it compatible with them? Are there conflicts? We turn now to these questions, which take up most of the remainder of this chapter.

HISTORICAL ROOTS

In attempting to grasp the missions of modern colleges and universities, we find nothing sharp, clean, or tidy. The mission statements of these institutions are one source of information, but they don't tell the whole story. For one thing, such pronouncements are necessarily broad and vague. When universities describe their missions, they often enunciate high-minded statements about a variety of goals, aims, and purposes with little guidance about how to interpret them, order them, or—where they conflict—render them consistent. Indeed, we don't find in them even hints of possible conflict or inconsistency. Mission statements are not things of beauty or rigor.

Even if what a university said in a few sentences or a few paragraphs was clear and unequivocal, its mission statement would provide only one piece of evidence for its central goals and roles. Just as, in understanding an individual's basic aims and purposes, we examine not only what she says but also her actions and her roles and relationships with others around her, so too with institutions. To understand the missions of colleges and universities we look not only to their mission statements but to other pronouncements, to important policy decisions, and, more broadly, to the functions these institutions perform and their relationships to other institutions in contemporary American society. It is largely by virtue of these functions and relationships that we ascribe responsibilities for social justice to universities—although, as we shall see, some mission statements make explicit reference to such responsibilities and many to the betterment of society.

We have used the plural word "missions." Despite the singular noun they often employ, modern colleges and universities are centrally invested in the pursuit of several fundamental goals. A brief look at the development of American higher education since the second half of the nineteenth century sheds some light on the evolution of the contemporary university.[13]

Before the late nineteenth century, American colleges served a tiny minority that was almost exclusively white and male. The watchword of the traditional philosophy of higher education, according to Laurence Veysey, was "mental discipline"—although moral discipline was also crucial.[14] Indeed, in the nineteenth century, educational orthodoxy was usually accompanied by the religious kind as well.[15] Even as late as 1884, it could be said that college "is a system of mental gymnastics, essentially nothing else."[16] Advocates of mental discipline prescribed a four-year course of study of the traditional subjects: Greek, Latin, mathematics, and some moral philosophy.[17]

College was a way of confirming one's respectability. But although colleges had thrived in the eighteenth century, the prestige they conferred had declined by the middle of the nineteenth. Enrollments fell as some potential students decided they could do as well or better by going directly into business or the professions. The status of the college professor was also at a low; he was badly paid and his job was tedious. Mostly, he listened to (and graded) memorized recitations in ancient languages or mathematics.[18]

Change came after the Civil War. Veysey offers three broad explanations: national wealth, concern about declining college influence, and "Europhilic discontent"—a yearning by a new class of American leaders for equality with Europe, where universities thrived. Mental discipline as the major theme of higher education—along with the moral and religious orthodoxy that accompanied it—began to decline, and three other conceptions began to ascend in importance. These centered "in the aim of practical public service, in the goal of abstract research on what was believed to be the pure German model, and finally in the attempt to diffuse standards of cultivated taste."[19]

Veysey labels these conceptions "utility," "research," and "liberal culture" respectively.

In their focus on the practical and vocational aspects of higher education, advocates of utility made much of the concept of "real life." The university should be a workshop rather than a cloister.[20] Students should be free to pursue whatever studies they believed beneficial; paternalism in education declined as the elective system replaced the prescribed curriculum. The practical dimensions of education were furthered by the Morrill Act of 1862, which provided aid from the federal government to states supporting colleges offering agricultural and mechanical instruction.[21]

By contrast, advocates of the research ideal of the university emphasized knowledge—or perhaps thought—for its own sake. In *The Higher Learning in America*, published in 1918, Thorstein Veblen stated this view—not unknown today among university professors—in no uncertain terms:

> A university is a body of mature scholars and scientists, the "faculty,"—with whatever plant and other equipment may incidentally serve as appliances for their work in any given case. The necessary material equipment may under modern conditions be very considerable . . . but all that is not the university, but merely its equipment. And the university man's work is the pursuit of knowledge, together with whatever advisory surveillance and guidance he may consistently afford such students as are entering on the career of learning.[22]

James Morgan Hart, an American who took a law degree at Gottingen in 1864 and wrote a narrative that became standard reading for students thinking of graduate study in Germany, argued that the chief task of university instruction "is the development of great thinkers, men who will extend the boundaries of knowledge." It trains practical men only indirectly, "by giving its students a profound insight into the principles of the science, and then turning them adrift to deduce the practice as well as they can from the carefully inculcated theory." German students evinced contempt "for everything that savors of 'bread-and-butter.' . . . All thought of practical life is kept in abeyance."[23]

The third conception, liberal culture, included aesthetic, moral, emotional, and social dimensions. It was essential, advocates thought, to develop students' taste by enlightening them about literary and aesthetic standards.[24] But liberal culture also included an important moral component: students must develop character. As one professor put it, the man of culture possessed "breadth of understanding and learning, breadth of sensibility and artistic feeling; breadth, both of aspiration and endeavor—of deference and charity."[25]

Yet culture also implied certain social assumptions. It demanded polish, elegance, and style.[26] Charles Eliot, president of Harvard for forty years, announced: "I have often said that if I were compelled to have one required subject in Harvard College, I would make it dancing if I could."[27] But Eliot acknowledged that other attributes, including hard work, had to accompany the social graces. Although such traits could perhaps be taught, they came more easily to the well-bred. According to Veysey, the leading universities stressed the aesthetic and social aspects of liberal culture; the smaller colleges emphasized the moral.

From the beginning the proponents of liberal culture were hostile "toward practicality and minute investigation."[28] So they stood in opposition not only to the increasingly vocational orientation of American higher education, but also to the research ideal, especially insofar as it took a scientific and empirical turn. Their main positive idea was that the study of man was intrinsically important in a way the study of nature was not.[29] Emphasizing the importance of literature and the humanities, advocates of liberal culture "ruefully . . . observed that in the Middle West literary courses had acquired a reputation of effeminacy among the students. 'The really virile thing is to be an electrical engineer.' "[30]

On the surface, this triumvirate of values—utility, research, and liberal culture—marks out clear lines of difference and even conflict. Consider, for example, the relationship between utility and research. Utility centers on the student's vocational interests and their effects on the larger society he will eventually join. The pure research ideal is, as we have seen, militantly un-, im-, and anti-practical; the German emphasis on *Lehrfreiheit* implies the researcher's freedom from utilitarian considerations and his passion for knowledge for its own sake. Students—if they are not actual impediments—play a distinctly secondary role. For liberal culture, on the other hand, the role of students is central, but here too advocates deemphasized education's vocational benefits. And the "minute investigation" characteristic of the research ideal was at odds with the broad aims of liberal education.

As these values played out in the development of the modern university, however, some of the conflicts among them were often more theoretical than real. For example, although the research ideal was shaped by the highly abstract philosophical idealism prevalent in Germany, whose universities served as a model, the domestic variety—in keeping with the pragmatic cast of the American mind—seemed always to have been more empirically oriented. Research meant scientific inquiry. With the growth of science and technology and the increasing "real-world" demand for specialization, research and vocational considerations did not necessarily conflict, and indeed often went hand-in-hand. Only in theory was research purely theoretical. Today, only in a few corners of the university—primarily in the humanities—do we find research wholly unconnected to the promise or at least the hope of concrete benefits.

Some of the confusion comes from the term "utility." The term is burdened with overtones deriving from its long career in both philosophy and economics, and as a result its meanings are varying and elastic. But "practicality," which appears to be a reasonable substitute for what proponents had in mind, does not fare much better, indicating that the problem is not simply terminological. We can approach the issues most easily by looking more closely at the third member of the trio, liberal education. It is more complex and multifaceted than the other two, and its features have altered more significantly over the last hundred years.

THE FACETS OF LIBERAL EDUCATION

In *The Invention of Love*, Tom Stoppard's play about the poet and Latin scholar A. E. Housman (and about life at Oxford in the nineteenth century), Housman describes the life of the scholar:

> A scholar's business is to add to what is known. That is all. But it is capable of giving the very greatest satisfaction, because knowledge is good. It does not have to look good or sound good or even do good. It is good just by being knowledge. And the only thing that makes it knowledge is that it is true. You can't have too much of it and there is no little too little to be worth having. There is truth and falsehood in a comma.[31]

Later, Housman once again defends "useless knowledge for its own sake. Useful knowledge is good, too, but it's for the fainthearted, an elaboration of the real thing, which is only to shine some light, it doesn't matter where on what, it's the light itself, against the darkness, it's what's left of God's purpose when you take away God."[32]

The idea of liberal education tempts us to distinguish, as Housman does, between knowledge-for-its-own-sake, or a realm of study that is *intrinsically* valuable, and knowledge-as-a-means, study that is *instrumentally* valuable. On this view, liberal education belongs in the first category and vocational education belongs in the second. But the distinction, familiar though it is, does not help very much—as we might conclude from Housman/Stoppard's faintly absurd idea that it doesn't matter where or on what we "shine some light," so that there's no difference between the value of knowing Catullus and the value of knowing the number of blades of grass on my front lawn.

From the beginning, advocates of liberal education were concerned to produce human beings with certain definite attributes—taste, intelligence, sensitivity—and they saw liberal education as a means to that end. Is the education they stressed, then, merely instrumental—a means to an end?

About anything we can know or study it is reasonable to ask why it's worth knowing or studying. Why study difficult and inaccessible (to most college students) masterworks of the past—the poetry of Dante, the key-board music of Bach? One might answer that they are intrinsically valuable. But in spelling out what this means one will make reference to some worthwhile effects that the *Inferno* and the *Goldberg Variations* have on those who become acquainted with them. The philosopher Brian Barry argues that "Education is a good thing in itself"—suggesting knowledge for its own sake—but he quickly adds: "more precisely . . . it provides people with the opportunity to live better lives."[33]

We do better if, instead of talking about knowledge for its own sake, we make finer distinctions among the various ends education can serve. As Nicholas Murray Butler (who would later become president of Columbia University) observed in 1895, "Utility . . . may be given either a very broad or a very narrow meaning. . . . There are utilities higher and utilities lower."[34] Butler was echoing John Stuart Mill's famous distinction in *Utilitarianism*, published three decades earlier. Using the term "utility" in the philosophical sense to mean pleasure or happiness, Mill argues against those who believe his theory of utilitarianism, according to which pleasure or happiness is the highest good and that toward which all action should aim, is "a doctrine worthy only of swine." "It is quite compatible with the principle of utility to recognize the fact, that some kinds of pleasure are more desirable and more valuable than others."[35] The debate between Mill and his critics (which continues to this day) is framed in terms of "higher" and "lower" pleasures, which derive respectively from human beings' "higher" and "lower" faculties.

It's possible, then, to explain why education is more than just a better way to the bottom line without resorting to the language of knowledge or study "for its own sake," which will satisfy no one not already persuaded of the value of the activity in question. The value of a liberal education is practical even though it is not merely materialistic. For its nineteenth-century defenders, the practical value lay "in the elevation of character, in the more lively sympathy with the true, the good, and the beautiful, and in the increase of mental power."[36] And these effects, they believed, made a person's life better.

But it is in the specification of these effects that we find a marked change in the understanding of liberal education—and its transformation from liberal culture—in the hundred or so years since the emergence of the modern university. The original proponents of liberal culture, as we have seen, emphasized aesthetic and intellectual appreciation and the development of character. They tended to be aristocratic in outlook and often scorned politics, democracy, and engagement in material life.

It is surprising to find this neglect of civic and political life even in thinkers like Alexander Meiklejohn, best known for his views about freedom of expression. Meiklejohn, a philosopher and one-time president of Amherst College, argued that the preeminent purpose of the First Amendment was to protect *political* speech because of its importance to democracy and democratic citizenship. Other forms of expression, he thought, such as advertising ("commercial speech"), did not deserve the same degree of constitutional protection. Yet Meiklejohn argued that "the primary function of the American college is the arousing of interests" in order that "life may be fuller and richer in content."[37] Although he emphasized the broad practicality of a college education, arguing that the whole college curriculum should "be unified and dominated by a single interest, a single purpose,—that of so understanding human life as to be ready and equipped for the practice of it,"[38] Meiklejohn did not specifically stress its civic and political importance.

Today, the explicitly aristocratic outlook has wholly disappeared from discussions of higher education; the closest thing to it is the claim of some selective colleges and universities to produce future leaders. But we find a much greater emphasis on the larger civic, political, and social contributions liberal education makes to the development of students and so indirectly to society. "The mission of Duke University is to provide a superior liberal education to undergraduate students, attending not only to their intellectual growth but also to their development as adults committed to high ethical standards and full participation as leaders in their communities."[39] The University of Texas says its core purpose is "to transform lives for the benefit of society."[40] Williams College is "Dedicated to the welfare of the great common life of the State."[41] The University of Michigan aims to produce students who will "recognize their responsibilities to society and their fellow man."[42]

This is not to say the other nonvocational purposes of going to college—the development of intellectual, aesthetic, and moral capacities—have disappeared. But in the rhetoric surrounding the roles of the university, its larger civic and political dimensions have assumed greater prominence. Indeed, the development of moral and intellectual capacities is conceived at least partly as serving civic and political ends. Enhanced knowledge, understanding, and ethical standards will enable and encourage college graduates, it is thought, to be better citizens—to be more effective deliberators about public affairs, but also to give something back to their communities. (In keeping with this goal, most selective colleges want to know whether and to what extent applicants have been involved in community service or charitable activities; presumably they believe these are predictors of future service.)

The purposes of liberal education, then, are more complex than they might at first appear. It's useful to divide them into three main categories. First is *education for work*. Leaving aside the purely vocational aspects of higher education—the *specific* training students undergo to pursue careers in science or business or journalism or teaching—a broad liberal education is meant partly to help people do their jobs better, whether they become middle managers or CEOs, by helping them think better, analyze better, communicate better, make better decisions. (So philosophy professors tell

students—or console their parents—when the students ask what a philosophy major is "good for.")

Next is *education for citizenship*, the development of students' skills,
understanding, and appreciation meant to enhance their roles as citizens—of
their nation and increasingly, it should be argued, of the world.[43] Liberal
education is supposed to help improve people's ability to understand complex public issues, evaluate arguments and information and those who pur-
vey it, and appreciate the points of view of those with different or even alien
outlooks.

Finally, there is (in Brian Barry's term) *education for living*: the idea that
developing one's mind, judgment, taste, and sensitivity opens doors to valuable aesthetic, intellectual, and emotional experiences and that these enhance
one's life.

All three—education for work, for citizenship, and for living—are evident, for example, in the University of Michigan's description of its teaching
mission:

> among its responsibilities the University has the obligation to . . . prepare stu-
> dents who . . . : have a mastery of a particular discipline; have an acquaintance
> with their society's past; have the training required to assume productive roles
> in society; have an awareness of the need for self-criticism; feel a responsibility
> toward the knowledge they have acquired; are prepared to question the uses to
> which their skills are being put; recognize their responsibilities to society and
> their fellow man; will preserve and enhance the legacy of the past; will continue
> to develop intellectually; respect and value intellectual rigor and intellectual
> freedom.[44]

Education for work, for citizenship, and for living are three aspects of *liberal* education. Liberal education, then, is not based on Housman's, or
Veblen's, idea of scholarship, and the admissions criteria that would be
appropriate for the research or the scholarly ideal—getting the cleverest students with the most refined sensibilities—are not appropriate for it. Liberal
education is a means toward various nonscholarly ends; it provides goods
not only for the smartest students but for all students, and for others whose
lives they affect as well. We want C students to lead good lives, be good citizens, and do their jobs well just as much as A students.

As we have seen, however, universities have other missions in addition to
liberal education. In courses in chemistry, accounting, education, and a variety of other subjects, they prepare students more directly and concretely for
jobs in particular fields. This is what the nineteenth century reformers meant
by "utility." Since both the research and the liberal education missions serve
useful, practical goals, it's less confusing to call this the *vocational* mission.
For many institutions—particularly larger public and private universities—

research, mainly fueled by the promise or hope of social benefits, also comprises an important part of their mission. And many have other social goals as well, often collected loosely under the idea of *service*, described by the University of Michigan as "helping to define and assist in the solution of the problems of society."[45]

Often, these multiple missions overlap and are not easily distinguished from each other. So, for example, Swarthmore College says its purpose "is to make its students more valuable human beings and more useful members of society."[46] On the other hand, colleges' various missions will—as we might already guess and will soon see more clearly—sometimes point in different directions.

CONSTITUENCIES AND THE WHOLE

When we think about the constituencies served by higher education, we naturally think first and foremost of students. Students constitute the largest and most conspicuous population within colleges and universities. They pay (typically) to attend the institution, and hope to take away some tangible (and possibly also some intangible) benefits. To the person-in-the-street, the idea that universities have any purpose other than educating students may seem surprising. Students, it seems, are what colleges are *about*.

Yet it's clear that universities have other purposes. Take for example, the research mission. It includes students only indirectly—as interlocutors, sparring partners, and critics with whom professors can discuss their ideas; as potential future researchers; as research assistants or experimental subjects. Faculty primarily committed to research tend to appreciate only the most intellectually capable students, those who could themselves choose (even if they don't) the scientific or scholarly life. Even if these students opt for business school instead, they serve as stimulating sounding boards for professors trying out new ideas or just attempting to stay in good intellectual shape. Less capable students, from this perspective, can be a distraction and a hindrance.

So different constituencies push for policies emphasizing different purposes. Students may demand more vocationally oriented courses. Faculty may want high-powered students, specialized courses fitting their research agenda, smaller teaching loads. Alumni want less research and more teaching.[47] Employers want faculty to grade students accurately so they can separate the wheat from the chaff; but virtually all faculty find grading the most onerous of burdens, and dislike giving bad grades.[48] Of course, the demands different constituencies press for don't necessarily have anything to do with the fundamental missions of the university. As Clark Kerr, former president of the University of California once explained, his primary administrative problems centered on the facts that the students want sex, the alumni want sports, and the faculty want parking.[49] But there can also be conflicts among constituencies concerning genuinely basic purposes of the institution.

It would be naive to think all such conflicts can be resolved. Universities have multiple missions, deriving from and aiming at multiple goods. There is no guarantee that all such goods can, practically, always be made compatible, and indeed strong reason to think they can't be. But we can take some steps to reduce the conflicts, or at least refine them, by stepping back from the standpoint of different constituencies with interests in the university to the more magisterial perspective of the institution as a whole, considering all its missions. As social institutions serving the interests of constituencies outside as well as within the university, colleges and universities cannot be made to serve the interests of students alone, or faculty alone, or staff, alumni, legislators, employers, or parents alone. All are important; none is decisive. The goals and roles of the university are determined by a complex negotiation among interests that is often best resolved by showing that an educational mission benefits multiple constituencies.

Take, for example, the development of a student's intellectual, aesthetic, moral, and civic capacities that liberal education hopes to achieve. It's natural to begin with the idea that the development of these capacities is good for the student, and thus serves her interests. Ironically, this is clearest in the case of education for living, typically conceived as the most irrelevant of benefits—the one whose value it may be hardest to convince students and their parents of. Defenders of liberal education often argue that exposing a student to Chaucer or the Mahabarata will make *her* life more satisfying—the supposition underlying education for living. In one way, making the student's life more satisfying should be reason enough for liberal education. But legislators, employers, and parents may demand that college do more than turn students into aesthetes and highbrows.

In fact, however, the development of the capacities with which liberal education is concerned also benefits others. People who appreciate art, science, literature, and philosophy often spread their delight to their friends, lovers, families, and particularly their children, whose lives are thereby also enriched. The case is even clearer with education for citizenship. A college that educates its students to become good citizens aims for benefits that will redound not primarily to them but to others. If liberally educated students become better informed and more intelligent voters who make superior political choices, that is a good for the polity as a whole. If liberal education broadens their sympathies from their own private preoccupations to the larger world, they will give more back to their communities.

The same can be said about education for work. The well (and liberally) educated student will, we expect, do his job better than the poorly educated student. That is probably a good for him, but it is at least as much a good for others. The point is obvious when we turn from liberal education to vocational education. Cardiologists and computer scientists, chemists and criminologists, put their education to work in ways that benefit society; presumably, they benefit as well. In the contemporary jargon, higher education through all its functions increases the stock of intellectual, political, and social capital.

Political theorists often point out that free speech—commonly thought of as a right of would-be speakers—benefits listeners and society at large at least as much as speakers, and that these benefits are central to the justification of freedom of expression.[50] We can make a similar argument for the benefits of education. A person's education benefits him—primarily in terms of vocational advantages and personal growth and self-realization—but it also benefits others, who gain from his becoming a brain surgeon or a public interest lawyer, and from the enhanced quality of his participation in the local, national, or world community to which his education contributes.

These observations do not imply that some entity called "society at large" exists over and above the individuals contained within it. The point is only that the benefits of education are spread widely, and that the beneficiaries of education are not always identical with its recipients. When we consider this fact, we see a fundamental ambiguity in statements universities make about their missions. "The mission of Wellesley College is to provide an excellent liberal arts education for women who will make a difference in the world."[51] Is it the well-being of the women educated, or the difference in the world they may make, that matters most? This question almost certainly has no straightforward answer. But when we consider the variety of differences education can make both to students and to the world, asking it highlights some of the complex choices universities face.

MISSIONS AND ADMISSIONS

One important conclusion to be drawn from this inquiry is that the missions of colleges and universities are inescapably connected with larger social goals, in at least two ways. First, as we argued at the beginning of this chapter, higher education is among the most important goods allocated in American society today, in virtue of its connection with other goods such as income, status, and rewarding work. Because colleges and universities are public trusts with the primary responsibility for distributing this good, they have the burden of making decisions fairly and consistently with the demands of justice. We enunciated two relevant principles of justice that we believe are widely accepted in our society. First, opportunities for advancement should be broadened to members of groups that have traditionally been deprived of such opportunities. Second, people should be neither helped nor hindered by factors irrelevant to the legitimate goals of educational institutions.

The missions of colleges and universities are connected with larger social goals in another way as well. Even apart from the de facto social role we have just described, most colleges and universities frame their missions with explicit reference to values such as "the benefit of society," "making a difference in the world," and engendering in students "responsibilities to society and their fellow man." As we have seen, it would be impossible to explain universities' central missions of liberal education, vocational preparation, and research in the absence of such larger social goals. Universities promote research and vocational preparation not simply so the individual students they educate can find interesting ways to occupy themselves, but because the fruits of their education will benefit others or the general good. The arguments for liberal education also rest in significant part on its civic and other benefits to people besides those students educated.

It's not that the goals of higher education are crudely utilitarian, always tied to merely materialistic concerns. The fruits of research, vocational training, or liberal education may draw upon and nourish what Mill described as human beings' "higher faculties." The point is not about the nature of education's benefits—whether they are merely material or more exalted—but about its beneficiaries. In educating students, universities shape society.

We argued in the last chapter that colleges' admissions decisions are not and should not be rooted in the aim of "rewarding" "deserving" students, but must rest instead on judgments about the extent to which students will serve the institution's larger purposes. These purposes, we have seen, are multiple and diverse—including vocational preparation, research, and liberal education. Each of these is itself complex, and each is inextricably tied up with large social goals.

Considering universities' purposes one by one, we would not necessarily expect to find convergence in their implications for admissions. So, for example, the research mission suggests favoring the most academically outstanding students; they are, on the whole, most likely to contribute to extending the boundaries of knowledge. Liberal education, on the other hand, implies a more democratic and less meritocratic approach. Above a certain intellectual threshold (almost certainly, we can assume, in the range of average intelligence), most recipients of liberal education can benefit, and there is no reason to think that more academically talented students benefit more than others. The vocational missions of universities suggest diverse criteria, in terms of students' qualifications, because of the tremendous variation in the kinds of work available and necessary in the world. As we have seen, professors often prefer to test their ideas on classes filled with brilliant students, but it would be folly to suppose that a more brilliant student body necessarily fulfills all the university's missions better than a less brilliant one.

For many jobs, the important credential is the college degree and the training it implies, not the stellar grade point average.[52]

Even within elite professions, we find important distinctions. The medical profession needs top-notch brain surgeons, but it also needs general practitioners; some communities, whether in rural Appalachia or inner-city Detroit, are underserved. African Americans fare much worse according to a variety of health indicators than white Americans.[53] Most people would agree that improving the health of African Americans (and thus of Americans) is a worthy goal. If this goal can be advanced by training physicians who will serve them, and if African American physicians are more likely to do so, then colleges have a legitimate, mission-related reason to admit black students they judge likely to be headed for medical careers, and medical schools will be justified in looking especially favorably on them. Such considerations apply not only to judging the specific career choices minority graduates may make, but also to their extra-vocational futures. The evidence that minority graduates of selective schools become civic leaders and activists at higher rates than their nonminority peers is not extraneous information; it bears directly on purposes central to the contemporary university.[54]

JUSTICE AND DIFFERENTIATION

These arguments show that virtually all institutions of higher education have good reason to consider admissions criteria beyond the narrowly academic. Because they are interested in producing not simply good students but good workers, good citizens, and fulfilled human beings, it's appropriate for them to consider a broad range of admissions criteria. What standardized tests and grades tell us about a student is one important aspect of what colleges and universities care about, but—no surprise here to anyone familiar with the college admissions process—it's not the only one. So far, psychometricians have not had much success in designing tests to measure these other qualities, such as reflectiveness, creativity, the capacity for leadership, or the propensity for civic involvement. That's why those who read college applications also look carefully at what students do outside the classroom, how they express themselves, what their teachers say about them, difficulties they have encountered or overcome, and anything else that sheds light on central personal attributes not captured by tests.

Many colleges and universities are eager to do what they can to broaden opportunities for advancement to individuals and groups—lower-income and minority students—that have lacked those opportunities. And although the "diversity" relevant to a healthy and fruitful campus climate includes many kinds of variety among students, in light of our country's legacy of racial discrimination racial diversity play a special role, not only in campus life itself but also in what happens after college.[55] This view does not commit us to believing that, for example, "all black students think alike." As Bowen and Bok argue in *The Shape of the River*, the conservative black student with high grades from an elite high school may challenge stereotypes as much as the black student from the inner city.[56]

But the impetus to broaden opportunities is qualified by considerations of practicability and consistency with other important goals. To see how these considerations affect and limit the aim of broadening opportunity, consider the broad outlines of the current system of higher education.

As we have seen, the American system offers an enormous range of institutions with different missions and widely varying levels of selectivity. The most selective schools generally admit less than a quarter of a very strong applicant pool. Other four-year institutions typically admit somewhere between a third and two-thirds of their applicants. Serving as gateways for the least prepared students are open admissions institutions, including especially community and junior colleges.

Consider state institutions. Over the second half of the twentieth century, typical state systems of higher education adopted a three-tiered form: one or more "flagship" research campuses with demanding entrance requirements; a second tier of less selective four-year state institutions more geared to teaching and service; and an array of inexpensive, commuter-friendly open admission community colleges that accept everyone (even those without high school diplomas). The typical state system, then, supplies a place for virtually anyone who wants to go beyond high school.

This division of labor seems rational and efficient. High achieving high school graduates can attend universities with other high achievers and find coursework that challenges their talents. Other good students can find places in excellent institutions just below the top tier that offer comprehensive curricula and many cultural amenities. For students who have not fared well in high school or who remain uncertain about their academic goals, local community colleges provide a point of entry to test the waters of higher education or to seize a second chance to remedy academic deficiencies and move into degree-granting programs.

A one-size-fits-all approach to higher education has little to recommend it. Before the middle of the twentieth century, a typical flagship state university accepted any state resident who graduated high school with a C average. As a result, its freshman class contained students at every level of academic capability. It resolved this extreme diversity by flunking out half the class at the end of the first semester. The university certainly didn't benefit from this policy, and neither did the low-achieving students whose first encounter with higher education was an experience of failure. Since that time, nearly all states have moved to a differentiated system, with different kinds of institutions for different kinds of students.

Of course, the different institutions are not all on a par. The flagship campuses are more prestigious than the second-tier schools, and the four-year institutions have more status than the two-year community colleges. And the differences in prestige are rooted in real differences in quality. The most selective campuses offer the richest cultural and intellectual climate. Moreover, graduating from one of them generates a payoff premium—recall our earlier discussion of employers who target their hiring at Ivy League graduates. Is it fair that one St. Louis high school student gets into the University of Missouri while her slightly less accomplished classmate must settle for Southeast Missouri State University, even though he might benefit just as much from Mizzou?

To answer this question at least two issues are relevant. One has to do with the costs and benefits of mixing students with a wide range of skills. Do the more qualified students benefit? Do the less qualified students benefit? Just how much variation is tolerable, and at what point do the differences make effective teaching impossible? Not a great deal is known on this subject at the level of higher education, but a developed literature exists on tracking in secondary schools.[57] This literature suggests that within limits, such intellectual integration benefits the students with lesser skills; whether better students benefit is less clear. Let's suppose, then, that the student who goes to Southeast Missouri State would have a better experience at the flagship campus.

Yet that benefit depends on the cultural and intellectual climate created on a campus with a substantial body of high-achieving students. The university can't provide this benefit if it admits all applicants at the margin who would benefit, or if it admits at random, or if it admits in any other way that doesn't yield the requisite high proportion of academic achievers.

Very selective institutions ought to leaven their student populations with applicants whose credentials are less stellar than the norm. This accords with our first principle of justice, and the point becomes clearer in chapter 10, where we argue that selective institutions, particularly public ones, have reason to choose students who represent the racial and socioeconomic character of the state and the nation. More purely educational arguments probably support such diversity as well. Students' intellectual, social, and moral development benefits from interaction with people of diverse social backgrounds. But the leavening necessarily runs up against severe limits if selective institutions are to remain selective. Thus, the threshold issue is whether a college is justified in choosing to be selective, or whether a state system is justified in creating selective campuses. (As we noted in chapter 1, selectivity is a relative thing and a matter of degree. But the point holds at every place along the selectivity spectrum.) We answer yes to these questions.

Not everyone agrees. Some critics regard the ubiquitous differentiated systems of higher education as deliberately class-stratified, designed to keep the lower and lower middle classes from the perks available to more privileged groups. Even critics who don't see in institutional differentiation a conspiracy may nevertheless note that it produces considerable class stratification—and they may find this effect intolerable.

In fact, few people today advocate bringing the walls of differentiation tumbling down, whatever their objections to the current system. Matters were different thirty years ago, as differentiation was moving into its mature phase. Indeed, at one important place, the walls did come tumbling down (for a while). In the 1970s, the City University of New York adopted an "open admissions" policy for its senior colleges. The classroom doors were thrown open to students who earlier would have been excluded by CUNY's admissions standards. How did this drama of open admissions play out? What lessons does it teach us about institutional differentiation and selective admissions policies? We examine the CUNY case, and its implications for the question of access to higher education for underprepared students, in the next chapter.

4

Open Admissions and the Community Colleges

In 1849, New York City launched the Free Academy, the country's first municipal college. The Academy—later renamed City College—was meant as a great experiment in "whether the children of the people, the children of the whole people, can be educated."[1] This populist mission of educating "the children of the whole people" informed the growth and development of City College (CCNY), which went on in the twentieth century to achieve a storied place in American higher education as the "Harvard of the Proletariat." It exceeded all other public universities in the number of its graduates who went on to win the Nobel Prize; it was second only to Berkeley in the number who obtained PhDs in the fifty-year period after 1920. Mid-century American intellectual life was strongly influenced by CCNY alumni such as Seymour Martin Lipset, Irving Kristol, Daniel Bell, Alfred Kazin, and Irving Howe.[2] For the better part of its history, City College (along with its sister institutions Hunter, Queens, and Brooklyn College) provided free high-quality public education to the sons and daughters of New York City's immigrant and working-class families.

By the last decade of the twentieth century, however, City College was in trouble. It suffered from persistent underenrollment and low graduation rates. A high proportion of its students sat in remedial classes, trying to pick up skills that would let them succeed in regular college courses. Many of those regular courses themselves had surrendered to an "ethos of mediocrity," according to one observer.[3]

What had happened?

OPEN ADMISSIONS AT CUNY

In 1970, calling CCNY the *Harvard* of the Proletariat was not altogether fanciful. After World War II, demand for higher education outstripped supply in New York City, and the academic threshold for entering City College rose and rose. At the end of the 1960s, an applicant needed high school grades of B-plus or better to get in. Indeed, an applicant needed at least a C-plus to get into one of the city's two-year institutions.[4]

However, calling City College the Harvard of the *Proletariat* had become something of a stretch. CCNY's student body no longer represented New York City's working classes. During the 1950s, hundreds of thousands of whites had left the city, replaced by an equal number of blacks and Puerto Ricans, mostly at the bottom of the economic ladder. Yet few children of these new residents got into City College or CUNY's other four-year colleges. Their high school grades weren't good enough.[5]

Those were racially tense times across America. Major urban riots in 1965, 1967, and 1968 left cities on edge and racial comity tattered. New York City was no exception. Indeed, the city was embroiled in a bitter struggle over political control of the schools that pitted black against white. A demonstration project in local control at the Ocean Hill–Brownsville school district, begun in 1967, resulted in a battle between the district's black governing board and the city's teacher's union. The union pulled its teachers out of the district's schools and then led a series of strikes against the entire school system. Racial politics had become a bareknuckled affair in New York.

There in the middle of Harlem sat City College. Although CCNY had a small percentage of blacks on campus, admitted through a new program for disadvantaged students (called SEEK—Search for Education, Elevation, and Knowledge), the college was an island of white in a sea of black. In 1968, black and Puerto Rican students, radicalized by the events of the day (and the rhetoric of H. Rap Brown and Stokely Carmichael), demanded that the college begin admitting minority students in numbers equal to their proportion in the city's high schools. To precipitate action on their demands, in April 1969 a group of protestors took over part of the campus. By May physical confrontations erupted among black and white students. The president closed the college and resigned.[6]

Within weeks the city's Board of Education announced that beginning in the fall of 1970, under a new "open admissions" policy, any student who graduated from high school with at least an 80 average in academic courses or ranked within the top 50 percent of his class could enter one of the city's senior colleges. High school graduates who did not meet these conditions were guaranteed a place in a community college or job-training program.[7]

The effect was instantaneous and dramatic. Whereas 20,000 freshmen had matriculated in one CUNY institution or another in 1969, over 35,000 registered in the fall of 1970.[8] The percentage of black and Hispanic freshmen nearly tripled.[9] Forty percent of the new students enrolling in the senior colleges were open-admissions students, possessing on average one-and-a-half fewer high school academic credits than regular students and grades 6 or 7 points lower (on a 100 point scale).[10]

At City College, the freshman class jumped from 1,750 to 2,750. The number of SEEK students tripled.[11] This last fact had particular significance. The newly relaxed admissions standards tilted the scales in favor of black and Puerto Rican students, but not dramatically so, because these groups were still disproportionately represented among high school students possessing less than an 80 average or ranked in the bottom half of their class. To include more blacks and Puerto Ricans on campus than the new standards generated alone, administrators expanded admissions through the SEEK program. However, whereas a pre-1970 SEEK student might enter from high school with a mid-80s average and possess reasonably good academic skills— credentials still not sufficient to qualify her for regular admissions because of the high threshold—the post-1970 SEEK students came to college with high school averages in the 70s and class rankings commensurately low.

Some of the new open admissions students and many of the SEEK students lacked the mathematics and language skills to succeed at college work. Deans and department chairs at CCNY—and throughout CUNY— scrambled to hire new faculty, find new classroom space, and create an extensive stratum of remedial writing and math courses to make up for the new students' deficiencies. Faculty divided sharply over the task facing them, some committed fervently to the proposition that all students can be educated, others alarmed at the decline in standards they saw ensuing.[12]

Open admissions rolled over CUNY like a tidal wave, without real advance planning or commitment of new resources. The faculty did its best with what it had, but conditions grew worse as New York City itself fell into financial crisis and near-bankruptcy. The university cut budgets, shed professors and programs, and finally closed its doors for two weeks in 1976 when money ran out altogether. Out of the turmoil, major policy shifts altered the face of CUNY momentously. The foremost shift was a bargain in which the State of New York assumed principal financial responsibility for CUNY and CUNY agreed to charge tuition. Free public education for the children of the people was gone forever. At the same time, CUNY raised academic standards. Now to get into a senior college, students had to possess a minimum average grade of 80 or a ranking in the top 35 percent of their class.

The effects of these changes? In 1980, two-thirds of the freshman cohort at the CUNY senior colleges took remedial courses, compared to one-third in 1970 when open admissions began. Their dropout rate after the first year was double. Their grades at the end of four semesters were a fifth of a grade lower than those of the 1970 cohort.[13] Why, if standards were higher, were students' achievements lower? The answer: tuition. Tuition dramatically changed the incentives facing the city's high school graduates. Although the point of open admissions in 1970 was to provide an avenue into the CUNY system for blacks and Puerto Ricans, and although it increased their rates of admission strikingly, the majority of open admissions students at the outset were whites who differed little from their regular admissions peers. The reason is easy to see. The very high admissions standards prevailing in 1969 at the Harvard of the Proletariat (and CUNY's other four-year campuses) excluded not only blacks and Puerto Ricans with limited academic preparation, but also middle-class Jewish and Catholic students with credible if not spectacular academic backgrounds. When open admissions began in 1970, the solid B, white high school graduate who would have gone to college in any case took advantage of it to gain a free education at CUNY. However, once CUNY began to charge tuition, middle-class white students no longer had as much reason to prefer it. Their enrollments dropped precipitously.[14] Academically promising middle-class minority students likewise faced changed incentives and increased opportunities to go elsewhere. When CUNY opened its doors in the fall of 1976, more than 10,000 fewer students showed up at the senior colleges.

Those who remained at CUNY were likely to be older, poorer, and academically weaker than their predecessors. They were more likely to work, to have family responsibilities, to struggle with English. As a result of these burdens, they started school, stopped, started again. They were less likely to take classes full time. They needed remediation. And their struggle for a degree became harder after 1976. As part of its elevation of standards that year, CUNY made passing skills tests in writing, reading, and mathematics—tests originally developed to decide whether entering students needed remedial classes—a condition for moving to the junior year. By the end of the 1990s, only 8 percent of CUNY students graduated after four years, only 32 percent after six years.

DILEMMAS OF REMEDIATION

After 1980, the demographic changes New York City experienced earlier accelerated and diversified. The city attracted waves of immigrants from all parts of the world. The flight of the middle-class continued. These changes are captured in a snapshot provided by James Traub, in his book *City on a Hill*, of City College's 1991 entering class. Half were born abroad; 39 percent were black, 28 percent Hispanic, 18 percent Asian, and 14 percent white.[15] The Hispanic students were no longer predominantly Puerto Rican and the white students were as likely to have been born in Russia as Rego Park.

This mosaic partly reflects City College's location in upper Manhattan. At Queens College, for example, many students come from the white suburbs on Long Island, and the College of Staten Island also draws from a less heterogeneous population. Still, the snapshot points to a systemwide phenomenon. Students entering CUNY today are less likely than those in 1970 to speak and write English as their native language. They are more likely to have completed their secondary education outside the United States. If they enter college from the city's high schools, they are less academically able than they were three decades ago. In 1998, two thirds of the Lehman College freshmen initially failed the writing skills test; less than 25 percent passed all three skills tests. Only 14 percent of the freshmen at Medgar Evers passed all three tests upon entry. Even at Queens College, perhaps academically the best CUNY campus, half the entering students failed one or more tests.[16]

In 1999, the Board of Trustees of CUNY embarked upon a radical course to remake the system. It voted to end all remediation in the four-year colleges and to deny admission to any student who had not passed the three skills tests.[17] The majority voted in favor of "raising standards" but not, it contended, against CUNY's historic mission of providing open access. Students unable to meet the new standards could enroll in one of CUNY's two-year colleges to begin their work toward a bachelor's degree.

The board adopted this sweeping policy because the majority saw in it only gains and no costs. Courses wouldn't have to be pitched to the lowest level in the four-year colleges, and the proficient students would get better instruction. Dropout rates would decrease. Graduation rates would rise. CUNY's degrees would increase in value.[18]

In addition, the city's high schools would be forced to change their ways and provide better preparation. Students would also have to become more diligent, taking more academic courses in high school and making sure their skills were up to par. As one critic of CUNY, Heather MacDonald, pointed out, less than 19 percent of New York City's students take a Regent's diploma, signifying that a student has taken a solid academic curriculum consisting of courses such as algebra rather than consumer math.[19] (Prior to 1970, possession of a Regent's diploma was a requirement for admission.) The importance of a solid high school academic curriculum to college success cannot be overemphasized. Educational researcher Clifford Adelman notes that the academic breadth and depth of a student's high school curriculum better predicts college success than either grades or class standing.[20] The CUNY board expected its policy to stimulate a new work ethic among the city's students.[21]

However, even if the city's schools did a better job and even if the city's students took more responsibility, inadequate preparation and language difficulties would remain a fact of life for many high school graduates who wanted a college degree. These students would need remediation. The board insisted they would get it, in the community colleges or elsewhere. From its perspective, the new policy brought about a range of improvements for

CUNY without imposing any costs on students. The Board of Trustees wasn't abolishing remediation, according to its chair, only changing its venue.[22]

Indeed, the board's policy might seem to represent common sense. Why not move students in need of remediation to the community colleges? Aren't these institutions the appropriate venue for preparing such students to go on to senior college? James Traub thought it "not unreasonable to ask students who complete high school without . . . [adequate] academic credits . . . [to] complete them . . . in a community college."[23] Theodore Gross, Dean of Humanities at City College from 1972–1978, voiced a similar opinion in *Academic Turmoil*, his reflections on the open admissions experience:

> Public colleges in a democratic society have an obligation to educate as many students as they can accommodate. And this means that within an institution like City University, the community colleges must be available to those who have the most severe problems. . . . The four-year colleges cannot perform this task and still maintain programs and departments that offer what we consider to be sophisticated education.[24]

In the abstract, the strategy of moving all remediation to community colleges makes sense. In practice, however, an important consideration speaks against it. Community colleges seem in fact to hold back rather than propel students toward the baccalaureate. Studies show that students who enter junior colleges have vastly lower rates of bachelor's degree attainment than students who directly enter four-year institutions. A good deal of this disparity, of course, is predictable, given that students often enter junior college aiming only for an associate's degree, not a bachelor's; that students who attend junior college are typically less academically prepared than those who enter senior college; and that junior college students are more likely to work part- or full-time than senior college students. Nevertheless, a significant gap in bachelor's degree attainment remains even when these variables are controlled for. Students who have the same degree aspirations, high school preparation, and work responsibilities succeed less frequently in getting their bachelor's degree if they start their academic careers in a two-year college.[25]

In his 1994 study *The Contradictory College*, Kevin Dougherty provides evidence and analyses suggesting that community colleges, on average, have a dampening effect on progress toward a bachelor's degree. Students with the same abilities, aspirations, and backgrounds who enter community colleges "receive 11 to 19% fewer bachelor's degrees" than those who enter four-year institutions.[26] Dougherty points to three institutional features of community colleges that account for this effect.

First, baccalaureate aspirants drop out of community colleges more readily than out of four-year institutions, for two reasons. One is that community colleges provide much less financial aid than four-year colleges. Although community colleges are cheaper, more students attending them foot the entire bill.[27] The other reason is that because they are commuter schools, community colleges do not integrate students into a common community life very successfully. A freshman at a four-year school typically lives in a dorm with other students and participates in easily accessible campus activities. His emotional investment in the institution is stronger, and dorm life can keep his morale high. A community college student visits the campus for classes, then leaves. He has less informal out-of-class contact with other students and enjoys fewer opportunities for extracurricular activities.[28]

Second, the community college student faces a hurdle at transfer time. He must apply to another school, negotiate to get credit for courses already taken, and uproot himself for the move to a different campus. Many community college students give up at this point. By contrast, the student at a four-year college moves effortlessly from sophomore to junior year.[29]

Third, once in a four-year college, community college transferees drop out at a greater rate than those who started there as freshmen. They often fail to get full credit for all their junior college courses, they have a harder time integrating themselves into campus life (by junior year, most students are living off campus and have already formed various social networks), and they experience "transfer shock" when their efforts in class yield lower grades than they received at their previous institution.[30]

These broad structural features mean that the barriers to a successful baccalaureate are higher if the same student begins in junior college instead of senior college. Studies by David Lavin and associates show that this effect operates in the CUNY system as well. They found that "two-year entrants were 19 percentage points less likely to earn a baccalaureate than comparable students who started college in a four-year school."[31] The gap arises partly from two-year entrants not proceeding onward to senior college and partly from their lesser success even when they do. Lavin and associates found in their study of the open admissions cohorts that "senior college natives did considerably better than community college transfers with comparable high school averages."[32]

Not only do certain factors in community college culture discourage bachelor's degree aspirants from pushing forward to senior college, but the quality of classroom instruction in junior college is generally inferior to senior college instruction. Transfer students from community colleges are therefore less prepared for senior college work. Thus, a CUNY policy of shifting the remediation burden to community colleges could mean that fewer of New York's "proletariat" will work their way into the ranks of the college-educated than they do now. The policy could exact a toll in the success rates of disadvantaged students.

The board's we-can-have-our-cake-and-eat-it-too attitude precluded an explicit discussion of tolerable trade-offs between toughened standards at CUNY and diminished opportunity. In this respect, the board's view was the perfect mirror image of the view expressed by some of open admission's early proponents. The goals of academic excellence and equal opportunity were not opposed, these proponents insisted; instead, they mutually reinforced one another.[33] Hard decisions about which goal to sacrifice needn't be made—on this the board joined hands with some proponents of open admissions.

No viable plan for academic reform at CUNY can ignore the special characteristics of the urban, polyglot, economically struggling population it serves. Both James Traub and Heather MacDonald provide portraits of CUNY students truly out of place on a college campus, continually failing their skills tests, mired in remedial courses, unable to read and write, wasting their own time and the resources of the city and state. Excluding these students would seem a legitimate first step in improving standards at CUNY. At the same time, both Traub and MacDonald provide examples of "diamonds in the rough," students whose initial academic records were checkered with deficiencies yet who seized the opportunity to proceed successfully to a degree. Given CUNY's historic legacy as a conduit of opportunity for New York City's "proletariat," a policy of raising standards ought not diminish opportunity for such enterprising students.

How can policy distinguish between the two kinds of students? One way is to differentiate among deficiencies. As the research by Clifford Adelman suggests, if a student is weak in math, say, but not in reading and writing, that lack usually can be remedied successfully in college. The same is true for a student deficient only in writing. Students who face remediation in more than one area, however, have a much rockier time. The amount of remediation matters. More importantly, the kind matters. Inability among native speakers of English to read well constitutes a far more serious impediment to a successful college career than deficiencies in math and writing. Observes Adelman: "When reading is at the core of the problem, the odds of success in college environments are so low that other approaches are called for."[34]

One option, then, in seeking to raise standards would be to exclude from the senior colleges native speakers of English who cannot pass the reading skills test. (Interestingly, the Board of Trustees, in excluding from four-year programs all students who fail the freshman skills tests, made an exception for students whose first language is other than English. These students were among those Traub depicted at City College as fighting, and often overcoming, high hurdles to getting an education.)

FROM POLICY VOTED TO POLICY ENACTED

Because the CUNY board's new policy meant amending the university's master plan, it had to be approved by the Regents of the "University of the State of New York" (not to be confused with the State University of New York), a body with the power to regulate all public education in the state from kindergarten to graduate school.

The deliberations of the Regents did not lack for input. They had three major studies to draw upon, all produced after the Board of Trustee's January 1999 vote. The first was the report of an advisory task force on the university appointed by Mayor Giuliani and led by Benno Schmidt, chairman of Edison Schools and former president of Yale University. The "Schmidt Report" was an exhaustive multivolume study of CUNY's financial, administrative, and academic condition, with many recommendations for making the university system more coherent, accountable, and stable.

In particular, the report was blunt about the "appalling educational deprivation of so many entering CUNY students" and its effect on the system's senior colleges.[35] Not a single one of these colleges, it noted, "was attracting a student body that would fall into the top half of student bodies nationwide in academic promise for college. CUNY is starkly unique among American public university systems of any size in having not a single senior college whose entering students are on average in the first or second quartile of academic achievement and promise.[36] The Schmidt Report urged CUNY to differentiate strongly among its many campuses. At least two of the senior colleges should "become flagship institutions which can attract student bodies of high academic promise."[37] Among the other four-year campuses, some should be more, some less, selective.[38] Finally, responsibility for remediating academic deficiencies should fall to the community colleges.[39] The Schmidt Report went on to recommend that CUNY scrap its skills tests because they had no scientific validity and replace them with nationally recognized assessment instruments. It further recommended using the SAT in the admissions process.[40]

The second study came from the Bar Association of New York City. It decried the rigidity of the board's policy and worried about its impact on minority students in particular. The Bar Association report feared that the new direction planned for CUNY would entail a real cost in opportunity, and that it was based on an unduly narrow view of "excellence":

Excellence [the report argued] should be measured by the achievements of the *graduates* of an institution, not by its *entrants*—an excellent university with CUNY's mission should *raise* the levels of achievement. It is relatively easy to take high-achieving incoming students and then graduate them with high achievement, but also important to take students who are ill-prepared and grad-uate them with high levels of achievement. This has been CUNY's contribution to this city.[41]

The report was silent, however, on the alchemy that produces high-achieving graduates from ill-prepared entrants.

The third report came from a consultant group commissioned by the Regents themselves. It endorsed the CUNY policy with reservations and, like the Bar Association report, deplored its inflexibility.

The actual, amended CUNY plan presented to the Regents in September 1999 had evolved from the bare bones simplicity of the trustees' January pol-icy vote into a baroque scheme that promised to affect adversely very few students. Whereas the January 1999 vote by the board seemed clearly to say, "Eliminate remediation at the senior colleges and put it in the community colleges,"[42] the actual plan didn't eliminate *remediation* in the senior colleges but only *remedial courses.* Even then the plan permitted these courses still to be taught on senior college campuses *in disguise,* so to speak.

Following the recommendation of the Schmidt Report, CUNY now allows applicants with the requisite high school grades or class ranking to pass the skills hurdle in several ways. One way is to pass CUNY's new skills tests. Another is to demonstrate competence in reading or writing by scoring 480 on the verbal SAT, 20 on the ACT, or 75 on the Regents English Exam. Finally, students can demonstrate competence in math by scoring 480 on the math SAT, 20 on the ACT, or 75 on the new Mathematics A Regents Exam or the Sequential II or III Exam.[43] This tripartite screen excludes fewer stu-dents, because some who might fall short on one might nevertheless succeed on another. Second, those applicants who "fail high" on a screen can be admitted to a new program called Prelude to Success. They begin their fresh-man year at a senior college but enroll in community college courses taught by community college instructors on the senior college campus.[44] At the end of the first term, those students who have passed all their classes, including remedial courses, are automatically enrolled in the senior college. Thus, tech-nically in compliance with the board's policy, all remedial *courses* are taught *by* (though not *at*) community colleges.

SEEK, ESL (English as a Second Language), and regular students enrolled in a senior college who need remediation now have available to them no remediation *courses,* to be sure, but they have expanded "tutoring centers, writing centers, math laboratories, and academic support services."[45] They are able to receive "supplemental instruction" as an adjunct to regular courses.[46] "We must continue to remediate at the senior colleges," insisted CUNY's Chancellor.[47]

Finally, CUNY anticipates that fewer and fewer students will find the screens an insuperable barrier. One reason is that the university campuses offer Summer Skills Immersion programs for high school graduates. Students who fail a skills test can join one of these free, intense training exercises to strengthen their reading, writing, and math. In recent years, enrollment in Summer Immersion has doubled, serving 18,000 students in 1999, 80 percent of whom, according to CUNY's Chancellor, passed through the program successfully and enrolled at a senior college in the fall.[48] Aspiring applicants can also take intersession, fall, or spring versions of this program.

These immersion opportunities have diminished the number of senior college aspirants who can't overcome the skills hurdle, especially when taken in combination with two further initiatives, one by CUNY and the other by the state of New York. The state is toughening high school graduation requirements and will eventually require all students to pass Regents examinations in several core academic subjects. In addition, the university is expanding its high school/college partnership program, College Now. Begun nearly two decades ago, community and senior college campuses join forces with high schools, offering diagnostic tests to juniors and providing free skills instruction, either at the high school or the college campus. Currently about half the city's high schools participate.[49] Aggressively utilized, the College Now program can intervene years before students graduate from high school, encouraging them to consider college, enroll in academic subjects, participate in special sessions with college faculty, and, if they are succeeding, take further college credit-bearing courses on one of the college campuses.[50]

The new policies at CUNY have raised academic standards without apparently diminishing opportunities for New York City students.[51] Students, high schools, and CUNY's constituent campuses have all lifted their performance to meet the new bar. But the new bar is not very high. A combined SAT score of 960 as a minimum threshold will not change the fact, noted by the Schmidt Report, that the CUNY senior colleges enroll large numbers of mediocre and struggling students. Through the creation of an Honors College and "flagship programs," CUNY hopes to attract more bright city high school graduates. But even if it is wildly successful, their added numbers will not raise any of the campuses to the level of top public universities elsewhere in the nation.

While in 1960 City College stood second only to Berkeley in many respects, the two schools have since taken very divergent paths. In 1960, California adopted a master plan for public higher education that called for sharp differentiation in the roles of different institutions. The campuses of the California State system would enroll the top 30 percent of high school graduates; the campuses of the University of California system would enroll the top 12.5 percent. For the rest, the community college system would constitute the portal to a bachelor's degree. The basic terms of this plan have shaped higher education in California for the last forty years.

In the 1960s City College and its sister campuses enrolled the top 20 percent of New York City high school graduates; after open admissions they generally have been far less selective. This is not a criticism. CUNY could not have followed a path much different from the one it did. What constrains CUNY is not misguided policy gone awry—although some of the shibboleths of open admissions enthusiasts were dubious—but the very nature of the constituency it serves. The population of New York City is very different than it was forty years ago. Nor is it politically feasible to cut loose one or two of the CUNY four-year campuses from the rest and turn them into flagship institutions taking students with average SAT scores between 1200 and 1450 (Berkeley's numbers). CUNY shows both the possibilities and costs of admitting students who range widely in academic competence. Students who would never have gotten a college degree found their way into CUNY after open admissions and—although it took many of them as long as fourteen years—ended up with bachelor's degrees.[52] The price of educating students at very different levels of academic preparation, however, was to make CUNY campuses less attractive to New York City's highest achieving high school graduates.

REMEDIATION, SECOND CHANCES, AND COMMUNITY COLLEGES

CUNY has not been alone in wanting to confine remediation to the community college level. Remedial classes are ubiquitous not only in community colleges; 80 percent of public four-year colleges offer them as well, as do 60 percent of private colleges. Nationwide, 30 percent of all first-time freshmen in college are enrolled in one or more remedial courses.[53]

Many state systems have begun phasing out remediation at the senior college level. Georgia, Florida, Massachusetts, and California have all undertaken plans to limit or eliminate altogether the remediation available to students in their four-year institutions.[54] Students needing remedial courses will have to seek them out in community colleges.

As the work of Dougherty as well as Lavin and his colleagues has shown, however, funneling all baccalaureate aspirants who need remediation through community colleges may effectively diminish opportunities for some students, because the barriers are higher when students start out in junior instead of senior college.

This broad-brush portrait doesn't hold in all cases, of course. For example, the CUNY student who transfers from Manhattan Community College to Hunter College is moving from one nearby commuter school to another. Moreover, the "articulation" between her courses at Manhattan CC and the requirements at Hunter may operate more smoothly than in other cases.[55]

Community colleges could do better in facilitating transfer to further institutions. For example, while 24 percent of community college students overall transfer to four-year institutions (compared to 11 percent of urban community college students), at Palo Alto College in San Antonio, 55 percent of the students move on to four-year institutions. Ninety percent of its students enroll in transfer-oriented programs.[56] However, Palo Alto's success points to the general problem that prompts Dougherty to call the community college a "contradictory" institution. Unlike most community colleges, Palo Alto limits its vocational offerings. It remains heavily oriented toward a liberal arts curriculum. By contrast, the vocational emphasis at most community colleges crowds out liberal arts offerings and demoralizes both faculty and students in nonvocational tracks.[57]

However, the vocational emphasis of community colleges is not simply an evil to be remedied. These institutions are supported in considerable part by local taxes, and their offerings reflect the desires of both local employers and students. A great many potential community college users—in fact, the great majority—want no more than an associate's degree or a study certificate, or even less. For example, more than 800,000 students take classes in the North Carolina community college system, but fewer than 150,000 take courses for credit toward a degree. The rest are local workers upgrading their technical skills with a noncredit course or two. Moreover, of the credit-enrolled students, if they follow the national pattern, 60 percent are pursuing associate's degrees in some area of vocational studies.[58]

Although not all community college systems mirror the North Carolina pattern, all comprise institutions heavily weighted toward vocational training. This weighting reflects a legitimate and significant local demand for postsecondary training that falls short of "higher education" as we've been (perhaps prejudicially) characterizing it. Unfortunately, this weighting also produces institutional cultures that impede progress toward a baccalaureate.

Thus, in thinking about increased opportunities for postsecondary education, one appropriate entering point is reform at the community college level. It is not a law of nature that vocational and liberal arts curricula cannot jointly flourish in one institution. Or that community colleges are unable to provide broad financial support for students who are already more hardpressed than the average college-goer. Or that four-year institutions set their course requirements without thought to the transferability of credits from local community college courses. Or that arts and sciences courses offered in the community college must be inferior to those offered in comparable four-year colleges. All these features of community colleges are amenable to policy intervention—some costing more money, some not. Indeed, reform efforts are already underway in many states to make the community colleges better springboards to the baccalaureate.

The community college system represents the most widely accessible "starting line" on the path to higher education, a line that almost any high school graduate can toe. The system doesn't equalize financial barriers to higher education—the financial barriers faced by the rich and the poor will always differ[59]—but it considerably attenuates their impact. For example, Prince George's Community College, near the University of Maryland, tells prospective applicants that it operates on the "philosophy that no student should be denied access to an education because of financial need," and then lists the various forms of aid, from Pell Grants to campus work opportunities, it can provide to the determined but financially hard-pressed aspirant. The financial obstacles can often—though not always—be reduced or overcome.

The more intractable problem for students from poor families is what happens years earlier that discourages them from aspiring to a college education in the first place and that leaves them unprepared for college work by the time they leave school. These outcomes can be tempered by various kinds of outside intervention, such as those in CUNY's College Now program and in a new federal government program, GEAR UP (Gaining Early Awareness and Readiness for Undergraduate Programs). Federal funds subsidize partnerships composed of colleges, allied middle and secondary schools, and community-based organizations. The resources of a partnership are directed toward intervening at the middle school level to elicit interest in college from sixth, seventh, and eighth graders; mentoring and guiding interested students along the path through high school; and guaranteeing financial support for their college work.[60] Although GEAR UP is only a few years old, it shows promise, already reaching out to more than a million students in low-income communities.[61] It and other "intervention" approaches are so important that we devote a chapter to them at the end of the book.

However, not all the barriers lower-income students face involve inferior preparation for college. In the next chapter we examine other obstacles such students confront.

5

How the Academically Rich
Get Richer

In chapter 1 we alluded to some unsurprising facts about the correlation between socioeconomic status and rates of going to and graduating from college. Students from lower-income families are underrepresented and those from higher-income families are overrepresented in institutions of higher education. At four-year institutions, the disproportion is particularly striking. In 1989–1990, entering students from the highest SES quartile outnumbered those in the lowest by more than 10 to 1.[1] At the most selective colleges, "only 11 percent of students are from the lower end of the economic spectrum."[2]

The most important reasons have been discussed in previous chapters. More affluent students typically grow up in households possessing greater financial resources and favored with other advantages that contribute to academic success. As a result of such advantages, affluent students on the whole learn more and acquire the skills necessary for higher education more readily than do students from less privileged backgrounds. These differences are reflected in a variety of measures of academic performance: test scores, grades, class rank, and breadth and depth of academic curriculum. Even though we may lament the educational disadvantages under which lower-income students labor, it's hard to deny that these handicaps render them on the whole less qualified academically than more affluent students who have had superior educational opportunities.

This last statement needs to be qualified in at least three ways. First, as we argued in chapters 2 and 3, which bundle of characteristics makes a person most suitable for a place in a college class, all things considered, is a complex question having to do with more than simply academic merit. It might include athletic or artistic talent, entrepreneurial ability, grit and determination, or the contribution a student makes to a school's diversity or overall composition.

Second, to the extent that attendance at or a degree from a selective college functions as a credential that opens doors to other desirable situations, or as a locus of networking opportunities that serve the same purpose, the academically less well-prepared can benefit just as much as the better-prepared. As far as the credentialing and networking functions go, what matters is possession of a status-conferring degree or a useful set of relationships, rather than academic traits acquired before or in college.

Third, insofar as students with lesser skills benefit from interacting with those who have more developed skills, students' suitability for selective institutions may not correlate directly with the level of their academic skills.[3]

Nevertheless, even if we acknowledge these points, it's clear that, other things being equal, students possessing better developed academic skills are more qualified for selective colleges than those whose skills are inferior, and that these traits correlate with socioeconomic status.

IRRELEVANT ADVANTAGES

But other advantages affluent students possess are not relevant in the same way: they do not genuinely enhance students' qualifications for admission. That these students possess what we shall call *irrelevant advantages* compounds the inequities in the college admissions process.

Irrelevant advantages are those that do not enhance students' real qualifications yet give them a leg up in admission to selective institutions. In chapter 2 we discussed some general and pervasive advantages of this kind: connections, old-boy networks, and the "rational search procedures" employers and admissions offices may use to simplify the tasks before them, such as giving less weight to the applications of students from less stellar high schools. In this chapter we discuss more specific examples of irrelevant advantages: money and financial aid; legacy preference; early admission policies; disparities between rich and poor students in the use of special accommodations for disabilities in test-taking; inequities in the quality of college counseling and, more generally, the competitive college culture in which privileged middle and high school students grow up. (We postpone discussion of one important issue that readers may think belongs here—coaching and test preparation—until chapter 7, for two reasons. First, its complexities are better understood once we have examined some of the technical issues concerning standardized tests and the SAT. Second, we argue that the advantages gained by coaching are in fact more modest than either the coaching companies or the behavior of large masses of students who flock to them would lead one to believe.)

The line between relevant and irrelevant advantages isn't always sharp. For example, more affluent students have much greater access to internships and other enriching experiences than do lower-income students. Their parents can and will pay to send them on exotic and educational summer adventures that, for $5,000, will buy a month of (choose one or more) community service, language immersion, and personal growth. These students are networked, through their parents, their parents' friends, and their friends' parents, to those in positions to dispense internships and jobs at leading media outlets, scientific, political, and cultural centers, and universities. They know scientists, journalists, fashion designers, TV personalities, and professors willing to take on high school interns. Poor students are not likely even to imagine such possibilities, and rarely have the connections to realize them.

But these experiences can produce both relevant and irrelevant advantages. When student interns learn useful lessons or acquire new skills, their qualifications improve. The advantage is relevant: they become more capable and more skilled than they were before. But fancy internships and summers abroad function partly as impressive lines on a resumé that can help students regardless of whether they have gained any skills. Observing ambitious high school students today, we find, not surprisingly, a mix of motives. Few act solely for strategic reasons: they want to gain the skills and experience that internships, work, and community service can bring. But they act (with their parents right behind them) partly for strategic reasons. They know that these credentials look good to colleges, whatever their real value. To that extent, the advantages produced are irrelevant.

We can disagree about which advantages are relevant—that is, which contribute to genuinely enhanced qualifications and which do not; and the line between the two categories is not always sharp. Nevertheless, some advantages are clearly irrelevant.

MONEY

Money is the most glaring example. However much socioeconomic status correlates with academic achievement, no one argues that having money or wealth in itself makes a student more qualified. Yet among equally able students, those who have more financial resources are more likely to go to college, and to graduate, than those who have less. High-achieving students who are poor are five times less likely to go to college than high-achieving students who are rich.[4] And the situation for low-income students has deteriorated over the last twenty years. Between 1980 and 1993, "the gap in enrollment rates between students from the lowest-income quartile and those from the other three quartiles grew by 12 percentage points."[5] The concentration of students from families with incomes below $30,000 at community colleges has increased, and low-income students are "increasingly rare" at four-year colleges.[6]

Three main factors account for the deteriorating financial picture for low-income students over the last two decades: college costs, the changing nature of federal aid, and the kind of aid provided by colleges and universities. We discuss them in order of increasing complexity.

College costs. The costs of going to college have increased sharply. Between 1981 and 2000, median family income in the United States rose 27 percent; tuition rose 112 percent at four-year private institutions and 106 percent at four-year public institutions.[7] In a recent survey, more than twenty-five public university systems reported raising tuition by between 10 and 20 percent in 2003–2004 over the previous year.[8] One central reason for this increase is that the contribution of both state and local governments to public colleges and universities has declined over the last fifteen years. In 1979–1980 "state governments contributed 45 percent of all of higher education revenues, almost all of it through direct support of state-run institutions. By 1992–1993, that share had fallen to 35 percent and has almost certainly fallen further since."[9] Offsetting these decreases are rises in tuition at state colleges and universities. In states whose public universities have high tuition rates, fewer students enroll, and the gap in enrollment between rich and poor students is wider than in states with lower tuition.[10] Although college enrollments are at an all-time high, lower-income students are, in economists' terms, "price-sensitive"; higher-income students are not.

The changing nature of federal aid. Although the federal government has contributed about the same share of public education revenues through aid to students since the mid-1970s, the nature of its aid has changed. Aid to students falls into three categories: grants or scholarships, loans, and work/ study opportunities. Over the last two decades, the proportion of federal loans has increased and the proportion of grants has decreased.

The primary source of federal grants to students since 1974 has been the Pell Grant program, which mainly serves low-income students and those from low-income families. Among students living with their families, 41 percent of Pell Grant recipients have families with annual incomes below $12,000 and 91 percent come from families with incomes below $30,000. Among independent students (those not living with their families), 73 percent have annual incomes below $12,000.[11] Independent students constituted a small minority of Pell Grant recipients when the program began, but since the mid-1980s they have been a majority.[12]

A 1995 study by the U.S. General Accounting Office shows that increasing subsidies to students through the Pell Grant correlates directly with decreasing the dropout rate, especially for minority students.[13] Yet the percentage of tuition covered by federal aid has decreased significantly, from 22 percent in 1986–1987 to 16 percent in 1992–1993.[14] In 2000–2001, the maximum Pell Grant was $3,300, covering about 40 percent of the costs at a four-year public college (compared to 77 percent in 1980) and about 15 percent at a private college.[15] The purchasing power of the Pell Grant is much less than it was twenty years ago.[16] And low-income students are often loath to take out loans and incur debts they're not sure they can repay.[17]

Aid from colleges and universities. Apart from federal loans, which account for about half of all student aid, the largest single source is colleges and universities themselves, which provide about 20 percent of student aid.[18] Here again, there have been changes in the way such aid is allocated, and on the whole these have not benefited lower-income students. Over the last decade, many four-year institutions, both public and private, have reserved an increasing proportion of their financial aid budgets for merit-based, as opposed to need-based, grants. In public institutions, more than half the aid given is not need-related; as a result, upper-income students constitute a larger share of students at state institutions than they used to.[19] These changes have occurred as admissions directors have been transformed into "enrollment managers," and as many colleges have begun to think of students as the airline industry conceives of passengers. Potential students are in the market for seats; like business travelers as compared to vacationers, they have different propensities to buy and thus varying "sensitivities to price," so colleges do well to charge them different prices depending on their willingness to pay.[20]

The issues surrounding merit-based versus need-based aid are complex, in part because of the varying circumstances surrounding different kinds of institutions. Here we summarize the most important developments.

According to a 1994 survey by the National Association of College Admissions Counselors (NACAC), 91 percent of the colleges who responded said they maintained a "need-blind" admissions policy until May 1. In other words, they did not consider students' ability to pay in making admissions decisions (until May 1). But only 20 percent said that they met 100 percent of the demonstrated need of students they accepted.[21]

The fifth who do meet students' full need are the most selective private colleges and universities in the country. With some exceptions, they practice "need-blind" admissions, they promise to meet the "full need" of students they admit, and they offer only need-based scholarships and no merit scholarships. (A few even among this select group, however, admit to taking a student's ability to pay into account for the last 5 or 10 percent of their classes.[22]) As economists Michael McPherson and Morton Owen Schapiro are careful to note, these colleges' need-blind and full-need policies do not demonstrate their moral superiority, rather their wealth and their surfeit of qualified applicants. Few institutions apart from the very richest and most sought after can afford *not* to balance students' financial need against other considerations in making decisions about admissions and financial aid.

Even institutions seemingly committed to need-blind admissions, meeting students' full need, and need-only scholarships sometimes depart from the purity of that model (this is even more true, of course, for the majority of schools not committed to these three principles). The most significant trend is "differential packaging"—providing more aid in the form of grant, less in the form of loan and work—to students a college especially wants to enroll, while offering less generous packages to students it cares less about attracting. Another practice is "gapping": offering aid packages that meet only some specified proportion of need. Under "admit/deny," admissions is need-blind, but students at the bottom of the admission pool are not offered financial aid. Such "merit-within-need" policies mean "the weakest students get saddled with loans and part-time work that make their already tenuous graduation prospects even lower."[23]

Important to the recent history of financial aid at highly selective institutions is a suit brought by the Justice Department in 1991 charging price-fixing against the Ivy League schools and MIT. Understanding its causes and consequences sheds some light on the nexus of issues surrounding financial aid, not only at elite institutions but at others as well.

After World War II and the Korean War, colleges began to see—in part through the G.I. Bill—the potential for increasing access to higher education.[24] But students were relatively scarce and colleges had to compete for them. In 1954 the College Scholarship Service (CSS), an offshoot of the College Board, was created with the aim of developing objective criteria for determining students' financial need. The working assumption was that a student with offers at several colleges that cost the same should, theoretically, receive roughly equivalent financial aid packages. Students could then choose their college on educational rather than on financial grounds, and the colleges could avoid bidding wars. For some years the Ivy League schools and fourteen other selective private schools—known as the Overlap Group—met every spring to discuss the financial situation of students admitted to more than one college in the group. In keeping with CSS's assumption that need is objective, they aimed to offer such students equivalent aid packages.

Such was the situation when the Justice Department expressed concern about antitrust violations in the late 1980s. The Ivy League schools eventually agreed to stop sharing information about particular students before making offers, although they were still permitted to discuss definitions of need in a general way. But the result has been a resumption of the bidding wars that CSS was created to avoid. Especially with the evolution of practices such as differential packaging, the concept of need has been interpreted in an elastic way, allowing different colleges to offer a given student varying financial aid packages and students in apparently similar financial situations different financial aid packages.[25]

The current situation clearly benefits students who are sought after by a number of elite schools. But many students gain nothing, and some—those who might have received aid that instead goes to a few stars—lose out. The colleges, meanwhile, find themselves in a financial arms race. To keep up with rivals in the competition for students, each college has to up the ante; in the end everyone ends up as they would have if no one had bid up in the first place. When everyone stands on tiptoe no one sees any better.[26]

Such "prisoner's dilemma" situations are not limited to elite colleges and universities. Schools down a notch (or two or three) from the most selective can find themselves in the same situation, bidding for students against other institutions with similar profiles. These schools—with smaller aid budgets, endowments, and applicant pools than the most selective colleges—can afford such wasteful expenditures less than their higher-ranked cousins. They make no claims to be need-blind or to meet students' full need, and they explicitly offer merit scholarships to attract desirable students.[27]

Yet for these colleges the decision-making is more complex than for the top-ranked schools. Not only are they trying to attract students away from colleges "in their league" (as are the most selective schools); they also aim to draw students away from higher-ranked institutions by offering them aid they would not receive at those schools. So, for example, a second-tier college might offer a generous merit scholarship to a student accepted without aid at a first-tier school.

The use of merit aid and "merit-within-need" aid is associated, then, with two kinds of competition among schools.[28] One is the attempt by colleges to recruit students away from more prestigious institutions. When they succeed, the result is that more qualified students are less concentrated in the most prestigious institutions and are instead distributed more evenly among colleges of different ranks. This, in turn, may have at least two kinds of benefits. First, insofar as less qualified students benefit from classroom and campus interaction with the more qualified, the educational climate at those institutions could be improved.[29] Second, one might speculate that over time the more even distribution of talented students among colleges could somewhat mitigate the name-brand, winner-take-all mentality that seems to characterize prevailing attitudes. Each of these effects is beneficial from an equity point of view because basic goods—quality education and status—would be more evenly distributed across students attending institutions at different levels.

But the other aspect of competition—schools vying with others in their league for the same group of students—benefits no one except the most sought-after students. Students in that group who are in need of financial assistance ought to receive it, of course, according to consistent criteria that dictate similar aid packages at similarly priced institutions. For example, either home equity should count among a family's assets for purposes of computing need, or it shouldn't. The same criteria should apply everywhere. But arms races in which institutions at the same level compete for students impose costs both on the institutions and on students for whom the price of an education makes a significant difference.

To summarize, several factors depress the college prospects of low-income students and others for whom the price of a college education enters into the decision about whether, or where, to attend. These include the rising costs of four-year colleges and universities; the declining proportion of grants relative to loans in aid to students from the federal government; the increasingly dominant commercial and consumerist vision of financial aid prevailing among institutions of higher education; and the dilution of the ideal of need-based aid at both public and private universities.

THE LEGACY OF LEGACY

Most selective colleges follow an admissions policy of legacy preference. That is, they accept children of alumni at a higher rate than other applicants. (They also favor siblings of students and alumni, as well as children of faculty.) Data from thirty selective colleges and universities (the data used by Shulman and Bowen in their study of college athletics, discussed in chapter 2) show that for the years 1976, 1989, and 1999, legacy applicants were on average 20–26 percent more likely to be admitted than nonlegacies, after controlling for SAT scores.[30] By contrast, the admissions advantage for minorities declined sharply during this period—for men, from 49 percent in 1976 to 18 percent in 1999; for women, from 51 percent to 20 percent. Moreover, the U.S. Department of Education Office for Civil Rights found that admitted legacies to Harvard and Yale in the 1980s had lower scores "in all quantifiable areas of admission criteria."[31]

The details surrounding legacy policies are often shrouded in mystery. Legacy, after all, is a form of hereditary privilege, and even to those without a particularly egalitarian bent it may seem out of place in a society that prides itself on rewarding merit. So it is hard to find out the exact parameters of legacy: who counts as a legacy and how much legacy counts. Most private universities consider as legacies only the offspring of graduates of the undergraduate college, and not the children of alumni of a university's graduate and professional schools.[32] Do grandchildren count, if no one in the intervening generation is an alumnus? Some schools say they give preference to legacies only if they apply early; others are silent on this matter. Equally difficult to discover—although of great interest to many students and their parents—is just how much of a difference being a legacy makes.

The argument for legacy preference takes two forms, which we might call the "soft" and "hard" versions respectively. The soft version rests on the value of community; it says that the identity and vitality of a university are partly constituted by tradition and human relationships and are therefore buttressed by the glue of family ties. As the father of a Harvard student whose college ties go back to her great-great-grandfather put it, "One of the salient characteristics of a college like Harvard is its history. Legacy students are a visible representation of that history and make it real for the students who are attending."[33] Stanford argued in 1958 that "strong family ties with Stanford are valuable in themselves."[34]

The hard version of the argument for legacy—generally thought to be its primary rationale—rests on the assumed financial benefits of admitting the family members, especially the offspring, of alumni. Universities believe that when they admit the children of alumni, the chances increase that parents and children will give money or other valuable assets to the institution. "Without legacy preference," according to Sheldon Steinbach of the American Council on Education, "there would be a significant decrease in giving from a core body of traditional support—families in which at least a second generation has gone to the institution."[35]

To put legacy in context, it's useful to see how it has evolved over time. Until well into the twentieth century, few colleges were selective. A survey in 1920 of the most famous colleges and universities in the country showed that only thirteen were turning away any applicants at all; Yale accepted everyone who satisfied its entrance requirements.[36] As late as 1950, Stanford University admitted 77 percent of all who applied; the following year it accepted 85 percent.[37]

In the late teens, Dartmouth College, at the time one of the most popular schools in the country, began to consider tightening its admissions standards. Its president, Ernest M. Hopkins, who spearheaded the effort, later recalled the reaction—to the contemporary reader barely credible—of one of the trustees of the college:

> When I got done, Mr. Streeter leaned over and said very seriously and without the slightest intention of being humorous, "Mr. President, do I understand rightly that you seriously propose sometime in the future to decline the application of somebody who really wants to enter Dartmouth? . . . Well, now I guess this is all right and I'll probably vote for it, but, by God, I've got to have a little time on it after forty years of watching Dartmouth grab and hogtie every prospect that wandered inadvertently into town with a hazy idea of sometime going to college somewhere.[38]

In 1922, Dartmouth became the first institution to institute a formal admissions process. "Exceptional scholarship" was the first of its nine criteria, listed as a "sufficient basis for selection." "High scholarship" was next— "prima facie evidence" for selection. Other criteria included "personal ratings," "the principle of occupational distribution," and "the principle of geographical distribution." Criterion number 7 read: "All properly qualified *Sons of Dartmouth Alumni* and *Dartmouth College Officers* [shall be admitted]."[39]

Colleges and universities became more selective beginning in the 1920s partly as a way to exclude Jews, whose increasing numbers and academic prowess threatened the WASP character of the best-known schools. Ivy League institutions, among others, tried to find indirect ways—in addition to explicit quotas—of limiting the numbers of Jewish students. Alumni in particular voiced the concern that Jewish students, if not restricted, would take up a great number of places in the class.[40] In 1925, Yale's board of admission decided that "any limitation on enrollment would not exclude any son of a Yale graduate."[41]

Obviously the climate of college admissions has changed a great deal since the 1920s, and especially over the last forty or so years.[42] A legacy with minimally respectable credentials could expect to be admitted even to very prestigious universities in 1960. (It was said that although legacy could not raise the dead it could heal the sick.) That is no longer true. University admissions offices today are more likely to say that a legacy connection is a thumb on the scale, or that between otherwise equally qualified candidates the legacy connection can make a difference in the outcome. In no sense is legacy status a sufficient condition for admission.

That seems a far cry from the old policy, and it is. But legacy still plays an important role in admissions to selective colleges, as the figures from Shulman and Bowen cited above show. As admissions has become more fiercely competitive, universities find many more highly qualified applicants than they can accept. For example, in 2001 Yale University had close to 15,000 applicants for 1,300 slots. It accepted 14 percent of applicants—about 2,100 students. Harvard, Princeton, Columbia, Brown, and Stanford boast similar acceptance rates, and each year the numbers of applicants increase. Over the last decade alone, applications—for approximately the same number of places—have increased at many colleges and universities by 50 to 100 percent.[43] In this climate, ambitious students have reason to be grateful for the mere thumb on the scale.

Is there anything wrong with preferences for legacies? Compare legacy with "development" cases, where a university admits a student whose family makes or is expected to make a large financial contribution to the institution.[44] (Similarly relevant are preferences for children of the famous—the senator's daughter, the movie star's son.) These cases seem to involve a direct tit-for-tat. Although it is easy to understand why colleges might admit the children of big donors, and while one might even think doing so is sometimes justified on pragmatic grounds, the practice makes us uneasy. The promise of financial gain seems an inappropriate basis for distributing the good of higher education;[45] in the worst case it smacks of bribery.

Universities suggest that they approach legacy differently—that they do not look at a family's past giving practices, or its wealth, when deciding whether to admit the children of alumni. Rather, the legacy advantage involves a general assumption by the institution ("Families of legacy admits tend to contribute more than others") rather than particular knowledge of a family's wealth and giving habits ("This family has given a lot of money, so we will give their child a significant boost"). That vaguer basis—the broad generalization as against the particular judgment about a family—seems less odious; it does not imply a clear tit-for-tat.

We say that universities *suggest* that this is how they approach legacy applicants. But suppose that, as some suspect, in deciding which alumni children to admit, universities do look at the family profile. Has the family made contributions before? How much? How rich are they? If calculations of this kind enter into the admissions decision, legacy begins to resemble the development cases that most people find troubling.

It is natural to reply that the question in both the development and the legacy cases (even those based on generalizations rather than on individual examination of the applicant's family) is whether the applicant is *qualified* for admission. If not, our doubts and worries are justified: the students and their families are *buying* their way in, and that's wrong. But if a student possesses the qualifications for admission and the preference is simply a thumb on the scale (a "plus factor," in the jargon of affirmative action), there's nothing wrong with giving preference to legacies (or to rich applicants). So it might be argued.

One problem with this response is that it conflicts with the claims by selective institutions—described in the previous section—to subscribe to "need-blind" admissions policies. In general, legacies at selective colleges come from privileged backgrounds; when the motive for admitting them is partly the prospect of financial gain, the admissions criterion is in effect not need-blind. More important, in the current climate of admissions, where enormous numbers of students can genuinely be said to "possess the qualifications for admission," the use of legacy makes more of a difference than the argument suggests. If we understand the decisive question to be *"Could* this student be admitted but for the prospect of financial gain for the university?"* this way of using legacy rules out the unqualified. But if the question is *"Would* this student be admitted but for the prospect of financial gain?" then it chooses a subset of privileged students on account of their privileged status from the set of qualified applicants.

If legacy policies make a contribution to the identity and cohesiveness of a college, that is an argument in their favor that may be mission-related. Colleges may, after all, have among their goals the aim to foster community.

(One may nevertheless remain skeptical that the presence of a legacy truly enriches the experience of the student body.) The financial argument has no such connection with the basic goals of the institution. It's not part of a university's mission to make money, even though financial health is necessary for it to carry out its missions. At best, legacy policies for gain are a concession to the vicissitudes of the real world.

One thing is clear. Both defenses of legacy preference—the soft as well as the hard—give a boost to those who need it least, for reasons having nothing to do with their qualifications.

EARLY DECISION

Early admission policies developed in the 1950s. Today many colleges have adopted them, and they exert a great deal of influence on the admissions process. Such programs fall into two categories. Early decision programs require students to apply by November 1 or November 15, in contrast with the January deadlines typical of regular admissions. In exchange for a decision from the college (acceptance, rejection, or deferral to the regular-admissions pool) by the middle of December, the student promises to enroll if accepted. It follows that students can apply to only one early decision school. Students who are deferred or rejected then have a few weeks to put in applications to other colleges.

Early action programs adhere to the same schedule as early decision but are nonbinding: students get an answer from the college in December but are free to apply elsewhere during the regular admissions process and make up their minds in the spring on the regular admissions cycle. The last few years have seen great upheaval in early admissions policies, with some colleges moving from early action to binding early decision, and others going in the opposite direction. For the 2003 admissions year Yale and Stanford switched from binding early decision to early action, with the proviso that a student apply early to no other school—a rule that until now has not applied to early action programs. At this point the only certainty is that the admissions landscape is in a period of instability and flux and that policies will continue to change for the foreseeable future.

The rationale for early decision policies from the colleges' point of view is obvious. The college can be certain of securing a proportion (increasingly, in some cases, a large proportion—30 percent or 40 percent or even more) of its entering class with enthusiasts for the school—students who require no wooing or stroking once they have been admitted. But colleges have even stronger reasons to favor early decision. They are in the business of "crafting a class," in the words of Elizabeth Duffy and Idana Goldberg[46]: not simply admitting a group of qualified students but finding the right mix and filling particular niches. Early decision enables the admissions office to lock in that much-needed French horn player or football quarterback (assuming they apply). From these perspectives, early decision is a rational and efficient approach to matching supply and demand.

There is also a less obvious, and more strategic, reason for colleges' interest in early decision. The more students a college accepts early, the lower its acceptance rate from the larger pool of regular decision applicants and the higher its "yield"—the number of accepted students who ultimately enroll. These factors have played a central role in an institution's ranking in *U.S. News & World Report*'s annual guide to colleges and other similar guides. Colleges zealously monitor the figures, which—because students zealously monitor them—can have powerful effects on an institution's fortunes.[47]

From the student's point of view as well, the reasons for preferring early admission seem clear. To gain admission to your first-choice college in December rather than April, after having filed only one application and waiting only a few weeks—instead of sweating over a half dozen or more and learning only months later of the results—what student wouldn't take that path if she could?

But serious drawbacks accompany these advantages of early decision policies. Some affect students as a whole, and some affect less privileged students in particular. Three general problems are commonly cited. One is the tendency of early decision policies to drive the preoccupation with college admissions to even earlier in students' high school careers, since those who apply early decision must commit to a college at the very beginning of senior year. Its clear that among higher-income families, the obsession with college admissions has been advancing to earlier and earlier in high school, and early decision policies probably contribute to this trend.

A second criticism is that early admissions policies cut short the high school educational experience, which for early decision applicants, it is said, ends by December of senior year. This complaint is probably exaggerated because all students are effectively finished with work that will influence their college chances by the middle of senior year. Some argue that early decision applicants have nothing to worry about after junior year. But the early decision college may look at mid-senior year grades; more important, students don't know until nearly the end of the first semester whether they have been admitted, and therefore have to continue to take schoolwork seriously at least until then.

A more serious problem is that early decision policies contribute to the "gaming" of college admissions—students' increasing reliance on strategic thinking in choosing a college. Why does early decision encourage gaming? The reasons have to do with the fact that, as a recent study has demonstrated, students who apply to college early decision have a significantly better chance—worth about 100 SAT points—of being admitted than do students who apply during the regular cycle.[48] Even if a senior hasn't completely made up his mind by the fall, he has an interest in committing himself to a particular college. Students may also strategize by applying early to a college that is not their top choice but to which they think they have a better chance of being admitted if they apply early.

These problems should not excite our pity. It's hard to feel sorry for the student who applies to Columbia early decision, although she would really rather attend Yale, because she thinks she's more likely to get into Columbia. If these were the only problems created by early decision, we might well conclude that its benefits outweighed its costs. Its most serious flaw, however, is that it gives already privileged students one more advantage in the admissions process—an advantage having nothing to do with superior qualifications. It does so for several reasons.

One has to do with information. More affluent students have better information, and they have it earlier, than less affluent students. Lower-income students are less oriented toward college admissions generally, less knowledgeable about the pluses and minuses of particular colleges and their own qualifications for them, and less likely to know of the advantages of applying early. Moreover, few students want to apply early decision—and thereby commit themselves to attending if accepted—to a school they haven't visited. Affluent students begin looking at colleges in their junior year (at the latest), and so are more likely to feel, and to be, in a reasonable position to apply by November. Lower-income students rarely make the junior year spring break tour to Amherst and Harvard and Brown, and would therefore be taking a risk by committing themselves so early to one college.

Most important are the financial aspects of early decision. Students admitted early tend to receive less financial aid because they lock themselves into matriculating and the colleges have no incentive to win their favor. (Students can be released from the commitment to attend if the school does not offer sufficient financial aid to make enrollment feasible. But the process is cumbersome and unpleasant—not how a student wants to spend her time while nursing more college applications.) Those who apply early deprive themselves of the opportunity to compare financial aid packages and negotiate with colleges in the spring.

These problems arise in part from the rules that now govern financial aid decisions at selective colleges. In the section of this chapter on money, we described how some selective schools (the Overlap Group) used to meet to agree on need levels for accepted students so that students received roughly equal financial aid packages from different schools and the colleges avoided bidding wars. When in the early 1990s the Justice Department struck down Overlap, these schools had to change their procedures. As a result, students accepted to more than one school can now receive very different financial aid packages. In one recent case we know of, a student who applied regular decision to both Yale and Princeton received a $3,000 financial aid offer from Yale and $19,000 from Princeton. (Since the Ivy League schools offer no merit aid, both were allegedly need-based scholarships.) Clearly, had this student applied early decision to Yale, he would have been significantly disadvantaged.

Colleges obviously gain from these student handicaps. And because the pool of early applicants is richer than the regular applicant pool, the greater the number of students a college accepts early, the lighter its financial burden is likely to be.

Members of minority groups, financial aid applicants, and public school students are in fact less likely to apply early, almost certainly for these reasons.[49] Early decision policies, then, create one more way for more affluent students to get a leg up over lower-income students in the college admissions process.

AN UNEVEN OUTBREAK OF DISABILITIES

Between 1992 and 1997, the number of students who took the SAT I with "accommodations"—special test conditions—as a result of disabilities doubled; the number of students taking the test with accommodations for disabilities has increased an average of 14 percent a year. From 1989–1990 to 1995–1996, the number of students who took the ACT with accommodations nearly tripled, from 8,519 to 23,463.[50]

A student may require special accommodations because he is blind and needs a Braille or cassette version of the test, or, as in a recent case, because he has no hands and needs a computer with a trackball.[51] But these are unusual cases. According to the College Board, "about 90 percent of all requests for accommodations are for students with learning disabilities and over two-thirds of these accommodations are simply for extended time."[52] The learning disabilities include ADD (attention deficit disorder), ADHD (attention deficit hyperactivity disorder), and dyslexia. Some students with disabilities receive time-and-a-half, some get twice as much time as nondisabled test-takers, and a few are permitted even more time.

Testing with disabilities raises several questions about fairness and justice. One concerns comparability. The aim of giving disabled students extra time (or other benefits) is to compensate them for their disabilities so that their opportunities to perform their best equal those of nondisabled students. But the question is how much extra time a particular learning disabled student should be given: too much time would give him an unfair advantage, too little would not compensate him adequately.[53] Testing agencies such as the Educational Testing Service (ETS) are under increasing pressure to pay close attention to this question, which has to be decided on an individual basis.

A second issue concerns disclosure of the accommodations made for disabled students. In 2000, Mark Breimhorst, the student without hands who took the GMAT on a computer with a trackball, brought a federal lawsuit challenging as discriminatory ETS's policy of sending out scores with the notation "Scores obtained under special conditions."[54] Breimhorst and his lawyers argued that this flag is a scarlet letter that stigmatizes disabled students and renders them more susceptible to discrimination. In July 2002, the College Board announced that as of September 2003 it would no longer flag the scores of disabled students. Some fear that the new policy will result in an increase in the number of students who apply for special accommodations—including requests from students who are not genuinely disabled.[55]

The problem of potential abuse is related to a third question of justice, which is most relevant to the subject of this chapter: the irrelevant advantages rich students have over poor. Students who take standardized tests with accommodations for learning disabilities—that is, who receive extended time—are much more likely to come from affluent families and schools, and the new policy of not flagging scores is likely to exacerbate the problem.

An audit by the state of California in 2000 showed "wide demographic disparities" among high school graduates in 1999 who took the SAT with extended time because of claimed learning disabilities. Students at private schools were four times more likely to get special accommodations than those in public school. The auditors found that "in six of seven school districts in wealthy areas," including Beverly Hills and Palo Alto, there were "questionable and potentially unwarranted cases of students receiving special treatment."[56] Claudette Sharpe, a guidance counselor at Eastern High School, a poor school in the District of Columbia, remembers only three students in twelve years who received extended time on the SAT.[57] According to the National Center for Policy Analysis, 10 percent of students at 20 New England prep schools got extra time on the SAT, while not one of 1,439 students at ten Los Angeles area high schools did.[58]

Affluent and educated parents often push to have their children classified as learning-disabled as early as elementary school. And as the California audit explained, "College admissions officers and high school counselors have been horrified to watch some parents shop around for a psychologist" who will give them documentation to show their child has a previously undiagnosed learning disability that will allow testing accommodations."[59] Parents of poor children and the teachers and counselors in poor schools are less likely to know about special services available for learning-disabled students and less likely to be aggressive in seeking them out.

It seems unlikely that the incidence of learning disabilities is greater among higher-income than lower-income students. Fairness may require that students with learning disabilities be granted extended time on standardized tests. Whether that means that more lower-income students should receive these special accommodations, or that fewer affluent students should, is a question we shall not attempt to answer here.

COLLEGE COUNSELING AND CONSPICUOUS
EDUCATIONAL CONSUMPTION

"College counseling" names a discrete activity performed by employees of high schools who inform and advise students about the college admissions process. But it also includes a much wider range of activities and information-sharing that shape students' college aspirations.

Begin with the formal college counseling process. In private and select public schools, a ratio of one counselor to fifty or sixty students is not unusual, and counselors may spend as much as six hours a year with each student. In most large public schools, the ratio may be one counselor to 300 students or more.[60] At Cardinal Hayes High School in the Bronx, a Catholic school serving many low-income students, the college counselor works with more than two hundred students while working a second job supervising custodians. When he explains the college admissions process at an assembly for juniors, most of them "have not given it a moment's thought." The college counselor at Grover Cleveland High School in Queens engages in a kind of academic triage, concentrating her efforts on the top third of more than 450 students, many of whom are impoverished immigrants.[61]

Among other things, counselors are responsible for writing a "counselor letter of recommendation" for each of their students. A counselor with hundreds of students will obviously be unable to say anything very meaningful about most of them, nor can she adequately advise so many students. These counselors are typically also responsible for other aspects of "guidance," whereas in elite schools counselors may be devoted to the college process alone. By contrast, letters from college counselors at elite schools tend to be rich with detail and nuance. These counselors are often extremely knowledgeable about the ins and outs of admissions (some may have been previously employed in the admissions offices of leading colleges and universities) and about students' prospects at different colleges. Such attention is almost unheard of at most public high schools.

Affluent students who demand more professional attention concerning their college prospects than their school counselors can provide sometimes avail themselves of the services of private college consultants. Admissions Consultants advertises a rate of $95 an hour on its website. Another company, College Admissions Consultants, offers a contractual relationship that provides ongoing access for a fee: four years of consultation beginning in ninth grade for $1,400, three years beginning in tenth grade for $1,200, etc.[62]

At least as important as the services provided by high school counselors or independent college consultants, however, is the general atmosphere in which more affluent students grow up and the very different environment in which lower-income students find themselves. There is strong evidence that by the ninth grade, and possibly as early as seventh grade, "most students have already developed occupational and educational aspirations," and that these are strongly related to socioeconomic status.[63] For affluent students, going to college—and more specifically going to high-status colleges—is in the air from the beginning of high school, or even earlier. They rely on various resources in addition to those provided by their schools: parents, other close adults, older siblings of friends and acquaintances who are already attending college, college guides, and an increasingly elaborate set of websites and online chat rooms. These students normally begin visiting colleges no later than junior year.

Ambitious high school students know that internships at scientific institutes, nonprofit organizations, and the like look good on one's college application. They know that colleges like to see a lot of Advanced Placement courses on the transcript. Until this year, affluent students knew they could employ "Score Choice," which allowed them to withhold SAT II results to colleges unless they were satisfied with their scores. As the College Board explained in its recent decision to abolish Score Choice, the policy "encouraged 'gamesmanship' and favored students wealthy enough to repeat tests."[64]

Lower-income students generally lack these resources and role models. Parental encouragement is the strongest factor predicting students' educational aspirations; parents' knowledge of financial aid possibilities is also crucial. But these factors are correlated with socioeconomic status. Poor students must rely mainly on their guidance counselors for information.[65] The guidance counselor at Grover Cleveland High School

> must micromanage everything for immigrant teenagers like Gerta, seeing that each deadline is met and that no piece of paper leaves her office stained with soda. An intact loving family is a blessing. But . . . [Gerta's parents] and others like them are helpless during college admissions season because they speak no English and know nothing of the American education system.[66]

Affluent students' problems are likely to lie at the opposite extreme: parents who believe that nothing less than a brand-name university will do and who exert enormous pressure on their children to attain the status to which the parents are or would like to become accustomed.

But these problems are not unrelated. Students who inflate their qualifications may squeeze out others who are equally qualified although not as slickly packaged. Admissions officers often deny that they are impressed by the slickly packaged student; they say they look for a student who is "simply being himself or herself."[67] The sentiment is surely sincere and admissions officers are no doubt savvy. But it is also clear that college-conscious students today expend a great deal of effort in their applications to "be themselves."

Happily, qualification-inflation and the mounting frenzy among the affluent surrounding college admissions may contribute to something of a leveling effect. With the rise in competition and college costs, and the growth of merit-based aid, the quality of students at less elite colleges and universities is rising. Students who might have attended fancy private schools may opt for state universities, many of which have introduced a variety of special programs to attract more talented students. The leveling effect also results from another otherwise unfortunate circumstance: the dismal job market for academics that has endured for the last thirty years, which has meant that talented scholars from excellent graduate programs have found jobs at colleges of lesser reputation than they might have hoped—if they have found jobs in their field at all and not changed careers because of poor prospects. As a consequence, the quality of education at those institutions, and in some cases their reputations as well, has improved.

There is also some evidence that students do not make material sacrifices to their long-term prospects in foregoing the high-status schools. Economists Stacy Berg Dale and Alan Krueger found that "students who attended colleges with higher average SAT scores do not earn more than other students who were accepted and rejected by comparable schools but attended a college with a lower average SAT score."[68] Krueger and Dale's findings run counter to conventional wisdom and to other evidence, some of which we cited in chapter 3, that going to an elite college makes a difference to one's later material prospects.

Certainly some equalizing of the prestige, and the quality, of different colleges would be a welcome (and paradoxical) side effect of the admissions frenzy among affluent students—a countertrend to the winner-take-all phenomenon that has received much attention of late. This evening out could help to mitigate the disparities in educational advantages between students at different socioeconomic levels.

THE RICH, THE POOR, AND THE REST

In the statistics cited in the first paragraph of this chapter, we compared students in the top and bottom socioeconomic quartiles; other studies divide people into quintiles. But the phenomena we have looked at also affect students—the majority—at neither end of the spectrum. If you want to make generalizations (and we do) it's hard to avoid terms like "rich" and "poor"—or substitutes like "affluent" and "low income"—and it's useful to make statements about the ends of the spectrum. But the terms are vague and the statements can obscure as much as they clarify. What we find is a continuum, a spectrum of differences, rather than sharp dividing lines; and different policies and practices affect people along the spectrum differently. For some purposes it appears that the very affluent are on one side and everyone else is on the other; for other purposes it looks as if the very poor are on one side and everyone else is on the other. Both ways of looking at things can distort reality, however. There isn't a neat and tidy way of describing or analyzing the phenomena.

Rarely are the rich and the poor pitted directly against each other. The student from a New England prep school with combined SATs in the 1500s is not competing for a place in the same institution as the low-income student from rural Appalachia with SATs in the 800s. So whatever irrelevant advantages benefit the prep school student, they do not directly disadvantage the kid from Appalachia.

But it doesn't follow that no one is harmed by these irrelevant advantages, nor even that the poor are never affected by advantages that primarily benefit the rich. One reason is that the system of higher education is an interconnected chain in which actions and practices in one location can ripple through the system, affecting individuals or institutions seemingly distant. If, as we suggested in the last section, the current college admissions frenzy means that qualified students are trickling down from the most elite institutions, then the institutions where they end up enrolling become more selective, pushing some students who would have otherwise been admitted to colleges down a notch, and so on. These cascading, trickle-down effects mean that policies that might seem to affect students only at some schools (for example, the most selective) may in fact have ramifications for other students down the line who are not competing for those same places.

In fact, the students most likely to be disadvantaged by policies such as legacy and early decision are middle-income students. We saw in the discussion of early decision that those for whom college costs are a significant factor are not well-advised to apply early decision because, by promising to attend a particular college, they lose the ability to negotiate financial aid packages. Savvy middle-class students who may have qualifications comparable to their more affluent peers realize they can't afford to apply early. Thus, insofar as applying early improves the odds of admission, these students are disadvantaged. Similar arguments can be made about the effects of legacy. A student from the lowest SES quintile who is highly competitive will (rightly) have a leg up in the admissions process for having overcome adversity. The competitive middle-class student, lacking both legacy and adversity, is likely to lose out.

We may not feel that sorry for these students. They haven't experienced serious deprivations growing up; by global standards they are extraordinarily privileged; and they probably won't be irreparably harmed by the irrelevant advantages we've described. But questions of justice still apply. Recall the second of our principles, introduced in chapter 1 and discussed in chapter 3: people should be neither helped nor hindered in their attempts at educational advancement by factors irrelevant to the missions of educational institutions. We have concentrated in this chapter on the ways that "helps" to some become "hindrances" to others. Wherever we find scarce resources (such as places in selective colleges), the two will be inseparable. In some cases middle-income students, in other cases lower-income students, are disadvantaged. Even apart from the harms to particular individuals, many people will find offensive the idea that individuals who begin with an embarrassment of riches (including the kind that genuinely enhance their qualifications) should benefit from other, irrelevant advantages that help to maintain and reinforce their privileged status.

6

The Test: Understanding the SAT

Each year, more than two million students take the SAT or ACT as stepping-stones to college, reenacting a ritual performed by decades of college-goers.[1] Scores on these tests play a prominent role in admissions decisions at selective institutions; at graduate and professional schools, so do the scores on their senior cousins, the Graduate Record Exam (GRE), Law School Admission Test (LSAT), Medical College Admission Test (MCAT), and Graduate Management Admission Test (GMAT).

The SAT in particular has attracted a long line of critics since the 1960s, both popular and academic.[2] Banesh Hoffman pioneered the way with his book *The Tyranny of Testing*, published in 1962. Attacks spiked again some twenty years later when Allan Nairn (associated with Ralph Nader) published *The Reign of ETS: The Corporation That Makes Up People's Minds* (1980) and David Owen published *None of the Above: Behind the Myth of Scholastic Aptitude* (1985).[3] A resurgent assault in recent years seems to be approaching a critical mass. *Time* magazine provided extended coverage in a special March 2001 report, "Should the SATs Matter?" Three recent books—Peter Sacks' *Standardized Minds*,[4] Lani Guinier and Susan Sturm's *Who's Qualified?*,[5] and Nicholas Lemann's *The Big Test*[6]—have raised the ante. The NAACP has undertaken a high-profile campaign to reduce the influence of the SAT.[7] FairTest (the National Center for Fair and Open Testing, a spunky advocacy group in Cambridge, Massachusetts) has maintained a steady drumbeat against the SAT, issuing "fact sheets" and position papers and supplying background assistance to groups that challenge the test's use. One such group went to court in 1999 to stop the use of the SAT in establishing college athletic eligibilty.[8]

In years past, FairTest could point to some success stories for its cause, to small liberal arts colleges like Bates, Bowdoin, and Muhlenberg that, although selective, stopped requiring applicants to submit SAT scores. Now it can point to a much bigger ally. In February 2001, the president of the University of California system, Richard Atkinson, proposed that it stop using the SAT for future admissions decisions.[9]

Atkinson was referring to the SAT I—a two-part instrument assessing verbal and mathematical skills. This is the ubiquitous hurdle over which millions of high school students must jump. The SAT II—a set of subject tests in writing, mathematics, history, languages, and other subjects—is optional at most universities though required by some selective campuses, including the University of California.

Atkinson's complaint was two-pronged. The SAT distorts learning, he charged, because it is not tied to the high school curriculum. Further, admitting students by their SAT scores, he declared, is "not compatible with the American view on how merit should be defined and opportunities distributed."[10]

This second complaint is the one seized on most vehemently by the SAT's critics, and the one we scrutinize in this chapter. According to Peter Sacks, the SAT is a "vicious sorter of young people by class."[11] Lani Guinier and Susan Sturm note the close linkage—to which we have already referred—"between test performance and parental income. Average family income rises with each hundred-point increase in SAT scores."[12] They point out that "the SAT . . . is a better predictor of family income than of first-year college grades."[13] This fact leads Julian Weissglass to conclude that "the SAT is a capstone of an education system that . . . serves to preserve privilege and economic inequality in this country."[14]

A casual look at our systems of higher education seems to lend credence to this view of the SAT. Consider the average combined SAT score at the University of Michigan at Ann Arbor: 1230. Note further that 16 percent of the university's students come from families earning more than $300,000 a year and 62 percent from families earning more than $75,000.[15] Now travel just ten miles east to Eastern Michigan University in Ypsilanti, where the average SAT score is 1006 and only 37 percent of the students have families earning more than $75,000 a year.[16] Farther east yet, at Wayne Community College in Detroit, the students don't even take the SAT and are on the economic ground floor. Or consider the California system. At UCLA, the average SAT score is 1277 and the average family income is $73,000. Seven percent of UCLA students come from families earning more than $200,000 annually. By contrast, at California State University at Stanislaus, the average SAT score is 949, and 20 percent of the students come from households where neither parent advanced beyond eighth grade. Eighty percent come from families earning less than $72,000 a year.[17] Further down the ladder, at San Joaquin Delta College—an open admissions institution—students attend from an area where the median household income is $38,000 a year and 30 percent of children live in poverty.[18]

A clear pattern stands out. Flagship campus = high SATs = high SES students.[19] Second-tier campus = mid-range SATs = mid-level SES students. Community college = open admissions = low SES students. Although the figures derived from Michigan and California may differ in other states, the pattern holds across the board. When we add private colleges of greater and lesser selectivity, the pattern repeats itself.

Critics make an even more serious charge: not only is the SAT riddled with class bias; it's also racially biased. Consider the SAT results for the year 2001. The average combined score for whites was 1060, for blacks 859, a 200-point disparity.[20] Does this 200-point spread reflect a real difference in academic potential? Not according to the critics. Some contend that the SAT is based on white supremacist views and biased against African Americans.[21] "So here is the great SAT test," offers Stanley Fish, "devised by a racist in order to confirm racist assumptions, measuring not native ability but cultural advantage . . . an indicator of very little except what money and social privilege can buy."[22]

THE REGATTA QUESTION

"Cultural bias" is the charge, and over the decades one example of this purported bias—a legendary question about *regattas*—has taken on almost talismanic properties, showing up in critique after critique. Richard Delgado, for example, writes that "until recently" the SAT "included items about polo mallets, lacrosse, and regattas. How likely," he asks rhetorically, "is a poor kid from the inner city to spend his or her weekend . . . attending regattas?"[23] Not very likely, we suppose—but then how likely is the middle-class white kid in Marshalltown, Iowa, to have attended a regatta? In fact, if the "poor inner city kid" lives in Philadelphia, Washington, or Boston, he has a much better chance of seeing a regatta than the kid in Marshalltown. But the point is not that either child is likely to have attended a regatta. What children (of any class) in Philadelphia, Washington, Boston, and Marshalltown have in common is access to libraries. Thus, the kid who latches onto *Making Waves*, #81 in the Nancy Drew series of mysteries by Carolyn Keene, or *The Regatta Mystery* by Agatha Christie, or—more ambitiously—*Vanity Fair* by William Makepeace Thackeray will learn what a regatta is.[24]

The SAT first came into use as an admissions tool in the 1930s. It was not geared to the prep school curricula of upper class students who then predominated in admissions to Harvard, Yale, and Princeton, and was valued precisely because it could reveal academic abilities that any youngster anywhere might display if he read widely.[25] Yet the critics charge that the SAT is "culturally loaded," favoring the cultural milieu of white upper class

Americans.[26] Its questions, they believe, don't reveal academic potential but class and race positions.

If the SAT is biased by class and race, there must be some important compensating gain for colleges and universities to persist in using it. But the critics deny there is any compensating gain. SAT scores are supposed to predict first-year college grades, but SAT score differences account for perhaps 15 percent of the variation in freshman grades, "a pretty slender achievement," writes Nicholas Lemann.[27] Susan Sturm and Lani Guinier report that the correlation between freshman grades and SAT scores ranges from 0.32 to 0.36, a correlation they take to be unimpressive, quoting David Owen's colorful assertion that "you would have a better chance of predicting a person's height by looking only at his weight than you would of predicting his freshman grades by looking at his SAT scores."[28] In their extensive and detailed examination, *The Case against the SAT*, James Crouse and Dale Trusheim conclude that the SAT is "statistically redundant"; it doesn't help college admissions officers make better selection decisions.[29]

Why, then, do so many colleges and universities continue to use the SAT? To explore this question, let's first set the foregoing arguments in some context.

Start with regattas. The complaint about the regatta question is a complaint about *item bias*. According to the critics, the questions—the "items"—on the SAT favor irrelevant knowledge possessed by some groups over others. Now, such item bias, where it exists in a test, ought to manifest itself in *predictive bias*. Since the SAT is supposed to predict first-year college grades, the presence of questions biased against blacks ought to result in underprediction of their academic success, forecasting lower grades for them than they actually get. After all, what does knowledge of regattas have to do with getting good grades in first-year college biology, economics, literature, and history? What does knowledge of regattas have to do with real academic potential? A test that underpredicts black academic performance underrates the true academic abilities of black students and thus potentially excludes those who would succeed just as well as white students possessing higher test scores. It is deeply unfair.

Underprediction of blacks' academic ability was one of the early charges against the SAT.[30] As it turns out, however, the SAT *overpredicts* rather than underpredicts the freshman grades of blacks. That is to say, blacks end up making college grades lower—not higher—than those predicted by their SAT scores.[31] Whatever we might make of this finding—long established in the testing literature—it doesn't square with the charge of pervasive item bias.

Further, if the black–white test score gap on the SAT were due to the "regatta problem" (too many "culturally loaded" test items), we would expect to find a gap only in the verbal half of the test. The mathematics part doesn't mention regattas and other matters that might be unfamiliar to black students. Rather, it utilizes concepts such as "greater than" and operations such as multiplication that are as common to African American as to white experience. Consequently, black students' scores on the math test ought to differ considerably from their scores on the verbal test and be more in line with scores achieved by whites. Yet the same score gap obtains whether we look at the SAT-Verbal or the SAT-Math. In 2001, whites scored 529 on the verbal part and 531 on the math part. Blacks scored 433 and 426—slightly worse, in fact, on the math than the verbal section. This parity between the math and verbal scores belies the charge that the verbal section is stacked with irrelevant, culturally loaded questions.

More important, if the SAT were culturally biased, we would expect its scores to stand in sharp contrast to scores on other tests, especially those that, unlike the SAT, are tied directly to school curricula. Consider, then, the results of statewide competency tests in Massachusetts, Texas, and California. In Texas, where passing the tenth grade TAAS (Texas Assessment of Academic Skills) is a condition of graduating from high school, 94 percent of white students passed the 2001 math test compared to 79 percent of African Americans.[32] On a California state math assessment, 53 percent of white eleventh-graders ranked at or above the fiftieth national percentile rank while only 25 percent of blacks did.[33] On the Massachusetts Comprehensive Assessment System math tests, 57 percent of tenth grade white students were "advanced" or "proficient" in the subject, while only 16 percent of black students were.[34]

The patterns in these state assessments are duplicated at the national level. The National Assessment of Educational Progress (NAEP) in the U.S. Department of Education conducts exams on particular subjects, each exam involving many thousands of students across the country. The results of these tests—of science and math knowledge in 2000, civics and writing in 1998—provide a "report card" to the nation of the educational progress of its children.

NAEP tests (like some of the state tests) are constructed differently from the SAT. The latter is a "norm-referenced" test. It measures the test-taker against other test-takers, and all the test-takers together against an original sample upon which the test is initially "normed."[35] The questions are designed to produce a normal distribution of scores in the sample—represented by a bell curve—so that two-thirds of the test-takers fall within one standard deviation in either direction from the mean score. To the degree that subsequent test-taking populations are like the original sample, their scores display the same properties.

By contrast, NAEP tests (and other similar assessments) are "criterion-referenced." The questions on the assessment are formulated to represent a level of knowledge a committee of educators and professionals thinks students at a certain level ought to possess. Thus, in theory at least, if schools were delivering uniformly outstanding teaching to uniformly dedicated students, the NAEP tests could display the "Lake Wobegon phenomenon," where all the students are above average—above, that is, the level set by the committee as an adequate command of the subject in question. (In fact, the results generally exhibit a normal distribution.)

The NAEP results show the same black–white gap noted in the other tests we've described. For purposes of illustration, here we use average scores rather than level-groupings ("advanced," "proficient," "basic," "below-basic"). The average scores of twelfth graders on the science assessment were: white = 154, Asian American = 153, Hispanic = 128, African American = 123; on the civics assessment: white = 158, Asian American = 151, Hispanic = 130, African American = 131; on the math assessment: white = 308, Asian American = 319, Hispanic = 283, African American = 274; and on the writing assessment: white = 156, Asian American = 152, Hispanic = 135, African American = 134.[36]

These results—and many others we haven't mentioned—present a striking picture of a black–white gap that persists across subject matter, grade level, region, age, and type of test.[37] Against this backdrop, the racial disparity in SAT scores doesn't stand out as an anomaly; rather, it fits in as a small instance of a larger pattern.

None of these observations disproves that the SAT is a culturally unfair test. They do, however, set the scene for a closer inspection.

IS THE SAT FAIR?

Behind the simple facade of the SAT lies a complex contraption even the Wizard of Oz couldn't have devised. For example, the test scores of the million-plus students taking the SAT (or the ACT) every year have to indicate the same thing about each of these test-takers and the same thing about test-takers in every preceding and succeeding decade. Otherwise, the scores are mere numbers without any significance. How is the uniform significance of scores achieved?

The scores on the SAT (and norm-referenced tests generally) exhibit a "normal distribution." On a graph with the horizontal x-axis marking off score intervals and the vertical y-axis indicating the number of test-takers residing at each score interval, the line connecting the dots on the graph has the shape of a bell curve. A few test-takers score very badly, a few score superbly well, and most cluster around the middle range of scores, with slopes down toward the extremes. That the scores represent a normal distribution is quite fortunate because a normal distribution curve has distinct and well-known mathematical properties that can be used to turn "raw scores"—

the number of questions correctly answered—into a common, informative metric. A line falling from the mid-point of a normal distribution's bell curve represents the mean score (and the median and modal scores, as well). A "standard deviation" *above* this mean is a line falling from the right slope at a point that includes roughly 34 percent of the test scores; a standard deviation *below* the mean is a line from the left slope at a point that includes roughly 34 percent of the test scores. In other words, 68 percent of the test scores will fall somewhere between the − 1 and the + 1 in the figure below; 95 percent will fall between − 2 and + 2 standard deviations.

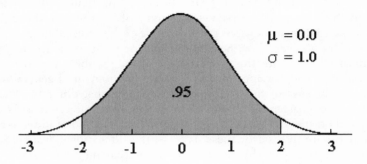

In this figure, μ is the mean and σ is the standard deviation. All test scores within this bell curve can be represented as a z-score somewhere between − 3.0 and + 3.0.[38] For example, suppose answering correctly 80 of 140 questions on the SAT yields a z-score of − 0.9 (a straight line dropping from the left slope of the curve striking the horizontal line just to the right of the − 1).[39] The administrators of the SAT could report this score, but it would distract and confuse the average test-taker and her parents. Scores with decimals and minus signs in front of them are hard to fathom. To eliminate these drawbacks, the SAT sets μ at 500 with σ of 100. Thus, students get scores ranging from 200 to 800. (ACT sets μ at 20 with σ of 5. Test scores typically range between 5 and 35.)[40] The SAT scores show exactly what the z-scores show, namely distance from the mean in terms of standard deviations, a ratio that remains constant no matter how it is described numerically.

SAT-takers also get a percentile ranking along with their score. For example, the student who scored 420 on the 2003 SAT Verbal (a score roughly nine-tenths of one standard deviation below the mean) fell in the 20th percentile, meaning that 80 percent of test-takers scored as well or better than she did.[41] Percentiles supply useful information to admissions officers and students alike but have a distorting feature: the distance between percentile ranks is not constant. While the distance between the 60th and 67th percentile on the 2003 SAT-Verbal is roughly the distance between scores of 540 and 560, the distance between the 95th and 99th percentile is approximately the distance between 700 and 760.[42] Thus, it is important for admissions officers to get reports of scores as well as percentiles.

The purpose of a test such as the SAT is to differentiate among test-takers. If every test-taker answered every question correctly, the test scores would have no value in the college admissions selection process. Similarly, the scores would be worthless if no test-taker answered any question correctly. So test constructors write test questions that span a range of difficulty: some easy, some hard, some in-between. The aim is to produce a set of questions that results in scores approximating a normal distribution.

With criterion-referenced tests—tests of a particular subject matter designed to ascertain the test-taker's mastery of it—the aim, through trial and error, is to devise questions representative of the subject "domain." (For example, a test of general mathematics proficiency that contained only questions having to do with the properties of prime numbers would not be a good test. It would not appropriately sample the domain of general mathematics.) In the case of the SAT, matters are somewhat different. The SAT doesn't test for mastery of a particular curriculum or subject area. The SAT was once characterized as a test of scholastic "aptitude," but ideas like aptitude and IQ are in disfavor these days, so the Educational Testing Service and the College Board shy away from saying that the SAT tests for such things. The letters "SAT" no longer represent an acronym for Scholastic Aptitude Test (its original name) or Scholastic Assessment Test (a subsequent name); "SAT" is now a proper name just like "George" and "Frances." Yet whatever the College Board's official view, the old idea dies hard. Part of the anxiety surrounding the SAT almost certainly derives from the widespread suspicion that it pretends to measure something putatively deep and largely immutable, whether it is called intelligence, IQ, aptitude, or innate ability.

The College Board currently calls the two parts of the SAT I "reasoning" tests, so we might say that they test for reasoning ability.[43] But we need not even say this. In a sense, the SAT need not test "for" anything at all if it produces scores that turn out to predict first-year college grades (which is its purported function). Suppose that admissions officers discovered that, oddly enough, the amount of chocolate pudding a student ate during his senior year in high school bore an uncanny relation to his freshman grades in college. Then colleges might start using a "pudding test" involving the collection of data about applicants' pudding consumption; and they wouldn't need to claim the data "tested for" any cognitive capacity at all. (Of course, the pudding test wouldn't work because, once students knew colleges were using it, its results could be easily manipulated. Students who badly wanted to go to Harvard would gorge themselves on hundreds of gallons of chocolate pudding in their senior year.)

The SAT isn't like chocolate pudding. Its questions draw on a test-taker's knowledge of basic mathematics, knowledge that most students should possess whatever the extent of their school's math offerings. Its questions also measure reading comprehension and vocabulary. The vocabulary questions and reading exercises don't presuppose a particular high school course of study. Rather, they reward the student who has read widely in literature, history, and other subjects.[44] The knowledge and comprehension measured by the SAT are not irrelevant to the tasks facing prospective freshmen in college.

A Fairness Review Steering Committee at ETS oversees a question-construction process to ferret out bias. Test-designers mechanically tally up group references to make sure that test materials "contain an appropriate representation of various populations" and that questions highlight "the achievements and contributions of different cultures and racial and ethnic groups."[45] Stereotyping, blatant or subtle, is rooted out. For example, the following passage would *not* do as the basis of a reading comprehension question:

> Khrushchev was the quintessential Russian peasant. He was cunning and sly. He was given to the charming fantastical Russian kind of lying called *Vranyo*, and to extremes, like the *Muzhik* who works hard and then spends days on a drinking spree. Coming at the moment of history when he did, Khrushchev's great contribution was his confidence in the Russian people and his effort to give them confidence in themselves.

What is the problem with this passage? It stereotypes Russian peasants.[46]

Apart from mechanical tallies of group references and subjective evaluations of stereotyping, ETS also engages in a more formal analysis. On any particular SAT exam, several questions are getting tryouts for future exams. Test-takers' answers aren't computed in their scores. Rather, ETS looks at the responses to see if they display certain patterns—for example, if everyone answers correctly, or if no one does. More importantly, suppose a particular question elicits a distinct pattern of wrong answers from girls who, by their other answers, show they are equal in ability to boys who answer the question correctly. This question will be flagged and likely rejected as containing some sort of irrelevant bias. So, too, will questions that show such patterns for ethnic and racial groups. Differential Item Functioning (DIF), as it is called, is used to spot questions in which particular groups perform inconsistently with their total performance on an exam. Such questions seldom survive to become actual test items.[47]

A related method is used not to detect bias in questions but to measure their power to discriminate among test-takers. For any particular question, ETS test-makers can look at the mean score of the test-takers answering it correctly and the mean score of all test-takers and plug these into an equation that tells them how good the question is. For example, if the test-takers who got the question right have overall lower scores than the test-takers who got the question wrong, then the question is a poor one.[48]

These matters, and many more, are handled through statistical analysis. Consequently, lying behind the question booklet and answer sheet in the hands of any particular SAT-taker is an elaborate structure of mathematical equations on top of mathematical equations. Indeed, we've only scratched the surface. The heavy-duty equations are brought to bear in determining the SAT's *validity* and *reliability*.

IS THE SAT VALID AND RELIABLE?

Validity and reliability are the cardinal virtues in a standardized test. First, the test has to measure what it purports to measure. When it does this well, it has high *validity*. Second, a test's results must be reproducible. When this requirement is met, a test is *reliable*.

We take up reliability first because this dimension of the SAT is less disputed than its validity. Suppose Sarah takes the SAT on a Saturday in December. Her baby cried all Friday night, so she arrives at the test site with little sleep; she had a flat tire on the way, causing her to arrive anxious and frustrated. She scores 550 on the verbal portion. Suppose now that the course of the world had gone differently. Sarah's baby slept through the night, her journey to the test was relaxing, and she started the test rested, calm, and focused. She might have scored 580 or 600. Play out these possibilities a bit more. On the Saturday Sarah took the test, she was unlucky. She knew only half the vocabulary words (though she's an avid reader); but had her test been the version administered a month later, she would have been very lucky, easily recognizing all the words. Different luck might have changed her score by forty points.

Now, if Sarah could take the test over and over (an infinite number of times) and if she learned nothing from each prior administration (she had amnesia right after each test), all these variable states of her environment would wash out, and the fluctuations in her scores would average out to her *true score*—a score free from *measurement error*. Of course, Sarah lives in only one world and takes the SAT on that fateful Saturday in December, scoring 550. Nevertheless, by estimating confidence intervals (or the *standard error of measurement*), ETS can give the user of SAT scores some sense of the *range* around Sarah's actual score and her true score.[49]

ETS can't subject Sarah and all other test-takers to an infinite (or even a large number) of retests, inducing forgetfulness after each administration. What it can and does do is divide every test taken into two halves and treat each part as a separate test, deriving correlation coefficients for the scores on each part.[50] It can do this for a horizontal time-slice, seeing how the hundreds of thousands of first-part scores obtained on Sarah's Saturday in December correlate with the hundreds of thousands of corresponding second-part scores; and it can do this vertically, seeing how the correlations go from version to version and year to year. It can do the latter because each version of the SAT is *equated* with other versions. This means that each version, in a very practical sense, is the *same test* even though each version contains a different set of questions. Equating is another feat of mathematical contrivance.

On every administration of the SAT, about 20 percent of the questions are *anchor items*, items used on past and future tests. By looking at performance on these items—which are not included in any test-taker's score—the test-designers can construct a mathematical model predicting how test-takers will do on the nonanchor items. They can then select new items accordingly and measure actual outcomes with predicted outcomes.[51] With experience, the test-makers can equate different versions of a test year after year with a high degree of confidence. Statistical analyses can be generated backward and forward for every anchor and nonanchor question in every test, and for every split-half score of every equated test down through the years. The numbers can add up to a high level of reliability. In the case of the SAT I, the reliability coefficients derived over time approximate 0.90 (where 1.0 represents the maximum).[52]

However, it is not the SAT's reliability but its validity that draws the sharpest criticism. The validity at issue here is *predictive validity*. Do the test scores generated by the SAT in fact predict first-year academic success in college? (In the next chapter we take up the question of whether predicting first-year academic success is a measure colleges ought to care about.) The two pieces of data—test scores and subsequently earned grades—are available to every college that requires the SAT, so each can calculate its own equation of correlation between the SAT scores of the students who matriculate and their GPAs at the end of first year.[53]

Such correlations suffer from a problem called *restriction of range*. If a college admits applicants with high SAT scores while turning away applicants with low scores, and then correlates the scores of the matriculated students with their subsequent grades, the correlation will underestimate the discriminating power of the SAT. Differences in SAT scores will explain very little of the variance between freshman GPAs. This doesn't show a defect in the SAT but an unavoidable skewing in the sample upon which the correlation is done. Consider a parallel case. Suppose a very demanding college admits only students with perfect 4.0 high school GPAs. High school grades will fail to explain *any* of the differences in freshmen year GPAs at that college. Yet we would not conclude that high school grades don't really discriminate between applicants who are academically capable and those who are not.

To appreciate the full power of SAT scores to discriminate academic promise, a college would need to admit every student that applied, then correlate scores and first year GPAs. Princeton, Stanford, Swarthmore, Michigan, Virginia, and Wellesley, which use SAT scores, obviously can't engage in such an experiment. However, some relatively unselective universities approximate this experiment by admitting nearly everyone who applies. The SAT/GPA correlation coefficients for these institutions are typically higher than those derived at selective institutions that reject many applicants.[54]

Since the SAT came into wide use forty years ago, ETS has encouraged and helped colleges do their own validity evaluations, and more than seven hundred institutions have produced thousands of studies. Hopkins et al. report the mean validity coefficient for freshman GPA in these studies to be 0.48.[55] The College Board itself reports a 0.42 correlation between the median SAT score and the freshman grades of an applicant at the median.[56]

We earlier quoted Sturm and Guinier reporting validity coefficients of 0.32–0.36.[57] Independent scholars have access to much of the data that colleges use and can make their own validity assessments. Reported correlations vary considerably, and it is often difficult to make useful comparisons because some correlations adjust for range restrictions and some do not. However, even if the correlations were consistently in the neighborhood Sturm and Guinier claim, this would not be evidence that SAT scores are not valid predictors. Consider the following results of a skills test (borrowed from an example used by Howard Lyman). The test scores are stated in bands, "Upper Third," "Middle Third," and "Lower Third." Subsequent proficiency ratings by supervisors assign performers to one of three categories.

	Proficiency Ratings		
test scores	*low*	*average*	*high*
upper third	18%	33%	50%
middle third	29%	36%	28%
lower third	53%	31%	22%

The correlation coefficient for this test is 0.38. Now, the test scores do not allow for fine-grained prediction. As we can see, some test-takers falling in the "upper third" band were subsequently judged to have low or average proficiency, and large segments of every band clustered in the average proficiency range. Nevertheless, when we look at the four corners of the table, we see a striking picture. Half of those who scored in the "upper third" band were highly proficient performers and more than half who fell in the "lower third" were below average performers. A selection officer who used these test results would make far better selections than if she chose randomly.[58]

If SAT scores correlate 0.36 with first-year college grades, as Sturm and Guinier report, they concede the predictive validity of the SAT. Their dismissal of the correlation as no better than that between height and weight speaks not to the predictive *validity* of the correlation but to its *utility*. They want us to believe such a low correlation can't help decision makers very much. But the skills-test example shows that this assumption is too glib. Measures with low correlation coefficients can be very helpful in the right circumstances. The usefulness of a predictor is relative to the other available information and the stakes at issue. If, for example, blindfolded, you had to rank several persons from tallest to shortest, paying out $50 for every wrong ranking, you would be quite grateful, in the absence of other information about them, to know their respective weights. Using this knowledge would save you a bundle.

HOW USEFUL IS THE SAT?

In fact, college admissions officers usually possess a lot of information about applicants besides their SAT scores. Leaving aside qualitative information gleaned from letters of recommendation and personal essays, they possess applicants' high school grades and (often) class rankings. High school grade point average (HSGPA) itself predicts first-year academic success in college. By the College Board's own estimates, while SAT scores correlate 0.42 with overall freshman GPA, HSGPA correlates 0.48. Why, then, do colleges use the SAT when they already possess an equally good or better basis for predicting first-year academic success? The answer is that the *combined* predictors are correlated 0.55 with freshman grades.[59] Employing the SAT adds information the admissions committees can use.

But how much information does the SAT add? According to the extensive critique by James Crouse and Dale Trusheim, it adds very little. In their words, SAT scores are "redundant."[60] Crouse and Trusheim did a retrospective analysis of 2,700 students from the National Longitudinal Survey of the high school class of 1972 who applied to college.[61] With data in hand about the students' SAT scores, high school grades, and college grades, Crouse and Trusheim looked back at the admissions decisions that colleges would have made using high school rank and SAT scores in combination versus the decisions they would have made using high school rank alone. (High school class rank is a better indicator of academic capability than HSGPA, but 20 percent or more of American high schools don't report class rank. Thus, HSGPA is the more common predictor associated with, or contrasted to, SAT scores.) They conclude that 74.2 percent of the college applicants would have been accepted and 16.6 percent rejected under either policy. The two prediction policies point in different directions for only 9.2 percent of the applicants.[62]

Thus, at most the SAT scores could tip the scales one way or the other in less than 10 percent of the cases.

Still, might not getting decisions right in these remaining cases be worthwhile? Crouse and Trusheim do not think adding the SAT contributes much to correct decisions in these cases (correct decisions are ones that select applicants who in fact succeed and reject those who would fail). They show that "when a college uses high school rank plus SAT, it will make . . . 2.7 more correct admissions forecasts out of each 100 than it would using rank alone. This is a proportional increase of 29.3 percent. Nonetheless, we doubt [they write] that most colleges would notice such a small increase in the number of correct forecasts."[63] But why wouldn't colleges notice, especially those that admit large classes? By Crouse and Trusheim's reasoning, we might ask why a college should even use high school rank to select students, when failing to do so decreases its correct decisions by only 20 percent. Would it notice such a small increase in mistakes?

These questions don't establish the SAT's utility, but they do suggest that the debate between Crouse-Trusheim and the SAT is a glass-half-full versus glass-half-empty quarrel. By the College Board's own calculations, two-thirds of all SAT-takers have "nondiscrepant scores." Their predicted first-year grades are the same whether HSGPAs or SAT scores are used.[64] This finding is hardly surprising. As Crouse and Trusheim point out, the College Board reports correlations between HSGPAs and SAT scores of 0.868. Kids who make good grades in high school also typically score well on the SAT. Thus, the SAT can shift an admissions decision one way or the other only in the one-third of college applications that exhibit discrepant scores. Even if the portion were one-tenth rather than one-third, the SAT might still have value under their selection model, Crouse and Trusheim acknowledge, if the test were cost-free.[65]

Taken in its strongest form, then, Crouse and Trusheim's argument doesn't show that the SAT has no utility for college admissions officers, but only that its utility may be outweighed by countervailing factors. (We consider these factors in the next chapter.) Moreover, their argument supposes unrealistic selection models in which admissions decisions take account only of first-year college grades as predicted by (i) high school rank and (ii) high school rank augmented by SAT scores. To assess how useful a tool SAT scores are in actual admissions decisions, we need to consider how they are actually used. For example, in the case of applications with discrepant scores, the SAT score may act as a red flag, triggering further inquiry by admissions committees. Since such inquiry may go in many directions—taking into account an applicant's full academic history, life circumstances, reported qualities of character, and the like—the utility of the SAT score lies in the fruitfulness of the inquiries it triggers, or in the availability of alternative triggers if it is absent.

CULTURAL BIAS AND UNFAIRNESS REVISITED

We began with a concern—forcefully expressed by critics such as Sacks, Delgado, and Fish—that the SAT is unfairly stacked against poor and minority students. The SAT, they contend in their less measured moments, merely rewards possession of culturally slanted information that is irrelevant to assessing a student's real academic potential.

Put this way, the charge doesn't survive. The SAT is a valid predictor of first-year college grades. This doesn't mean colleges should continue to use it or that matters of unfairness are disposed of. It does mean, in the words of Christopher Jencks, who himself would like to see the SAT relegated to the dustbin, that "the skill differences" the SAT and other standardized tests "measure are real, and these differences have real consequences both at school and at work."[66]

The SAT excites an animus out of proportion to the equity arguments brought against it. In part, this animus may arise because the SAT is, in the minds of critics, associated with claims about IQ and innate ability. Yet almost any basis of predicting academic success produces results similar to those produced by the SAT. Suppose all colleges used *only* HSGPA as a predictor of first-year success and used predicted success as a ground for admission. Socioeconomic and racial distributions would change very little. In fact, because HSGPA and SAT scores are so highly correlated, whatever exclusions the SAT produces, HSGPAs will produce nearly as well. If the "SAT is a vicious sorter by class," as Peter Sacks complains, HSGPA is hardly less so.[67]

To make this point clear, recall the original pattern displayed by the Michigan and California systems: flagship university = high SAT scores = high SES students; middle-tier university = mid-range SAT scores = mid-level SES students; community colleges = open admission = low SES students. Now take out the middle term—the SAT scores—and revise the descriptions instead using high school grades. At the University of Michigan at Ann Arbor, where 62 percent of the students come from families earning more than $75,000 annually, the average HSGPA of entering freshmen is 3.8, and 70 percent of them ranked in the top 10 percent of their high school class. At Eastern Michigan University, where only 37 percent of the students come from families making more than $75,000 a year, entering freshmen bring an average HSGPA of 3.0, and only 12 percent of them ranked in the top 10 percent of their high school class. At UCLA, where the average family income of students is $73,000 a year, incoming freshmen have HSGPAs of 4.1; at California State University in Stanislaus, where 80 percent of the students come from families making less than $72,000 a year, incoming freshmen average 3.3.[68] Finally, at the bottom of the pyramid, the grades and family incomes of students at Wayne Community College and San Joaquin

Delta College are modest, to say the least. Just as one could generalize the earlier pattern featuring the SAT to many other institutions across the country, one can generalize this pattern too, with grades taking the place of test scores.

Sacks is typical of many critics of the SAT who rail against it as a "vicious sorter" by class and race and then propose a substitute with the same sorting features. It is surely disappointing to the reader who has followed Sacks's extended diatribe against the SAT to find him recommending in its place "the best evidence" for predicting college success—high school performance.[69] The black–white high school grade gap is nearly as robust as the black–white SAT gap. Rebecca Zwick reports a 1995 analysis by the National Center for Education Statistics of high school seniors who would meet a very selective college's 3.5 HSGPA threshold, noting that "29 percent of Asian Americans, 21 percent of whites, 10 percent of Latinos, and 4 percent of African Americans had GPAs this high."[70]

The same anti-climax lies in wait for the reader of Crouse and Trusheim. They begin their book by framing the reader's expectations in a certain way:

> It has been known for a long time that one can predict fairly well where young children will end up in the competition for college admissions by knowing their race, the quality of their schooling, and their family background. If we can predict where young people will end up merely by knowing their race or family background . . . then the competition may be unfair to some people. . . . Assessment of qualifications with the SAT or other tests may simply perpetuate this pattern of unequal schooling.[71]

After this rhetorical framing the reader is treated to an elaborately detailed argument that SAT scores are not useful and that they come with a cost, namely a slightly higher rate of black exclusion at selective colleges.[72] This cost, too, is elaborated at length.

Given the initial framing, this cost is surely significant. Yet, after 145 pages of tables, charts, and dense discussion, what does the reader find at the end? Crouse and Trusheim report that the SAT II achievement tests predict first-year college performance just as well as the SAT I, and that if colleges used them instead of the SAT I, high school students would have added incentives to redouble their studies, while high schools themselves would have incentives to enrich their academic offerings.[73] University of California President Richard Atkinson's first complaint against the SAT contained a similar implication. These are good educational reasons for substituting the SAT IIs for the SAT I. But what of the initial equity concerns? Crouse and Trusheim admit that substituting the SAT IIs will not "lower the rejection of applicants from low-income and nonwhite backgrounds compared to the SAT."[74]

A PORSCHE HELD TOGETHER
WITH DUCT TAPE

We noted earlier that once you begin to look behind the SAT, you find an amazing contraption built of mathematical equations and models. Each equation and model offers clean-cut, powerful conclusions. Correlation coefficients can be piled upon correlation coefficients. In a way, this is a marvelous achievement of human ingenuity. However, no mathematical formula by itself generates any result at all—until values are assigned to variables, parameters established, and assumptions made about the world at large. At every stage, assumptions fill the spaces between equations—not necessarily unreasonable or implausible assumptions, but assumptions nevertheless. For example, the restriction of range problem we noted earlier represents one instance of sample bias. The correlations a selective college establishes between SAT scores and first-year grades apply to a sample skewed by the fact that only high SAT scorers got into the freshman class in the first place. As a consequence, the correlation coefficients derived by the college probably understate the real discriminating power of the SAT. Whether true or not, the soundness of the college's correlations assumes that "predictions of freshman performance based on nonrandom samples of students attending college are the firmest basis on which to make accurate predictions for applicants" as a whole.[75] Without this assumption, no numbers get crunched. So, too, in other cases: whether in estimating "true scores" or equating versions of a test or deriving reliability from split-half scores, the use of one equation or model rather than another depends upon certain assumptions, more or less empirically supportable. The SAT is like a Porsche held together with duct tape. Its engine is a flawlessly crafted masterpiece, its transmission transfers energy with unmatched efficiency, its suspension glues the wheels to the road, its body panels reduce wind resistance to the vanishing point—but engine, transmission, suspension, and body panels all are attached to one another with duct tape. As long as the duct tape (the assumptions) holds everything together, the other parts (the equations) combine to give you a breathless driving experience. But if the tape doesn't hold, the rest is so much expensive junk.

That the SAT is a masterpiece of psychometric ingenuity shouldn't seduce us into uncritical admiration. That the SAT is held together by a tissue of often contestable assumptions shouldn't lead us into derogatory dismissal.

Anything we would put in the SAT's place as a predictor also will be held together with duct tape. Deriving correlation coefficients between high school grades and first-year academic performance is equally a psychometric feat of equations and assumptions. SAT II scores, AP test scores, NAEP scores—the story is the same.

Crouse and Trusheim are right that we must weigh the value of the SAT against its costs, and among those costs is its impact on minority admissions. Also among the costs are the putative educational distortions alluded to by them and by Richard Atkinson. Finally, if, as we have seen, the alternatives to the SAT as a predictor turn out to have much the same effect for the racial and socioeconomic make-up of selective institutions, one might argue that admissions committees should abandon the predictive strategy altogether, as Lani Guinier and Susan Sturm advocate. We turn next to these questions.

7

Admissions Tests:
Uses, Abuses, Alternatives

In *The Case against the SAT*, Crouse and Trusheim compare two college admission models. In the first, students were admitted to college based on HSGPA alone; in the second, they were admitted based on HSGPA combined with SAT scores. For each model, any student predicted to get less than a specified freshman-year GPA was rejected and all others were admitted. According to Crouse and Trusheim, for any specified GPA cut-off, the two models reject or admit virtually the same students. The SAT, they conclude, adds little to the admissions process.

However, SAT scores do add something, and the bottom-line complaint by Crouse and Trusheim is not that the scores are wholly useless but that the costs of using them outweigh the benefits. In this chapter, we pursue this matter further. First, however, we need to get a better picture of the SAT's usefulness. No real-life college admissions scheme performs exactly like the models considered by Crouse and Trusheim. The actual utility of SAT scores will depend on their role in an overall admissions process. How, in fact, do colleges use SAT scores, and how should they use them?

THE SAT AND REAL-LIFE
ADMISSIONS CHOICES

As we have noted in earlier chapters, four-year institutions vary enormously in their aims, resources, and selectivity. Admissions procedures vary as well. Some are highly formulaic. Until recently, students applying to the University of California system campuses were automatically admitted if they fell in the top 50 percent of a composite ranking based on (i) HSGPA in core academic courses and (ii) scores on SAT I and SAT II exams. Remaining applicants were evaluated by adding to their ranking other factors such as extent and quality of extracurricular activities. In this scheme, SAT I scores represented one of five quantitative measures. All other things being equal, admission of the top 50 percent of applicants reflected the rank order of their SAT I scores.

At many other selective institutions, no such tight correlation holds between test scores and admissions. For example, in the year 2000 entering class at Brown University, only 30 percent of the applicants with SAT-Verbal scores between 750 and 800 were admitted although Brown could have filled its class twice over from this applicant pool alone. Seven percent of those admitted had SAT-Verbal scores between 500 and 540.[1] Obviously, Brown took account of much more than an applicant's SAT I scores, and many other institutions do too.

Brown receives fifteen thousand applications each year. Each application file contains a high school transcript, a school recommendation, assorted teacher recommendations, SAT scores (the SAT I and three SAT IIs), a personal essay, and interview information. (Many, although not all, applicants are interviewed by someone on the admissions staff or by an alumnus.) Every file is read at least twice by the admissions staff and given two numerical ratings (ranging from 6 for high to 1 for low), the first for academic qualities and the second for nonacademic qualities. The assignment of a rating reflects the file reader's overall assessment. There are no minimum SAT or HSGPA cut-offs, and no fixed priority among the several items in the file. Each reader completes her task by appending a paragraph summing up her impressions.

After this initial double-reading, some applicants are admitted without further review and some are rejected. Files falling in the middle get further consideration. The admissions committee reassesses the academic and personal achievements of each applicant, now in conjunction with other desiderata important to Brown (for example, an applicant's desire to major in an underutilized area, display of unusual artistic or athletic skills, or possession of an ethnic or regional affiliation underrepresented in the student body). Based on this process, the admissions committee makes offers to about 2,500 applicants to fill a class of fewer than 1,500 freshmen.[2]

An applicant's SAT I scores give the Brown admissions committee one snapshot of her academic ability, to set alongside several others: her HSGPA (and class rank, if available), SAT II scores, recommendations, quality of high school, rigor of courses taken, and extrascholastic awards and prizes. Does the SAT I play an indispensable role in Brown's decisions? As one of many pieces of information about an applicant's academic potential, it could probably be omitted without much loss, especially because Brown also requires

SAT II scores. Even so, Brown sees enough value in the test to continue to require it (or the ACT as a substitute).

Brown's admissions process is extremely labor-intensive. An admissions office that performs similarly must be sizable and command a budget that makes possible such intensive consideration of every single application. Institutions without Brown's deep pockets cannot—or will not—invest the same time and effort.

Consider, by contrast, the procedures in place at the University of Georgia in 1999. For each of the more than ten thousand applications it received, the university computed an Academic Index (AI) by combining an applicant's HSGPA and SAT I (or ACT) scores with a small additional weighting for quality of curriculum. If an applicant whose combined SAT scores were 1000 or above had an AI of 2.86 or higher,[3] he was automatically admitted; if he had an AI of less than 2.40, he was automatically rejected.[4] Roughly 85 percent of the freshman class was admitted in this manner.[5] Those applicants who fell between the upper and lower AI cut-offs moved to a second stage in which the university computed a Total Student Index (TSI) from points or fractions of points added on the basis of twelve factors. Three were factors already counted in computing the AI, namely HSGPA, SAT scores, and quality of high school curriculum.[6] The second set comprised "leadership/activity" and "other" factors: hours spent on extracurricular activities and out-of-school work; parental or sibling ties to the university; and first-in-family to attend college. The third set included "demographic" factors. An applicant could get 0.5 points for being nonwhite, 0.25 points for being male, and 0.75 for being a Georgia resident.[7] After the TSI was computed, those with a score of 4.93 or higher were admitted and those with a score below 4.66 were rejected.[8] The remaining applications—only a small percentage at this point—proceeded to the third stage, Edge Read (ER). At ER, the applications were actually read by members of the admissions staff—read, as opposed to merely skimmed to note and record the presence of AI and TSI factors.

These details about the University of Georgia's 1999 procedures were included in a lawsuit complaining that the university's mechanical assignment of points for being nonwhite violated the Constitution. This point-assignment took place only in the second, TSI, phase of consideration, where only about fifteen hundred files were still in play. In defense of its automatically assigning racially based points instead of treating race as one among many plus-factors to be considered in an applicant, the university pleaded that it could not practicably provide personalized analysis of applications.[9] Thus, while Brown could carefully double-read fifteen thousand applications, Georgia insisted that it could not read fifteen hundred even once.

Obviously, the SAT I played a larger role in Georgia's procedures than in Brown's because the bulk of Georgia's admissions were based on an index

combining HSGPA and SAT I scores (with an addition for difficulty of curriculum). Georgia had to revise its admissions scheme after 2001 because the
Court of Appeals for the Eleventh Circuit found it unconstitutional; in 2003
the U.S. Supreme Court reached the same decision in *Gratz v. Bollinger*
about a similar admissions process at the University of Michigan.[10] The university can no longer mechanically assign points for race (and gender). Georgia's current admissions website indicates that "demonstrated academic
achievement" counts most heavily in admissions decisions, and in measuring
this achievement, "GPA and rigor of curriculum weigh roughly two-to-one
to standardized tests." Thus, "a student with a 4.0 GPA in a superior curriculum" might be admitted with an SAT score at or below 1000" while
another "with a 3.0 GPA and an SAT score of 1400" might not be.[11] In the
AI phase of assessment, then, three measures, all predictors of academic success, determine the fate of an applicant. SAT scores and HSGPA predict first-
year grades. According to Clifford Adelman, the third measure—the quality
of the applicant's high school curriculum—is by far the most significant
because it predicts degree completion better than anything else.[12]

Many variations are possible along the spectrum lying between the intense
personalized attention of each application at Brown and the largely mechanical processing at Georgia. A cursory look at a range of institutions shows,
however, an interesting uniformity. First, colleges seldom use the SAT (or
ACT) as a sole exclusionary device. Second, they almost always read high
school grades and test scores in light of the academic intensity of the applicant's high school curriculum. Indeed, almost unfailingly, the first thing a
potential applicant finds when she visits a college's admissions website is a
description of a minimum required or recommended college preparatory
curriculum.

For example, Brown recommends that applicants take four years of high
school English with "significant emphasis" on writing, three years of college
preparatory mathematics, three years of a foreign language, two years of a
laboratory science beyond the freshman level, two years of history, and one
year of music or art. With only small variations, this recommendation holds
good at such institutions as the University of Tennessee at Knoxville, Lewis
and Clark College, Santa Clara University, Johns Hopkins University, Kenyon College, University of Cincinnati, Boston University, University of
Nebraska at Lincoln, Smith College, Northwestern University, Arizona
State University, Claremont McKenna College, Butler University, Elon College, and the University of Alabama at Tuscaloosa.[13]

At James Madison University, for example, of the six elements in an
admissions selection, quality of the high school curriculum comes first, then
HSGPA and class rank, SAT (or ACT) scores, record of extracurricular activities, recommendations from high school teachers and counselors, and statement of personal aims.[14] All these items together give an institution the best

picture of a student's ability to profit from admission and to contribute to the overall institutional climate, both cultural and intellectual.

The SAT I does not play an irreplaceable role in this picture. Other national *standardized* measures could take its place. Brown could easily omit the SAT I because it requires three SAT II subject area scores. Richard Atkinson's proposal that the University of California system eliminate the SAT I involves using in its place SAT II scores already required of UC applicants (or scores from some achievement test yet devised). Atkinson did not propose dropping standardized tests themselves.

While the strength of an applicant's high school curriculum is important to an admissions committee, no committee would admit blindly based on strength alone without looking at the applicant's grades. But individual high schools differ so much from one another—in the quality of their teachers, the strictness of their grading, and the like—that an admissions committee is justifiably reluctant to rely on high school grades alone, even when it can augment them with information about high school quality. What a standardized test such as the SAT I or the ACT provides is an objective measure based on a comprehensive national cross-section of college-goers. The test scores add one useful element to an overall estimation and decision by an admissions committee. Because the SAT I and the ACT have been in use for decades, they provide a vertical as well as horizontal national context for assessing a college applicant's complete file. The admissions committee can act on the basis of substantial past experience with the test scores.

Even after their extensive criticisms of the SAT, Crouse and Trusheim hesitate to endorse an immediate across-the-board abolition of the test. Such an action could have long-run effects that hurt colleges, they caution.[15] For example, applicant pools might rearrange themselves in unforeseeable ways if all institutions dropped the SAT. Moreover, like many other critics of the SAT, Crouse and Trusheim do not support elimination of standardized tests as part of the college admission process. Tests based more solidly on high school achievement, they believe, would create more productive incentives for students and schools alike.[16]

The SAT I is not without its usefulness but its usefulness comes at an educational price. Sociologist Christopher Jencks emphasizes this price:

> No other country uses a test like the SAT to screen university applicants. Other countries use tests that cover (and largely determine) what prospective applicants have studied in secondary school. These tests resemble university examinations more closely than the SAT does, and they predict university grades more accurately. By relying on achievement tests to choose among applicants, universities abroad also reap other benefits. First, weak secondary schools know what their best students must learn in order to get into a good college. This probably improves the courses offered by weak schools. Second, because admis-

sion is contingent on how much applicants have learned, ambitious teenagers have more incentive to study hard.[17]

Thus, according to Jencks, the widespread use of the SAT provides the wrong kind of incentives to secondary schools and their students. This was what the University of California's president Richard Atkinson meant when he claimed that the SAT "distorts learning."

The SAT may indeed distort learning, although Jencks's, Atkinson's, and Crouse and Trusheim's conclusions are speculative. If the University of California begins relying only on the SAT II subject area tests—or develops its own standardized tests geared directly to the California secondary school curriculum—the state will become a laboratory for experimentation and information-gathering about these matters.

What will not be much affected by the substitution of the SAT II battery for the SAT I is the predictive power of the test scores. Crouse and Trusheim point out that ETS's own studies over the years suggest "that, on average, SAT and achievement scores predict freshman grades equally well, though the pattern varies from college to college. In most colleges, scores on ETS's achievement tests are almost interchangeable with SAT scores."[18] Interchangeability is further confirmed in a recent study by Saul Geiser and Roger Studley commissioned for the University of California system. Because the University of California requires applicants to submit three SAT II subject area scores as well as SAT I scores, Geiser and Studley had access to data that allowed them to see how the various tests predicted first-year grades for 78,000 freshmen who entered the university between 1996 and 1999. They conclude that the SAT II composite scores do a better job than the SAT I of predicting freshman grades. When SAT IIs are added to HSGPA, the combination explains about 22 percent of the variance in first-year grades, a figure slightly higher than when the SAT I is added to HSGPA. Adding the SAT I to the SAT II/HSGPA combination does not further augment predictive power.[19] If the SAT IIs equally or better predict first-year success, then only transition costs (and they may not be small) stand in the way of supplanting the SAT I with a battery of achievement tests that *may* generate more desirable educational incentives for high school students and their institutions.

THE REAL COSTS: RACE REVISITED

The speculation by critics that significant educational costs are associated with using the SAT I supports a reasonable though not conclusive case for moving to standardized achievement tests. When weighing up the SAT I's educational costs and benefits, the scale may tip against it.

However, the SAT has not been a thirty-year lightning rod for attack because of the undesirable educational incentives it possibly produces. For example, while Crouse and Trusheim dwell in their concluding chapter on the educational pros and cons of using the SAT, in two preceding chapters they hammer home a seemingly more telling cost—that using the SAT adversely affects admission of blacks and low-income students. As we saw in the last chapter, it is the *equity* cost, not the educational cost, that draws the most vociferous complaints about the SAT.

Yet when they turn to their proposals at the end of their book, Crouse and Trusheim concede that using "achievement tests would not be likely to lower the rejection of applicants from low-income and nonwhite backgrounds compared to the SAT."[20] Earlier in the book, this rejection rate seemed to indict the SAT. Why doesn't it indict achievement tests?

Likewise, when Richard Atkinson proposed scrapping the SAT I at the University of California, he gestured toward *both* the educational and equity costs of using the test. However, the Geiser and Studley study done for his office shows clearly that substituting the SAT IIs for the SAT I would not have "any substantial effect on the demographic make-up of the UC admissions pool." African Americans applicants fall .71 standard deviations below the mean for all UC applicants on the SAT I composite Verbal and Math score while falling .70 standard deviations below the mean on the SAT II composite Writing, Math, and Third Test score.[21]

Still, there is an aspect of the SAT I's unevenly distributed burdens that may seem to disqualify it. We consider it here at some length.

Suppose the SAT I is a valid and reliable predictor of first-year grades and adds some real value to admissions decisions. Using it might still be unfair to blacks. The reason is that the SAT does not predict equally for all subpopulations. In particular, it does not predict first-year grades for African Americans as well as it does for whites. We noted a dimension of this phenomenon in the last chapter when we pointed out that the SAT *overpredicts* the grades of black students. However, it does not overpredict black performance as badly as HSGPA alone, which is the reason that, when the SAT is combined with HSGPA as a predictor, the combination cuts harder proportionately against African Americans.[22] Now, as it turns out, in the California study the SAT II composite scores overpredict black grades less markedly that the SAT I. This has prompted some in California to oppose Atkinson's proposal, for fear that SAT II combined with HSGPA will cut against black applicants even more strongly than the SAT I.

Overprediction seems to favor black students—they get admitted at SAT score levels that make them look more capable than their subsequent performance bears out. Yet overprediction derives from a further fact, namely that the SAT doesn't predict the academic performance of black students quite as well as it predicts the performance of whites. This further fact works against black applicants. To illustrate, consider the following two scatter plots representing two groups of applicants. Line Z represents perfect correlation between SAT scores and predicted grades (given on the X and Y axes, respectively). Every dot in the scatter plots—representing first-year grades—would fall on this line in the case of such perfect correlation. Of course, the correlation between SAT scores and grades isn't perfect, and the actual grades applicants would attain are dispersed on either side of the line. Nevertheless, in Scatter Plot W, the dispersed dots are clustered fairly near to Z. Let's say that the score-grade correlation coefficient in W is 0.6.

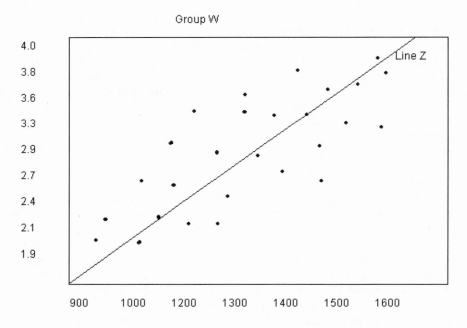

In Scatter Plot B, the dots are more widely dispersed, indicating a lower correlation coefficient (let's say 0.45).

Suppose a (very small) college wants to admit students who will achieve at least a 2.4 GPA in their freshman year and uses only SAT scores as predictors. Accordingly, it will accept applicants with scores at or above 1200 (the point where a horizontal line drawn from 2.4 intersects Z). Let's see how this policy plays out in the two different cases.

In W, the policy results in two false positives (acceptance of two students who fail to achieve a 2.4) and three false negatives (rejection of three students who would have surpassed 2.4).

In B, the policy results in six false positives and five false negatives. If the college wants to decrease its false positives, it can move its selection line to

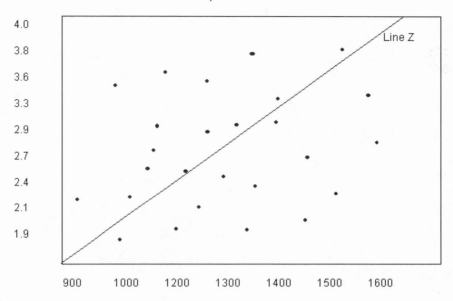

Group B

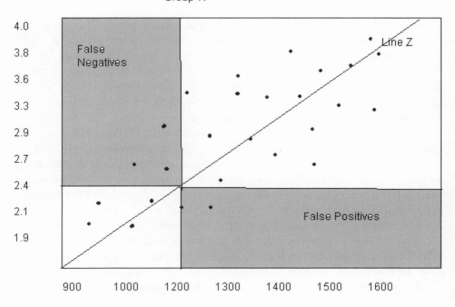

Group W

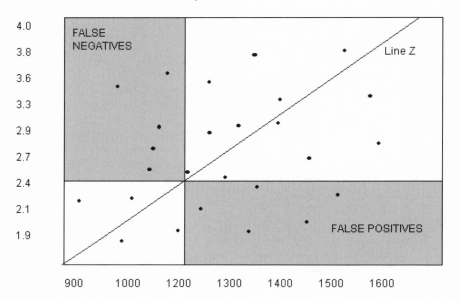

Group B

the right, using higher and higher SAT scores as cut-offs. But in doing so, it will increase its false negatives. In case B, this result is more extreme than in the case W.

The fact that SAT scores do not predict first-year grades for blacks as well as they do for whites means that scatter plots comparing SAT scores and attained grades will differ for whites and blacks much in the way Scatter Plots W and B differ. Using the SAT as a filter will, among other things, reject proportionately more blacks who could have succeeded than whites. Put the other way around, the odds of acceptance by a black applicant who could succeed in college are smaller than those of a similarly situated white.[23]

Surely, then, on the assumption that like cases should be treated alike, this upshot reflects a kind of unfairness that ought to preclude using the SAT. But this conclusion is too hasty. The question is what colleges would use in its place. Recall that HSGPA also has different predictive powers for white and black students. Indeed, it is worse in this regard than the SAT.[24] Redrawing our initial scatter plots using HSGPA instead of SAT scores to predict a 2.4 first-year average would show an even wider dispersal in B. However, because the level of overprediction is greater than with the SAT, using HSGPA as a filter is more lenient to blacks because it admits more black false positives. Taking steps to decrease those false positives (by raising the HSGPA hurdle) increases the number of false negatives.

If SAT IIs come into widespread use, they too will likely predict less well for African Americans than for whites, although if the results of the University of California study hold for the larger universe of college applicants, the SAT IIs may minimize the difference. This would provide an additional reason for substituting them in place of the SAT I (although not one that necessarily points to any benefit for black applicants).

This substitution may not take place, however, since, in response to the University of California's threats to abandon the SAT I, the College Board has announced plans to revise it considerably, aligning it more closely to high school curricula.[25] The new SAT may yield more accurate predictions for both blacks and whites, or it may yield the same pattern displayed by the present SAT. Since the ACT, which has always been more closely aligned with high school curricula, produces outcomes not very different from those produced by the present SAT I, there is not much reason to think the new SAT I will make a marked difference in any of the matters discussed in this chapter and the last.

To what degree does use of the SAT *really* produce unequal probabilities of acceptance for similarly capable black and white applicants? We cannot answer this question directly from the account just given because it relies on an artificial admissions system. No actual selective college admits solely on the basis of an SAT cut-off score. The effects of the SAT in real admissions decisions are cushioned by the other factors—and their weights—that colleges use. However, some of these other factors filter out blacks from college eligibility even when they don't treat like cases differently. For example, the legitimate emphasis colleges place upon an applicant's having taken a solid college preparatory curriculum in high school cuts adversely against blacks because they are far less likely than whites to have taken the requisite math, science, and language courses.[26]

A RADICALLY DIFFERENT APPROACH?

Our focus so far has been on the SAT's power to predict academic success as measured by first-year grades. One complaint lodged against the SAT is that "academic success" ought to be construed much more broadly than simply getting adequate first-year grades, and when it is, the SAT ceases to be a predictor of success at all. Academic success broadly conceived, goes the charge, should focus on a student's entire educational career, including his degree completion and his subsequent use of the skills and maturation picked up along the way.

This way of thinking seems to focus on what is important. After all, no one really cares about college students' first-year grades except insofar as they indicate something about other outcomes. What matters is how students fare throughout college, whether they graduate in a timely fashion, and what they do with their lives afterward.

The flaw in this line of reasoning for decision makers who must choose among applicants is that there are no reliable predictors of academic success in this broader sense, or even half-way good ones. What would admissions committees put in place of standardized test scores and HSGPA? Letters of recommendation? Applicant essays? Personal interviews? Gut-level hunches? As we have seen, admissions officers consider all these factors and more, often in a subtle and sophisticated way. Their decision making reflects the fact that the missions of most colleges and universities are multiple and diverse, and academic success narrowly construed is but one goal among several. Yet the judgments of admissions officers are leavened by numerical measures that predict first-year grades. Without that leavening, how would judgment proceed? Degree completion or years in school might serve as alternative benchmarks to first-year grades, but apart from the influence of high school curriculum noted by Adelman, "surprisingly little is known about the predictors of college graduation," observe Frederick Vars and William Bowen.[27] More remote postcollege outcomes such as personal intellectual growth and contribution to the community are too ill-defined to serve as targets for measuring predictive success. As much as decision makers and critics might like the matter to be otherwise, predictive success seems tethered to standardized test scores and HSGPA.

For those dissatisfied with this response, another route beckons: abandon the very attempt to predict academic success. Lani Guinier and Susan Sturm aim to cut the tether by suggesting a wholly different approach to selection. In their view, institutions should adopt a performance-based, as opposed to a prediction-based, model: if we want to know whether someone can do a job or pass a course, we let him try. His success or failure at the task is the best proof of his ability. (Of course, this option assumes that success and failure in doing the job or completing the course are themselves measured fairly.)

How, then, could we operationalize such an idea in the context of college admissions? In their book *Who's Qualified?*, Guinier and Sturm offer few concrete answers.[28] Guinier has subsequently amplified their ideas, but only barely. She writes:

> Some colleges might abandon the SAT . . . entirely. . . . Other institutions, such as large universities with tens of thousands of applications, might consider using tests only as a floor—accepting no students with scores below which no one previously succeeded in graduating. Above that floor, applicants could be chosen by several alternatives, including a lottery. Concerns about a lottery's insensitivity to an institution's particular needs or values could be dealt with by increasing the selection prospects of applicants with the skills, abilities, or back-

grounds that are valued by the institution. For example, a weighted lottery could enhance the chances that certain students will be selected by putting their names in two or three times. Depending on the state's or locality's needs, the institution could weight the names of students who come from underrepresented communities or demographic groups, or students who make five-year public-service commitments to work in disadvantaged communities upon graduation.[29]

To this lottery proposal Guinier adds two further ideas. First, noting that the University of Georgia's mechanical approach to diversity fared badly in court because it did not "assess each applicant as an individual rather than as a member of a particular racial group," she suggests that, as a "confirmative action" alternative, the university could require each applicant to write a "diversity essay" describing "how the applicant would contribute to the diversity of the intellectual community that is dedicated to preparing its graduates to function consistently with the institution's democratic mission."[30] The diversity essay could show "evidence of a long-term commitment to public service, leadership, and group problem-solving skills—especially those involved in overcoming obstacles or working with diverse communities—and an ability to contribute to a successful multiracial educational experience for other students.[31] Second, Guinier proposes that flagship campuses might reserve space in the sophomore or junior classes "for students who have maintained B averages at community colleges, where admission would be open to all."[32]

These ideas fall far short of charting a course for a boldly different approach to college admissions. For one thing, although Guinier and Sturm claim to reject the predictive approach to admission, the very point of the diversity essay Guinier proposes is to provide evidence an admissions committee can use to predict which applicants are genuinely committed to public service, leadership, and group problem-solving approaches. Moreover, Guinier doesn't tell us how admissions officers would weigh the diversity essay alongside traditional indicators.

A lottery, of course, is not predictive: it chooses blindly. But how exactly would a lottery work? According to Guinier, the lottery pool for a college should comprise every applicant who gets equal to or more than a "floor" score on the SAT, where the floor score is defined as the lowest score any previous graduate of the college has ever had. This clearly sets the floor too low. Suppose that in the last fifty years one student with an SAT combined score of 900 graduated from Brown. The next lowest score was 1020; and 75 percent of students scoring between 1020 and 1100 who graduated did so with GPAs of 2.1.

Obviously, under Guinier's lottery system, every low-scoring high school senior in the country would have an incentive to apply to Brown. The admissions committee would need to select 2,500 individuals to be tendered offers of admission by flipping a coin among not 15,000 but, say, 75,000 applicants. The outcome would inevitably produce a high number of extreme mismatches between Brown's academic demands and its new students' capabilities. Of course, Guinier allows Brown to weight the lottery. For example, if an applicant had straight As in high school, might not Brown put her name in the pool three times? Suppose 10,000 applicants fit this description. This means that Brown would randomize over a pool of nearly a 100,000 applicants (since some are now triple-counted). Chance alone will still throw a lot of academic duds Brown's way. Could Brown, then, do the same weighting for applicants who score over 1500 on the SAT? Since many of these will have been the straight-A students, several thousand applicants will get listed six times in the pool. What about class rank and scores on SAT II achievement tests? Can Brown weight them separately as well? If so, the pool is going to approach 250,000, with several thousand individuals holding 20 or 30 tickets each. By iterating this process, Brown could give a chance to every applicant with an SAT score of 900 or slightly above—a vanishingly small chance—while retaining a student profile much like the one it currently exhibits. The lottery would be rigged.

That Guinier's lottery idea can be lampooned does not mean that a lottery is out of the question as a selection mechanism. It does mean that Guinier has not thought through the tough questions a serious lottery proposal would pose. More to the point, a lottery is a bad vehicle for conveying what is distinctive about Guinier and Sturm's own approach, namely their brief for the superiority of performance-based over prediction-based models of selection. Indeed, the lottery proposal diverts attention from the main issue.

Let's return, then, to the idea of performance-based selection in higher education. Recall Guinier's proposal that flagship campuses reserve places in their sophomore and junior classes for community college students who maintain a B average. Community colleges "would be open to all," she writes. Her use of the conditional here is odd. Almost all public community colleges *are* open to all. Moreover, university systems already *do* reserve places for high scoring community college students.

California provides an example. Two of the University of California campuses—Riverside and Davis—guarantee admission to students at a large array of California's community colleges. The guarantee is made through the form of an individualized contract signed by the student, the community college transfer counselor, and the university's transfer counselor. The contract specifies a list of course and grade requirements the student must meet. The requirements are more stringent than those for regular transfer but provide an assured place in the university once they are met. A student with a B average in core academically demanding courses—the standard identified by

Guinier in her third proposal as a possible threshold—would be a good candidate for one of these programs.

California is not alone. In Massachusetts, a community college student, through a joint admissions program, can get a conditional acceptance at a state university that turns into actual acceptance once the student has met all associate's degree requirements.[33] In Washington, community college students can execute a direct transfer agreement, which ensures their admission to the University of Washington if they complete their work with at least a B-minus average.[34]

When the higher education systems in California, Massachusetts, Washington, and other states are viewed as a whole, they all provide a performance-based mode of entry. No student in any state is barred by a bad high school record or low admission test scores from proving, *by actual college performance*, that she is capable of doing college work. And in some states, at least, the well-performing community college student is assured a pathway to a flagship university where she may complete her baccalaureate.

In other states—Pennsylvania, for example—community colleges have transfer agreements with state colleges below the flagship level.[35] And in most states, flagship campuses give some priority to well-performing transfers from their state's own community college campuses.

However, performance-based admissions need not proceed through the community college system alone. Consider the options available to students who want to attend Texas Tech University. Like most other selective universities, it uses standardized tests and high school rank as a partial basis for admission. For example, a student falling in the lower half of her high school class would need an SAT composite score of 1270 to gain admission. If she fails to meet this standard for assured admission, her application can still be "reviewed in order to evaluate other factors that could influence success at Texas Tech." Suppose, however, that even this additional review fails to gain her acceptance. She can still seek entry through "provisional admission." She can enroll at Texas Tech in the summer or spring after her high school graduation and achieve a C-plus average in 13 hours of basic courses. She will then be admitted as a regular student. Finally, there is the community college option: she can complete 24 or more hours of core requirements with a 2.25 average and transfer from community college to Texas Tech. Thus, she has three "performance" options in addition to the traditional "predictive" option. She can show her mettle through an intensive summer program, through a spring semester try-out, or through community college coursework.

Performance-based models can be integrated into regular college admissions procedures without resort to pie-in-the-sky lottery schemes. Whatever their missions, colleges achieve them by a particular route. They subject students to an academic curriculum. When that curriculum is demanding, a college has to predict which of its applicants can meet the challenge. Of course, actually performing a task is one sure way for a student to show he can do it, even if he fails to show it in other ways. Thus, all else being equal, ample opportunities ought to be available through the community college route or through provisional admissions programs, such as Texas Tech's, for students who don't initially succeed in proving their worth to a four-year institution.

Guinier and Sturm premise their performance-based model on a commitment and an assumption. The commitment is to expanding opportunities for those from lower socioeconomic groups. They attack the SAT as an unjust barrier to lower-income kids getting a college education. Their assumption is that performance-based methods of admission would actually boost the inclusion of such kids. The commitment is commendable but the assumption is dubious. In a study done by Steve Chatman, director of student affairs research at the University of California, Davis, transfer students from community college who best succeeded at Davis were found to (i) be from families with high incomes, (ii) have clear goals, (iii) possess strong motivation, (iv) develop early aspirations, (v) stay the course without interruption, (vi) establish contact with a four-year school before transfer, (vii) follow a rigorous program of study, (viii) achieve high grades, (ix) transfer a high number of credit hours, and (x) hold an associate's degree.[36] Thus, the performance-based way of getting into a University of California campus looks more like an avenue for well-focused, middle-class kids than one for the low-income students Guinier and Sturm have in mind. We shouldn't be surprised. After all, when CUNY became an "open admissions" institution thirty years ago, the students who benefited most were middle-class Jewish and Catholic kids whose grades were just below the high cut-offs swept away by open admissions.

TEST PREP

One aspect of the public debate about the SAT we haven't yet touched on deserves discussion. Critics of the test point to the flourishing test prep industry in this country as evidence that the test is bankrupt (what test could be valid if its results are coachable?) and unfair (only those whose families can lay out substantial sums of money get the benefits of test preparation). Today the test prep industry includes prominent companies such as Kaplan and The Princeton Review, which offer six- to eight-week courses all over the country that cost over $800. It also includes smaller, local versions of these companies, some of which are much less expensive, and companies offering individual tutors, which can charge as much as $150–$350 an hour. Not surprisingly, students who take coaching and tutoring sessions come from wealthier families than uncoached students.

Is the SAT coachable? The test prep industry makes large claims for itself. The Princeton Review, for example, says that students who enroll in their SAT courses "improve an average of 140 points, and the top 25 percent improve by a whopping 256 points!" It guarantees that if a student's SAT scores do not improve by at least 100 points, it will "work with you again for up to a year FREE."[37] Kaplan, the Princeton Review's major competitor, claims that "the average SAT score increase of all Kaplan SAT students" is 120-plus points, with the top 28 percent improving 170 points or more.[38]

The Educational Testing Service and the College Board, who make and administer the SAT, deny that coaching produces substantial gains. Obviously, familiarity with the test format can help a test-taker maximize her performance. She can get right to work on the test questions without wasting time figuring out what to do. The College Board publishes its own test prep materials, including *10 Real SATs* and "SAT Prep Center" on its website, and encourages students to rehearse with these materials before taking the test. Moreover, students who take the SAT and then retake it tend to show some gain. The question, then, is whether, beyond the advantages accruing to test familiarity (or "testwiseness"), intensive coaching classes such as those run by Kaplan and The Princeton Review produce additional substantial gains.

In a 1999 research note, "Coaching and the SAT I," Donald Powers (of ETS) and Wayne Camara (of the College Board) report that overall the studies on the "coaching effect"

> suggest that formal test preparation programs are likely to result in an increase of between 9 and 15 points on the verbal [SAT] scale and 15 to 18 points on the math [SAT] scale. . . . These figures are increases attributed to coaching that are beyond the average increase found across groups of students who did not attend formal coaching programs.

For students who attend the Kaplan or Princeton Review programs, according to Powers and Camara, the average gains are slightly higher.[39]

Powers and Camara base their estimates on a detailed survey of 4,000 SAT test-takers in 1995–1996.[40] Their findings are in line with the few large-scale "meta-analyses" social scientists have performed over the years on the proliferating studies and experiments on "coaching effects." (Meta-analysis is a second-order enterprise that looks at a broad range of studies on a topic and uses statistical techniques to offset or correct, where possible, the methodological limitations of individual studies.) The main meta-analyses are by Samuel Messick and Ann Jungeblut (1981),[41] Rebecca DerSimonian and Nan M. Laird (1983),[42] Betsy Jane Becker (1990),[43] and Donald E. Powers (1993).[44] We also include here the survey article by Lloyd Bond (1993),[45] written for a handbook on educational measurement sponsored by the National Council on Measurement in Education and the American Council on Education.

Like any complicated cause-and-effect question, devising the perfect study for coaching effects on SAT scores—one that assures the detected effects are effects of the cause being investigated and not some other factor—proves very difficult. Some studies don't use control groups. The better studies do. However, using control groups brings problems of its own. For example, control groups can be contaminated. If a study aims to see if a special program improves "testwiseness," it cannot be certain that members of the control group don't familiarize themselves with test format and test-taking techniques in informal ways. This kind of contamination is less likely in studies where the "treatment" group is subjected to special academic content not accessible to the control group, or where the control group is given a delayed "treatment." Even so, many other problems remain. For example, in an experimental setting, students may be less motivated to take tests seriously or to take the coaching seriously. Members of control or treatment groups may drop out midway through a study. Control groups and treatment groups may not match in significant ways (in class rank, for example, or level of math courses taken).[46] Some studies overcome this problem by randomizing assignment to control and treatment groups, but many others do not.

Apart from the problems in setting up studies are problems in definition. What counts as "coaching"? As Messick and Jungblut note: "Some writers restrict their usage of the term to practice on sample [test] items and last-minute cramming . . . whereas others include under the same rubric virtually full-time instruction at specialized preparatory schools for periods of 6 months or more."[47] Thus, anyone investigating coaching and coaching studies must beware of comparing apples and oranges.

Further difficulties concern the different test–retest mechanisms and adjustments in different studies. Many studies use an administration of the PSAT (preliminary SAT)—which high school students typically take in their junior year—as the initial test, and then an unofficial administration of the SAT (often in nonstandard or shortened form) as the second test, but some studies use made-up tests at both ends. Since the PSAT is shorter than the (unmodified) SAT, the scores from the two administrations have to be equated before they can be compared. Moreover, the resulting raw score increase has to be adjusted. First, because there is a typical test–retest learning effect, a coaching study has to estimate the gain in test scores that would result without any coaching and discount the gain by that amount. Second, if the coaching lasts for a considerable period—say six months—the study has to further estimate the gains that maturation and normal course work over that period would produce and do a similar discounting.

Nevertheless, despite the muddied waters of coaching studies, certain conclusions emerge from the meta-analyses. DerSimonian and Laird conclude that when coached students are simply compared to national norms as in uncontrolled studies, the mean gains in verbal and math scores [from coaching] are about 40 and 50 points. For controlled, but unmatched and unrandomized studies, the mean gain is about 15 points for both math and verbal scores, and is reduced to about 10 points for matched and randomized studies.[48]

Likewise, Bond speaks of the "10–20 points [gained through coaching] typically found in well-designed studies of the SAT"[49] and Becker concurs in this conclusion.[50] Thus, the *average* gain from going through the Kaplan or Princeton Review programs is probably on the order Powers and Camara suggest: 10 points on the SAT-Verbal score and 22 points on the SAT-Math score.[51]

Of course, not every test-taker reaps the average gain and some coached retest scores can be high. Anecdotal evidence abounds of enormous improvements, especially within the circles of upper middle-class students and parents. No doubt some of the anecdotes are true. In any case, for ambitious—and affluent—families, $800 is a small price to pay for a chance at greatly improved scores. Consequently, Kaplan, Princeton Review, and their smaller cousins thrive.

Powers and Camara report that most students spend some time preparing for the SAT I, mostly by buying how-to books, using the College Board's own familiarization materials, or at least taking the PSAT. The riches Kaplan, Princeton Review, and the other test-prep companies sweep in come from only 12 percent of students planning to take the SAT.[52] Let's assume that some or even many of that 12 percent make score gains greater than the academic studies indicate and closer to the gains claimed by the coaching companies. Do they have an unfair advantage, and if so, over whom? On the one hand, the child of working-class parents, white or black, is likely aiming at a second- or third-tier state school nearby, where a few points on her SAT score may not matter, or the local community college, where the score won't matter at all. On the other hand, most kids, minority and white, competing for Stanford or Duke or Amherst are middle- or upper-middle class and can afford to pay Princeton Review for its services. Those most likely to be disadvantaged by the test-prep opportunities of affluent students, we surmise, are some middle-class kids whose parents can't afford the sizeable outlay for a full-blown prep course or to whom it seems an extravagant indulgence.

To some extent, the advantage, if any, that Kaplan and Princeton Review afford well-to-do students can be tempered if not altogether neutralized. Rebecca Zwick notes a 1996 survey showing that slightly over half of American high schools offer SAT coaching. In the years since then, state legislatures have begun funding aggressive test-prep efforts. California, for example, has embarked on a multiyear program (the College Preparation Partnership Program) to coach all college-bound students from low-income families on taking the SAT or ACT. Indeed, Princeton Review has won state contracts to tutor a third of these students, according to Zwick.[53]

It is important here to reemphasize the fundamental dynamic at work in the admissions scramble: too much demand, too little supply. An overabundance of smart and well-credentialed students is competing for a limited number of prestigious slots. If colleges and universities abandon the SAT and rely on achievement tests instead, the competition for the winning edge will shift its focus to enhanced achievement (more than it already has). The advantages that advantage buys will not go away.

As a lesson in perspective, it's valuable to contrast the American admissions scramble with another. In Japan, every step of the educational ladder is reached through achievement tests. Students cannot move on to high school without passing an entrance exam, and they cannot move on to college without passing another. Getting into one of Japan's national universities is especially hard because the spots are limited and the scramble is extraordinarily fierce. Graduating from a prestigious university is the only ticket to the top ranks of government, law, finance, business, and education in Japan.

Thirty to 40 percent of junior high students in Japan attend commercial "cramming schools" after the regular school day, from 5:00 to 8:30 or 7:00 to 10:00 in the evening. They do additional cram schooling on Saturday evenings. High school students use the cram schools even more frenetically because the stakes are enormous, and Sundays are gobbled up, along with all other free time, in studying for college entrance exams. *Yobiko*, as the cram schools at this stage are called, run year-round. Students who fail to get into college become *ronin* (from "samurai who've lost their masters")—full-time students at a *yobiko*, studying for the next year's round of entrance exams. Imagine yourself after graduating from high school attending Princeton Review sessions all day, every day, every week, all year to get ready to score 1550 on the SAT. That is the daily lot of the *ronin*. Worse yet, imagine yourself first taking a cram course to pass the *entrance exam* to get into the Princeton Review cram course! Competition to get into the better *yobiko* in Japan is so intense that many of them admit only by entrance exam.

It is not unusual for *ronin* to spend a second full year at a *yobiko*, and in some cases a third. As many as 36 percent of college matriculants in Japanese universities are *ronin* who have spent at least a year of extra full-time study after high school.[54]

The commercial sector in Japan devoted to test preparation completely dwarfs American efforts. Recently, the Japanese government, in an effort to ease the burden on students, eliminated school on Saturday. The shift is producing the opposite effect, however. Japanese parents, convinced that less school exposure means a child less prepared to compete, are rushing to enroll their children in the already jam-packed cram schools. Share prices of cram companies on the Osaka and Tokyo stock exchanges are at all-time highs.[55]

SOME CONCLUSIONS

Many of the most vociferous attacks against the SAT are misplaced. There is no question that students' scores are closely correlated with the incomes of their parents. But so are grades, class rank, achievement test scores, rigor of curriculum, and other measures colleges use. The SAT may be marginally worse in this respect, but only marginally so. The real question of interest is the causal mechanism that produces these correlations. The mechanism is complex and many-faceted, but the University of California study we referred to earlier hints at some of its features, describing the path of transition from junior college to a UC campus. Middle- and upper-middle-class kids grow up expecting to go to college, guided by parents and schools into demanding courses and monitored in their academic progress. The parents have been investing in state tuition annuities or other college savings programs for years. The students read books, play musical instruments, participate on youth sports travel teams, and know something of the world outside their immediate circle. They are prepared for the opportunities offered by a demanding four-year college, whether those opportunities are prediction-based or performance-based.

Changing or even abandoning the SAT I won't alter the prospects for low-income students, who will still find themselves on the lower rungs of the admissions ladder. To change that fact something different is required. We return to this point in chapter 11.

8

The SAT on Trial

It's no surprise that criticism of the SAT as a discriminatory instrument has transmuted into litigation. The test has been hauled before the bar of legal judgment and has not fared well. Prevailing law and regulation might seem ripe to support an all-out assault against it. The story about the legal peril to the SAT is complicated, and we must defer its conclusion to the next chapter. Here we make a beginning.

A FIRST ATTACK: THE SAT AND
THE REGENTS SCHOLARSHIPS

For most of the twentieth century New York State dispensed Regents Scholarships to worthy high school students. Until 1974, the students were chosen through their performance on a six-hour examination. That year, a Select Committee on Higher Education bridled at the inegalitarian consequences of the exam, charging that it "can be criticized for actually rewarding family background and upbringing that enables students to study and perform well, rather than an objective kind of merit."[1] The legislature then created a two-tier system, awarding students tuition assistance based on need and Regents Scholarships based on achievement. It also created a new award, the Empire State Scholarships of Excellence, to be granted to the top one thousand Regents Scholarship winners. Finally, as a cost-cutting measure, the legislature directed the State Education Department to discontinue the Regents exam itself and substitute a "nationally established competitive" test.

The department subsequently adopted the SAT as the screen for Regents Scholarships because most college-bound New Yorkers would be taking that test in any case. However, the use of the SAT immediately prompted objections. Men have always scored higher on the exam than women. This differential was reflected in New York's scholarship awards under the new policy. In 1987, for example, 72 percent of the Empire State Scholarships and 57 percent of the Regents Scholarships went to male students.[2]

Of course, if women were consistently inferior students in high school and college than men, the disparity in awards would be an unfortunate but faithful reflection of reality. Such is not the case, however. As we noted in earlier chapters, the SAT does not predict equally for all subpopulations. In the last chapter we focused on the SAT's *overprediction* of black students' college grades. By contrast, the SAT *underpredicts* the first-year college grades of female students. In college, women typically outperform comparable male students, and they get grades belied by their SAT scores. Underprediction is a very serious defect in a test such as the SAT. When SAT scores are the sole criterion for a reward, the exclusionary effects of underprediction can be stark, as the male–female ratios of the Regents award-winners exhibit.

In 1987, the New York legislature passed a law requiring that Regents Scholarships be awarded on the basis of both SAT scores and high school GPAs. As a consequence, the list of 1988 award winners was less markedly skewed toward male students. However, after this one-year experiment, the legislature failed to extend its mandate and the State Education Department returned to using the SAT as the sole measure of meritorious achievement. A female student, Khadijah Sharif, then brought suit in federal court.

Sharif prevailed. The law was sufficiently clear in 1988 that the State Department of Education should have known better than to use the SAT as the single basis of scholarship awards. The judge in *Sharif* applied several common standards. Did the New York policy have a "disparate impact" on females? Yes, it did. Even so, was the New York policy necessary to promote a legitimate end? New York's end—to encourage and reward good high school performance—was wholly within its discretion. Was the tool it used to further its end appropriate? No, it was fatally flawed. New York used the SAT in a way its makers and sponsors—ETS and the College Board—did not sanction. As the court observed, both these institutions "specifically advise against exclusive reliance on the SAT, even for the purposes for which the SAT has been validated—predicting future college performance."[3] And the SAT had never been validated as a test of high school *achievement*. Therefore, New York could not plausibly claim that using the SAT was a proper and necessary means for furthering its concededly legitimate goal.

The legal standard applied in *Sharif* went back twenty years. After the Civil Rights Act of 1964 was enacted into law, federal courts and federal agencies had to give concrete meaning to its broad prohibitions of racial discrimination. Employment cases arising under Title VII of the act soon pushed courts and agencies toward an "effects" test for discrimination, a test ratified in the Supreme Court's 1971 decision in *Griggs v. Duke Power Company*.[4] The legal standard established in *Griggs* prohibits an array of practices and actions whose effect—not purpose—is to discriminate. In brief, any employment practice amounts to discrimination if it disproportionately hurts the prospects of minorities or women *and* cannot be justified by "business necessity."

Paralleling this development under Title VII, federal departments and agencies charged with enforcing Title VI of the act ("No person . . . shall, on the ground of race, color, or national origin, be . . . subjected to discrimination under any program or activity receiving federal financial assistance")[5] formulated similar interpretations barring "disparate impact" practices. These interpretations were widespread and well-entrenched by the time the Department of Health, Education, and Welfare (HEW) completed its rule-making under Title IX of the Education Amendments of 1972 ("No person . . . shall, on the basis of sex, be . . . subjected to discrimination under any education program or activity receiving Federal financial assistance"),[6] which joined gender and racial discrimination under one concept.[7] "Disparate impact" theory as applied to educational institutions meant that schools and colleges receiving any federal aid had to justify exclusionary practices by invoking "educational necessity."

Equally well established by the time *Sharif* went to trial was the legal cloud hanging over tests. In 1978, the Equal Employment Opportunity Commission issued "Uniform Guidelines for Employee Selection Procedures," imposing upon employers the burden of proving through specific validation studies that their employment tests were good predictors of job performance. "Under no circumstance," declared the guidelines, "will the general reputation of a test . . . be accepted in lieu of evidence of validity."[8] Like the idea of "disparate impact," this demand on tests migrated to Title VI law and regulation.[9] Thus, when New York, against the warnings of ETS and the College Board, used the SAT as a measure of high school achievement (a purpose for which it was not designed) without performing any specific validation studies of its own, it virtually invited an adverse legal ruling.

A SECOND ATTACK: THE SAT AND THE NCAA

In March 1999, a federal court in Philadelphia enjoined the National Collegiate Athletic Association (NCAA) from enforcing Proposition 16, its rule for determining whether a high school student athlete can be recruited by Division I colleges and universities. Under Proposition 16, a student becomes a "full qualifier"—and thus eligible to receive an athletic scholarship and immediately play a varsity sport—by posting high school grades and admission test scores that match or exceed a sliding-scale minimum. For example, a high school graduate with a 2.0 GPA in core academic subjects becomes a full qualifier by scoring 1010 on the SAT. If his GPA is as high as

2.5, he can qualify with an SAT score of 820. (A student can offer comparable ACT scores instead.)

A high school graduate can score as low as 720 on the SAT and still become a "partial qualifier" if the sum of his test score and GPA is at least as high as that of a full qualifier. In other words, he can partially compensate for a below-minimum test score by making very good grades. As a partial qualifier, he is eligible to receive an athletic scholarship but not to play during his freshman year. Any high school student who fails to satisfy one of these two conditions can enter a Division I institution only as a paying, regular student.

When Proposition 16's predecessor, Proposition 48, took effect in 1986, it drew protests from black coaches, who deemed it unfair to minority athletes. When the slightly more rigorous Proposition 16 replaced Proposition 48 a decade later, black coaches were so incensed that they toyed with the idea of boycotting NCAA events. The gravamen of their complaint: Proposition 16's disparate impact on black students, who fail to reach the SAT cut-off score in markedly higher proportions than whites. John Chaney, Temple's basketball coach and an early critic of Proposition 16, offered a common view among black coaches in a *New York Times* editorial. Proposition 16, he insisted, had excluded students who could make it in college. He referred to one of his own players, Rasheed Brokenborough, who was raised in a poor part of Philadelphia and had scored too low on the SAT to be even a partial qualifier.

> That meant we could not provide him with any scholarship money, much as he needed it, during his freshman year, and he had to accumulate 24 credits or face expulsion. Rasheed was a serious student and finished his course work in four years plus summer school. . . . He is now doing student teaching in a Philadelphia school. He is also deeply in debt. He was punished for a crime he did not commit.[10]

Proposition 16 eliminated too many Rasheed Brokenboroughs, in Chaney's view, and most of them were black. In the words of the Black Coaches Association, "minority and low-income student athletes, academically qualified as measured by their classroom performance," have borne the brunt of a misguided effort to set academic standards. Let a student's high school grade point average suffice for admission and athletic participation, the Black Coaches Association insisted.[11]

The core narrative in *Cureton v. NCAA* is simple enough.[12] Tai Kwan Cureton and two other students denied full eligibility by Proposition 16 sued the NCAA under Title VI of the Civil Rights Act of 1964, which prohibits institutions who receive federal funds from discriminating on the basis of race. The judge determined that the NCAA fell under the scope of the title.

As we observed in discussing *Sharif*, Title VI case law establishes a two-part test of discrimination. Any practice by a covered institution is discriminatory if (i) it creates an adverse, disproportionate impact on minorities and (ii) it is not justified by "educational necessity." The second conjunct of the test itself divides into two. "Educational necessity" is established when (iii) the challenged practice is shown to bear a "manifest relationship" to a legitimate educational goal and (iv) no other practice producing less disproportionate impact serves the goal equally well.[13] In Title VI litigation, the burden of proof moves backward and forward. First, the burden lies with the plaintiff to show that the defendant's practice produces disproportionate impact. When that burden is met, the defendant must then show that the challenged practice bears a "manifest relationship" to a legitimate goal. If such a showing is made, the burden returns to the plaintiff to offer evidence of alternatives that can serve the goal as well as the challenged practice without generating the same adverse impact.

The judge's decision in *Cureton* tracked this formula. The plaintiffs established "disparate impact," in his opinion, by showing that, of those students who requested eligibility certification in 1997, 21.4 percent of African Americans were denied while only 4.2 percent of whites were.[14] Turning, then, to the defense of this disproportionate effect, the judge observed that the NCAA justified Proposition 16 as a device "designed to discourage the recruitment of athletically talented, but academically unprepared students." The NCAA used college graduation rates as a proxy measure of its success in achieving this goal. It further argued that the graduation rate for student athletes has, indeed, increased since Proposition 16 was put in place. Finally, the NCAA contended that using the 820 SAT score as a minimum for full eligibility bears a "manifest relationship" to raising graduation rates for student athletes. Its own research, it insisted, shows that SAT scores plus HSGPAs predict academic performance *and* graduation rates.[15]

The judge conceded to the NCAA that the goal of raising graduation rates of student athletes is legitimate but challenged the association's contention that the 820 cut-off bears a "manifest relation" to this goal. There were four parts to his challenge. First, he argued that the NCAA's evidence indicated a temporal relationship between the implementation of Proposition 16 and improved graduation rates for athletes, but fell short of showing causation. The evidence did not distinguish the many variables that influence graduation so that the contributory effects of Proposition 16 could be isolated.[16]

Second, the judge observed that the use of the SAT to predict graduation rates was questionable. The test has not been formally validated for that purpose; it has been validated only as a predictor of first-year academic performance. That the NCAA's own research (and the research of others) indicated a stronger or weaker correlation between SAT scores and graduation rates didn't change the fact that the test was being used for a purpose it wasn't designed for. As *Sharif* and other cases have made clear, using a test beyond its intended purposes is legally treacherous.[17]

Third, the judge could find in the NCAA's evidence no argument for the 820 score as a "logical break point." Why was this the disqualifying score rather than some adjacent one? The NCAA's reference to informal impressions that scores below 820 indicate reading problems in students wasn't sufficient.[18]

Finally, the judge noted that the NCAA's own evidence showed that partial qualifiers graduate at the same rate as full qualifiers, calling into question the contention that a score of 820 represents a true minimum below which students are at risk of academic failure.[19]

For these reasons, the judge refused to grant the NCAA's claim that the 820 score was "manifestly related" to the goal of raising student athlete graduation rates. Moreover, he argued that the plaintiffs would prevail in any case because they could point to alternative eligibility criteria that would generate a less adverse impact while not appreciably degrading achievement of the NCAA's goal. According to projections developed by the NCAA itself, weaker eligibility rules would impose smaller disparate impact on black athletes, yet still yield a student-athlete graduation rate as high as 59.8 percent. The NCAA "has not demonstrated there is anything special about" the 61.8 percent graduation rate, wrote the judge, and so it cannot insist that weaker eligibility rules do not substantially realize its goal.[20]

Thus, the judge found for the plaintiffs and enjoined the NCAA from using Proposition 16.

On appeal, the NCAA won its case—but only on a technicality. The Court of Appeals for the Third Circuit ruled that the district court's threshold finding was in error: The NCAA is *not* subject to Title VI because it receives no federal funds.[21] This ruling, however, left unchallenged the *substance* of the district court's application of Title VI to Proposition 16.

A PERFORMANCE-BASED SOLUTION

Both coach John Chaney (implicitly) and the judge in *Cureton* (explicitly) drew a fallacious conclusion from Rasheed Brokenborough's emblematic college success. Recall that the judge argued that because partial qualifiers (who scored at least 720 on the SAT) were graduating at the same rate as full qualifiers (who scored at least 820), the NCAA could not claim that 820 reflected "minimum competence" to succeed at college. And recall that John Chaney indicted Proposition 16 for excluding Rasheed Brokenborough altogether, though he went on to enroll and graduate from Temple, financing his first year through student loans.

Both the judge and Chaney make the same error. The success of partial qualifiers in general, and of Rasheed Brokenborough in particular (not even a partial qualifier), points to the wisdom of the NCAA's rule, not its folly. The partial qualifiers and nonqualifiers such as Rasheed Brokenborough succeeded under very different conditions than full qualifiers. A full qualifier is given an athletic scholarship and thrown immediately into intense, high-powered competition, practicing long hours, playing frequent games, traveling long distances—all this as a freshman trying to make the transition from high school to college, a transition difficult no matter what a student's academic credentials or background. Despite tutoring assistance and other services provided by the athletic department, the athlete's transition remains very challenging.

On the other hand, the partial qualifier also receives an athletic scholarship and can avail herself of all the tutoring help the regular athlete receives. But because she does not play her first year, she can concentrate on adjusting to the academic rigors of college life. It is no surprise, then, that partial qualifiers go on to succeed academically as well as full qualifiers. We certainly cannot conclude—as did the judge in *Cureton*—that the partial qualifiers would have done as well had they been thrown immediately into competition as freshmen.

As for Rasheed Brokenborough, the stirring story of his college success may have had everything to do with the fact that he was held out of competition on John Chaney's high-powered basketball team his first year. Suppose he had been thrown immediately into the maelstrom of constant practice and competition while facing a panoply of demanding college courses. Coming from a background devoid of real preparation for college, Rasheed would have faced a high prospect of failure that even his earnest character and diligent work habits couldn't have stayed.

In fact, Rasheed Brokenborough's case can illustrate quite a different conclusion than John Chaney meant us to draw. Chaney's complaint—and the complaint of the Black Coaches Association—focused on the false negatives (students eliminated by the cut-off who could have succeeded academically) generated by the NCAA's eligibility standards. Yet any selection system that predicts future academic success will generate false negatives because no prediction system is perfect. Such selection systems generate false positives as well (admitting students who fail academically), a fact that both Chaney and the *Cureton* judge ignore, although colleges and universities cannot. The dilemma for colleges and universities is how to strike a balance, making as few mistaken rejections as possible without opening the floodgates to seriously mistaken acceptances.

It is precisely this dilemma—and the unavoidable fact of false negatives—that Lani Guinier and Susan Sturm aim to obviate by moving universities from a prediction-based model of admissions to a performance-based model. Whatever its prospects and virtues as a *general* substitute for current university practices, the performance-based strategy provides a neat and compelling solution to the question of athletic eligibility. The answer is simple: don't let freshmen play varsity sports.[22]

Freshmen were not eligible to participate on varsity teams for most of the twentieth century. When this norm was abandoned in the 1970s, the change had nothing to do with academic concerns. It derived largely from pressures arising out of developments in college football. With the advent of the two-platoon system in the 1960s, teams needed to carry greatly enlarged squads. Coaches—and college presidents—looked at the quarter of their scholarship athletes who couldn't suit up and saw a way to leverage huge squads without further expense: make those ineligible freshmen eligible. The basic consideration today against barring freshman play remains cost: to maintain the current level of competition, teams will need more athletic scholarships, which universities cannot afford. No one advances an academic reason for maintaining freshman eligibility; no one advanced an academic reason in 1970 for adopting it.

Ending freshman eligibility would undercut the objection to Proposition 16 made by John Chaney and other black coaches. They complain that Proposition 16 denies to some disadvantaged kids the chance to prove they can succeed at college work. Eliminating both Proposition 16 and freshman eligibility together would let colleges take chances on such kids, who could then prove they can succeed at college work—by actually succeeding. Then let them play ball.

LEGAL THREAT TO THE SAT?

Does *Cureton* auger a clouded legal future for the SAT? Could similar suits be mounted directly against university athletic programs that adhere to the NCAA standards? The short answer is no. As a result of a recent Supreme Court ruling in *Alexander v. Sandoval*, there can be no more lawsuits like *Cureton*.[23] No future Tai Kwan Cureton, aggrieved at the disparate impact an educational practice imposes on him and others like him, can take his complaint to court. Why this is so requires tracing out the Byzantine contours of Title VI case law, which means opening the file on affirmative action and exploring one of its peculiar contents, the foundational case of Allan Bakke against the University of California, decided in 1978. This is the subject of the next chapter.

Institutions that use the SAT no longer have to worry that an aggressive federal judge, unwilling to defer to the judgment of educators, will put their admissions practices under a microscope. Such institutions are not home free, however, at least in theory. The Office of Civil Rights in the Department of Education could move on its own against colleges or universities it thought were misusing the SAT in the sense we have itemized in this chapter: disproportionately excluding black students without a justification sufficiently rooted in educational necessity.

The legal standard of discrimination attached to Title VI and Title IX—the disparate impact standard—is worth considering for a moment in its own right. Charges of "discrimination" and "bias" swirl around the SAT, and their meaning is not always clear. Some critics take the bare fact that the SAT scores of blacks are disproportionately lower than those of whites by itself to prove discrimination and bias. On the other side, some defenders of the SAT seem to dismiss the disproportion in scores as irrelevant because they believe that the test is a neutral assessment of academic skills reflecting real differences in preparation and ability.

The disparate impact standard strikes a sensible balance between those for whom any exclusionary effect counts as discrimination and those for whom neutrality in form and intent is all that matters in measuring fairness. The disparate impact standard imposes a certain asymmetry. It demands that institutions bend over backward to show their exclusionary practices to be adequately justified. Given our national history of racism and racial oppression, this is not an undue demand. By requiring institutions to provide clear and convincing arguments showing that their present practices are "necessary," the disparate impact standard gives institutions a strong incentive to find alternatives that both serve their ends *and* reduce the exclusion of African Americans and other groups. It gives institutions a strong incentive to find win-win solutions.

However, by requiring too much—for example, by insisting on demonstrations of "logical break points" in test scores—the burden on institutions to justify their practices could become virtually insurmountable. Now that judges have been put out of the picture by *Sandoval*, it is not likely that the U.S. Department of Education itself will be inclined to ride roughshod over universities' opinions about the SAT and its appropriate role in their admissions procedures. Indeed, when, in May 1999, three months after the *Cureton* decision, the Office of Civil Rights (OCR) in the Department of Education circulated a draft of guidelines on testing, it stirred up a hornet's nest in academia. Although OCR claimed it was merely offering a synthesis of well-settled law, many colleges and universities saw it differently.[24] The draft's emphasis on disparate impact theory made them exceedingly nervous. The College Board responded to the OCR in a June memorandum insisting that the draft had erred in suggesting that "'educational necessity' can only be established by rigorous scientific proof of validity and reliability. In fact, common sense and educators' good judgment are often the appropriate measure of educational necessity."[25] The insistence that "good educational judgment" could not be taken out of the equation was, perhaps, a backward glance at the *Cureton* judge's dismissal of the NCAA's "abstract rationality" and his demand for proof of a "logical break point" for using a particular SAT score. The Office of Civil Rights tried to smooth the waters in the summer of 1999, but its eventual guidelines, called *The Use of Tests as Part of High-Stakes Decision-Making for Students: A Resource Guide for Educators and Policy-Makers*, still leave room for conflict. The guide clearly warns institutions and states against using tests for purposes for which they were not designed, and it emphasizes that important decisions (such as scholarship awards) should not be made solely on the basis of a single test score. It allows a variety of types of evidence to count toward a test's validity and allows validity in some uses to be inferred from validated uses in other instances. It does not threaten colleges with a heavy hand. Nevertheless the inherent vagueness of the disparate impact standard means that conflict of (reasonable) judgment is inevitable.

9

Affirmative Action and the Legacy of *Bakke*

When applicants' standardized test scores, high school grades, and rigor of high school curriculum serve as (partial) screens to admission into selective colleges, blacks, Hispanics, and Native Americans are disproportionately screened out. On average, they do less well than whites on the SAT or ACT, their high school grades are lower, and their high school coursework is less demanding.

Selective colleges, aware of this reality, factor race into their admissions decisions. They give racial preferences. Sometimes the preferences are crude and explicit, like the University of Georgia's past practice of assigning 0.5 points to an applicant's Total Student Index if she was African American (or like the University of Michigan's point system, invalidated by a 2003 Supreme Court decision discussed below); sometimes they are subtle and visible only in their results—a consistently greater percentage of black students on campus than one might expect from the application of race-blind criteria.

Consider what happened at the University of California at Berkeley when the University System's Board of Regents under Governor Pete Wilson voted to stop allowing universities to consider race and ethnicity in their admissions decisions, a policy that went into effect in 1998.[1] In the years before 1998, black enrollment at Berkeley ranged between 6 and 7 percent of each freshman class. In 1998, it plunged to 3.3 percent, rising slowly to 3.7 percent in 2001, still about half its earlier level.[2] The same thing happened at UCLA, which had been averaging 6.7 percent black enrollment in its entering classes before 1998. Since then it has been averaging 3.6 percent.[3] Both schools, like the University of Georgia and many other institutions, had been putting a thumb on the scales for African American, Hispanic, and Native American applicants.

Since 1998 fewer black California resident freshmen have enrolled at all of the university campuses—Berkeley, UCLA, San Diego, Riverside, Davis, Santa Barbara, and Santa Cruz—except Irvine, where a miniscule 2.9 percent enrollment in 2001 topped the 2.2 percent enrollment in 1995. The drop in enrollments reflects a drop in admission offers caused by taking the racial thumb off the admissions scale.[4] Since no campus in the university system enrolls more than 5 or 6 percent of out-of-state freshmen, the modest representation of blacks will continue until African Americans students living in California increase their standardized test scores, raise their high school grades, and beef up their coursework—or until they find an alternative transfer route. Perhaps all these things will happen. One immediate effect of the colorblind policy put into effect in 1998 was to stimulate the California legislature and the university system to create or augment "outreach" programs: partnerships between university campuses and school districts to improve K–12 teaching, identify and mentor promising students, strengthen particular high schools, and further facilitate transfer from community to senior colleges. We talk more about these initiatives in chapter 11.

The black students who lost out at Berkeley and UCLA after 1998 didn't necessarily leave the University of California system; they just dropped down to less selective campuses like Riverside or Irvine.[5] Those who lost out at Riverside or Irvine dropped down to one of the California State University campuses. And those who lost out at one of these campuses still had the community college system to fall back on. The race-blind admissions policy generated a "cascading" effect. It deprived no California resident of an opportunity for higher education, but it meant some would start on a lower rung of the ladder. That may not prove such a severe hurdle in the long run. Already, underrepresented minorities are substantially increasing their transfer rates out of the community colleges to UC campuses.[6]

Even so, if UCLA and Berkeley have good reasons for wanting to enroll 6 or 7 percent African Americans each year, why shouldn't they put the racial thumb on the scale? Is anything wrong with affirmative action?[7]

THE LEGAL FOUNDATION

In the late 1960s and early 1970s, on the heels of the Civil Rights Act of 1964 and the momentous changes it brought about, selective universities sought to open their largely white and sometimes entirely male classes to formerly excluded minorities and women. This transition occasionally proved tumultuous, and it wasn't going to succeed at incorporating some minority groups unless institutions altered their standards. This they did. Some openly—

others less openly—reserved positions in their entering classes for African Americans, Hispanics, Native Americans, and (back then) Asian Americans. Professional schools were in the forefront of this movement.

Open racial preferences, however, would not long go unchallenged. In the great debates leading up to the Civil Rights Act, the voices for change had all sounded an unqualified "nondiscrimination" theme. Likewise, court decisions and government policies at the time consistently condemned existing racial classifications. Carl Cohen, a contemporary critic of affirmative action, likes to quote Thurgood Marshall's encomium to colorblindness, given before the Supreme Court in the *Brown v. Board of Education* case, decided in 1954: "Distinctions of race [wrote Marshall to the Court] are so evil, so arbitrary and invidious that a state, bound to defend equal protection of the laws, must not invoke them in the public sphere."[8] If *all* racial distinctions are wrong—and if that principle is embedded in our Constitution and (after the Civil Rights Act of 1964) in our statute books—how could a public university justify policies that depend precisely on making "distinctions of race"?

Courts were soon enough called upon to answer. The first case to work its way up the judicial ladder was *DeFunis v. Odegaard.* The case involved a complaint by Marco DeFunis against the University of Washington Law School, which had denied him admission. The law school used a two-track approach by segregating applications submitted by "Blacks, Chicanos, American Indians, and Filipinos" and measuring them only against one another, not against the applicant pool as a whole. DeFunis charged that such a dual system violated the Equal Protection Clause of the Fourteenth Amendment to the Constitution because it employed a deliberate racial classification. A trial court agreed in 1971 and ordered the law school to admit DeFunis. A Court of Appeals later reversed but let DeFunis stay in school. When the matter reached the Supreme Court in 1974, DeFunis was weeks away from graduating and the Court decided to dismiss the case as moot.[9]

Even as DeFunis was graduating, however, another applicant—this time to a medical school—was being rebuffed by a selection system that he too thought unfair. The applicant, Allan Bakke, had applied to the medical school of the University of California at Davis. The medical school, like the University of Washington law school, used a dual system of admission, assessing "special" applicants (blacks, Chicanos, Asians, American Indians) only against one another until it filled sixteen of its one hundred places in the entering class. Bakke charged that this scheme violated his rights under the Constitution and under Title VI of the Civil Rights Act. By 1978, his charge, vindicated by the California Supreme Court, lay before the United States Supreme Court.

The stakes were high. Amici curiae briefs showered down upon the Court. Urging it to turn back Bakke's challenge were the Association of American

Law Schools, the Association of American Medical Colleges, the National Medical Association, the Law School Admission Council, the Society of American Law Teachers, the American Medical Student Association, and the American Association of University Professors; Columbia, Rutgers, Harvard, Stanford, and Howard Universities; the American Civil Liberties Union, the NAACP, the NAACP Legal Defense Fund, and the National Council of Churches of Christ; the state of Washington and the United States. Urging the Court to side with Bakke's grievance were the American Federation of Teachers, the American Jewish Committee, the Anti-Defamation League of B'nai B'rith, and the U.S. Chamber of Commerce.[10]

We provide here an extended analysis of the Supreme Court's decision in *Bakke* for three reasons. First, upon the slender and fragile basis of *Bakke*, colleges and universities across the nation created or expanded existing affirmative action programs that have persisted for thirty years and that have come under increasing legal attack since 1994.[11] Many institutions after *Bakke* not only tipped the admissions scales in favor of race; they also established racially reserved scholarships, permitted racially exclusive dormitory arrangements, and the like. Second, today's debate about affirmative action on campus uses themes and concepts that flow directly from *Bakke*. To understand why the debate takes one form rather than another, one needs to understand the Court's decision. Indeed, the main moral and legal positions on affirmative action mirror the various opinions—deciding, concurring, and dissenting—delivered by the justices of the Court in *Bakke* (there were six opinions rendered in all). Thus, in closely rehearsing the arguments in *Bakke* for and against the medical school's policy, we see the main lines of contention and the broad principles to which the protagonists and antagonists of affirmative action, past and present, have pinned their arguments. Finally, the Supreme Court's decisions in the summer of 2003, upholding an affirmative action program at the University of Michigan's law school while striking down a second program at the university's undergraduate college,[12] relied on Justice Powell's lead opinion in *Bakke* without further clarifying or augmenting it. Its strengths and weakness were carried over into the new decision.

BAKKE: FRACTURED LAW, OPAQUE GUIDANCE

We characterized the legal basis for affirmative action provided by *Bakke* as slender and fragile because, until the summer of 2003, academia's use of racial preferences was supported by the arguments of a single justice, Lewis Powell. His views carried the day in 1978 because the nine justices in *Bakke* split three ways.

One bloc of four, led by Justice Stevens, thought the case was easy: the medical school's policy violated Title VI of The Civil Rights Act. Title VI declares: "No person in the United States shall, on the ground of race, color, or national origin, be excluded from participation in, be denied the benefits of, or be subjected to discrimination under any program or activity receiving Federal financial assistance."[13] (The rest of Title VI directs agencies that dispense federal financial assistance to enforce this antidiscrimination mandate and makes their enforcement actions subject to judicial review.) Compared to the long and involved text of Title VII, which covers employment discrimination, Title VI is brief and simple. Its language seems as plain as can be—or so thought the members of the Stevens bloc. They concluded that the medical school's use of an explicitly segregative selection policy violated the "crystal clear" terms of Title VI.[14]

A second bloc of four, led by Justice Brennan, sought to thwart the drawing of any such inference from Title VI. Brennan wanted to save the medical school's policy from a legal death sentence. To succeed, he needed to shift the legal evaluation of the policy onto a different terrain, away from the words of Title VI. After all, the simple injunction in those words "Do not discriminate" left very little wiggle room if embraced directly. So Brennan argued that the words of Title VI didn't mean *anything* by themselves. He reasoned as follows. When Congress enacted Title VI, it invoked as its authority the need to make sure that federal spending accorded with the requirements of "equal protection" imposed on the states by the Fourteenth Amendment and, through "incorporation," on the federal government itself by the Fifth Amendment.[15] As a consequence, contended Brennan, the language of Title VI has no independent meaning. Its meaning is "absolutely coextensive" with the Constitution's understanding of discrimination.[16] And the Constitution's understanding? Well, that was still up for grabs. The Constitution's language is accommodatingly vague and general. It does not say, as the Civil Rights Act does, "Do not discriminate on account of race." It says only: "Do not deny to any person the equal protection of the laws."[17] Since the "equal protection of the laws" is compatible with all sorts of government-imposed inequalities and classifications, there is room here to argue that constitutional equality is compatible with some racial classifications made for some worthy purposes. This was the opening through which Brennan tried to salvage the medical school's program.

Brennan only partly succeeded. He brought on board Justice Powell, who agreed that the language of Title VI had to be construed through the prism of the Fourteenth Amendment. That made a majority of five in favor of measuring the medical school's program against the demands of the Constitution. However, unlike the Brennan bloc, Powell still thought the Davis program *violated* the Constitution. Hence, that made a majority of five in favor of keeping Bakke in the medical school—the Stevens bloc plus Powell.

Since Powell was the swing vote, he got to write the Court's holding, and he based it on considerations absent from any other justice's opinion.

Justice Powell first rejected the medical school's claim that the Court should judge its program in the way it would judge any ordinary classification—say a tax code that differentiates between sources of income, or a regulation that imposes a safety requirement on passenger trains but not on passenger buses, or a law that makes only those above a certain age eligible for a driver's license. In such cases, the Court simply ascertains whether the classification is enlisted on behalf of good public purposes and leaves it at that. The medical school urged the Court not to apply to "benign" uses of race, such as those in its special admissions program, the kind of "strict scrutiny" the justices had been using for nearly two decades to strike down one Jim Crow law after another. Rather, the Court should defer to the medical school's worthwhile effort to compensate for the paucity of minorities in medical training and medical practice, a shortage due to our national history of racial injustice.

Powell would have none of it. Discrimination against Allan Bakke must be measured by the same standard the Court had used in its other race cases, he declared. "The guarantee of equal protection cannot mean one thing when applied to one individual and something else when applied to a person of another color. If both are not accorded the same protection, then it is not equal."[18] For the Court even to take a step toward a variable standard of review invited folly, Powell thought. If government institutions could "benignly" boost the prospects of some groups because they were victims of past discrimination, where would the process stop? All manner of groups would claim eligibility for such boosting. But, Powell argued,

> there is no principled basis for deciding which groups would merit "heightened judicial solicitude" and which not. Courts would be asked to evaluate the extent of . . . harm suffered by various minority groups. Those whose societal injury is thought to exceed some arbitrary level of tolerability then would be entitled to preferential classifications at the expense of individuals belonging to other groups. Those classifications would be free from exacting judicial scrutiny. As these preferences began to have their desired effect, and the consequences of past discrimination were undone, new judicial rankings would be necessary. The kind of variable sociological and political analysis necessary to produce such rankings simply does not lie within the judicial competence.[19]

No, the job of the Supreme Court, declared Powell, is to "discern 'principles sufficiently absolute to give them roots throughout the community and continuity over significant periods of time, and to lift them above the level of pragmatic political judgments of a particular time and place.'" The Court must use a single, *constant* standard of justification.[20] And that standard is this: in order to justify a "suspect classification" (such as a racial one), a public authority must proffer a substantial, legitimate purpose and, further, show the classification it uses to be *necessary* to serve that purpose.[21]

Against this standard, how did the medical school's policy fare? The medical school asserted four reasons to justify its use of preferences. Its program aimed at "(i) 'reducing the historic deficit of traditionally disfavored minorities in medical schools and in the medical profession' . . . ; (ii) countering the effects of societal discrimination; (iii) increasing the number of physicians who will practice in communities currently underserved; and (iv) obtaining the educational benefits that flow from an ethnically diverse student body."[22]

Powell considered each reason in turn. As to the first, he was dismissive.

> If . . . [the medical school's] purpose is to assure within its student body some specified percentage of a particular group merely because of its race or ethnic origin, such a preferential purpose must be rejected not as insubstantial but as facially invalid. Preferring members of any group for no reason other than race or ethnic origin is discrimination for its own sake. This the Constitution forbids.[23]

What about the second reason? California "certainly has a legitimate and substantial interest in ameliorating, or eliminating where feasible, the disabling effects of identified discrimination," Powell wrote, but the Supreme Court has "never approved a classification that aids persons perceived as members of relatively victimized groups at the expense of other innocent individuals *in the absence of judicial, legislative, or administrative findings of constitutional or statutory violations*"; and the medical school "is in no position to make . . . [such] findings. Its broad mission is education, not the formulation of legislative policy or the adjudication of particular claims of illegality."[24]

On the third reason: the medical school said its policy would improve the "delivery of health-care services to communities currently underserved," noted Powell, "but there is virtually no evidence . . . [that] the program is either needed or geared to promote that goal." The medical school "has not carried its burden of demonstrating that it must prefer members of particular ethnic groups over all other individuals in order to promote better health-care delivery to deprived citizens. Indeed . . . [the medical school] has not shown that its preferential classification is likely to have any significant effect on the problem."[25]

The first three reasons disposed of, Powell turned to the fourth aim, attaining the benefits of educational diversity. This aim, he concluded, is

> clearly . . . a constitutionally permissible goal for an institution of higher education. Academic freedom, though not a specifically enumerated constitutional right, long has been viewed as a special concern of the First Amendment. The freedom of a university to make its own judgments as to education includes the

selection of its student body. . . . The atmosphere of 'speculation, experiment, and creation'—so essential to the quality of higher education—is widely believed to be promoted by a diverse student body.[26]

If the medical school's interest in educational diversity is constitutionally compelling, "the question remains whether the [school's use of racial preferences] . . . is necessary to promote this interest."[27] Powell answered no. In fact, the medical school's use of racial preferences

> misconceives the nature of the state interest that would justify consideration of race or ethnic background. It is not an interest in simple ethnic diversity, in which a specified percentage of the student body is in effect guaranteed to be members of selected ethnic groups, with the remaining percentage an undifferentiated aggregation of students. The diversity that furthers a [school's] compelling state interest encompasses a far broader array of qualifications and characteristics of which racial or ethnic origin is but a single though important element. [The medical school's] . . . special admissions program, focused solely on ethnic diversity, would hinder rather than further attainment of genuine diversity.[28]

The medical school's program failed the second prong of the constitutional test. The school's fourth aim was certainly legitimate, but its mechanism for serving the aim was not only unnecessary but also actually subversive of it, properly understood. The school's program, according to Powell, was unconstitutional.

Justice Powell could have let matters rest there. His conclusion—on constitutional grounds, added to the conclusion of the Stevens bloc on statutory grounds, that the medical school wrongfully excluded Bakke—meant there was a majority of five for keeping Bakke in school, thus disposing of the specific issue before the Court. However, Powell went on to amplify his remarks about diversity. Since the medical school had got diversity wrong, he would show universities how to get it right. As an exemplar, he pointed to the "Harvard College program."

The Harvard admissions program took a full range of "diversity" factors into account in selecting its freshmen, noted Powell, and those diversity factors could, and did, *include* race or ethnicity:

> When the Committee on Admissions reviews the large middle group of applicants who are "admissible" and deemed capable of doing good work in their courses [explained a Harvard University memo], the race of an applicant may tip the balance in his favor just as geographic origin or a life spent on a farm may tip the balance in other candidates' cases. A farm boy from Idaho can bring something to Harvard College that a Bostonian cannot offer. Similarly, a black student can usually bring something a white person cannot offer.[29]

The racial or ethnic background of an applicant might make him or her attractive to the college in the same way an applicant's special talent as a musician, or background traveling with the circus, or experience living in a foreign land, or extraordinary efforts overcoming a debilitating illness, or exceptional record of providing leadership might make him attractive:

> This kind of program treats each applicant as an individual [reckoned Powell]. The applicant who loses out on the last available seat to another candidate receiving a "plus" on the basis of ethnic background will not have been fore-closed from all consideration for that seat simply because he was not the right color or had the wrong surname. It would mean only that his combined quali-fications, which may have included similar nonobjective factors, did not out-weigh those of the other applicant. His qualifications would have been weighed fairly and competitively, and he would have no basis to complain of unequal treatment under the Fourteenth Amendment.[30]

The problem with the medical school's program, then, was that it excluded Allan Bakke from competing for every seat. The California Supreme Court had properly invalidated the program. It went too far, however, when it ordered the medical school not to consider race or ethnicity in *any* fashion. Thus, Powell voted to set aside that part of the order, and his vote, combined with the Brennan bloc's vote to preserve the medical school's program in its entirety, meant there was a majority of five on the Court for the proposition that colleges could not altogether be forbidden from taking race into account in their admissions decisions. Within this majority, however, there was no common view about *why* colleges could not be forbidden.

This, then, was the legal basis upon which colleges created, or modified, their affirmative action plans. There is much that was not entirely clear in Justice Powell's holding but one thing certainly was: what colleges after 1978 could *not* do was create positions or benefits for which some—on grounds of their race or ethnicity—were excluded from competing. Yet by the end of the 1980s many colleges and professional schools had reestablished dual-track admissions schemes and created racially reserved scholarships. Against Justice William O. Douglas's admonition in *DeFunis*, they had set about using race "in order to satisfy [their] . . . theory of how society ought to be organized."[31] *Bakke* had given them a green light, and they were not too particular about the fine points. As a result, when lawsuits came their way in the 1990s, many found their affirmative action programs legally vulnerable.[32]

THE OTHER SIDE

When Justice Powell dismissed the medical school's plea that its program be viewed under a less demanding legal test than the Court imposed on Jim

Crow legislation, he was also taking aim at the argument of the Brennan bloc. Brennan had succeeded in getting Powell to join his interpretation of Title VI but he failed to move Powell further. Well aware that, as Powell had emphatically noted, the Court's earlier approvals of racial preferences had been confined to instances where there had been judicial, legislative, or administrative findings of prior discrimination, Brennan sought to set the medical school's policy within the same remedial context, arguing that the medical school could appropriately use race to offset the effects not only of its own but of *society's* past and continuing discrimination.[33] Powell was unpersuaded, however, seeing this move as an invitation to an unseemly contest of minority groups lining up to claim victimization by "society."[34]

Brennan also wanted to soften the scrutiny the Court gave the medical school's program. The Court, conceded Brennan, should not use the same kind of relaxed standard of scrutiny it uses for state classifications such as those illustrated earlier by the tax code or the safety regulations or the age-eligibility rule for driver's licenses. A racial classification is inherently dangerous, however good its purpose and benign its intent. Rather, Brennan hoped the Court would approach the medical school's classification with the middle level of scrutiny it had come to apply to gender classifications. Government, in order to use gender differentiations, had to demonstrate an "important" purpose to which the differentiation is "substantially related."[35]

Despite Brennan's hopes, Powell was unrelenting. However, the latter's insistence that the Court must apply a single, absolute principle of equality meaning the same thing whether applied to black or white missed the point.[36] He and Brennan were *not* at odds on this particular proposition. Moreover, Powell's claim that there was no principled way to distinguish between "benign" and vicious uses of race showed he hadn't understood Brennan's argument. Brennan *had* offered a principled way.

Brennan, like Powell, embraced a principle of constitutional equality that meant the same thing whether applied to blacks or whites. The "cardinal principle" in the Fourteenth Amendment, contended Brennan, precludes "the use of racial classifications that stigmatize—because they are drawn on the presumption that one race is inferior to another or because they put the weight of government behind racial hatred and separation."[37] By construing the meaning of the Fourteenth Amendment in this way, Brennan was following in the steps of the famous dissent by Justice John Harlan eighty-two years earlier in *Plessy v. Ferguson*.[38] Opponents of affirmative action are fond of quoting Harlan's assertion that the "constitution is color-blind," but they don't attend to his actual argument against the Louisiana statute under challenge, which required black and white citizens to ride in separate railway cars. Immediately before his oft-quoted assertion, Justice Harlan construes the Fourteenth Amendment as a bar on legislation that creates or maintains *caste*: "But in the view of the constitution, in the eye of the law, there is in this country no superior, dominant, ruling class of citizens. *There is no caste here.*"[39] Thus, the problem with the Louisiana law was not an abstract inequality engendered by it or an incidental separation by race. The problem was that the law "was conceived in hostility to, and enacted for the purpose of humiliating, citizens of the United States of a particular race."[40] The clear, public message of the law was that "colored citizens were so inferior and degraded that they cannot be allowed to sit in public coaches occupied by white citizens."[41] The clear, public intent of the law was to maintain and fortify the caste system Southern states had put in place after the Civil War ended slavery. Thus, Harlan's indictment of Louisiana's law turned on its *purpose*, which was to throw the weight of government behind race hatred and caste subordination.

In the same way, Brennan wanted the Court to focus on the *purpose* of the medical school's racial classification. Was it, like the Louisiana law in *Plessy*, meant to separate and stigmatize a hated and politically powerless group? To the contrary:

> It is not . . . claimed [by any party, wrote Brennan] that . . . [the medical school's] program in any way stigmatizes or singles out any discrete and insular, or even identifiable, nonminority group. . . . Bakke [is not] in any sense stamped as inferior by the Medical School's rejection of him. Indeed, it is conceded by all that he satisfied those criteria regarded by the school as generally relevant to academic performance better than most of the minority students who were admitted. Moreover, there is absolutely no basis for concluding that Bakke's rejection as a result of . . . [the medical school's] use of racial preferences will affect him throughout his life in the same way as the segregation of the Negro school children in . . . [*Brown v. Board of Education*] would have affected them. Unlike discrimination against racial minorities, the use of racial preferences for remedial purposes does not inflict a pervasive injury upon individual whites in the sense that wherever they go or whatever they do there is a significant likelihood that they will be treated as second-class citizens because of their color. This distinction does not mean that the exclusion of a white resulting from the preferential use of race is not sufficiently serious to require justification; but it does mean that the injury inflicted by such a policy is not distinguishable from disadvantages caused by a wide range of government actions, none of which has ever been thought impermissible for that reason alone.[42]

Following in Harlan's path, Brennan would not have the Court accept the medical school's "mere recitation" of a worthy purpose; the Court should give the special admissions program searching scrutiny.[43] But after assuring itself that the program was not a pretext for an illicit purpose and not so badly designed that it would bring in its trail the very evils it was meant to remedy, the Court should give way to the medical school's judgment.

The Court, Brennan argued, should bring to this kind of case the careful but nuanced scrutiny it was then bringing to gender cases. While the Court had recently invalidated legislation differentiating between men and women when that legislation was based upon paternalistic stereotyping of women as weak, inferior, and confined to certain roles thought appropriate to their sex, it did not treat all gender classifications as automatically illicit. Not every gender differentiation betrays a demeaning and disrespectful view of women. For example, the signs "men" and "women" on the separate courthouse bathrooms are not in any way like the signs "white" and "colored." The former pair acknowledges a genuine privacy interest of women (and men) while the latter declares to the world the "dirty" and "degraded" status of black people.

The anticaste principle condemns state action expressing hate and bestowing stigma, whether that action is directed toward blacks *or* whites. Thus, it conforms to Justice Powell's insistence that there must be a single principle of constitutional equality consistently applied. Since the medical school program is not based on hate and does not bestow a "badge of inferiority"[44] on those it excludes, this single principle consistently applied ought not put it in peril. So Brennan argued.

MISSED OPPORTUNITIES

Justice Powell took note of Brennan's argument only in passing, relegating to a footnote his view that "stigma" isn't a useful legal concept.

> The Equal Protection Clause is not framed in terms of "stigma." Certainly the word has no clearly defined constitutional meaning. It reflects a subjective judgment that is standardless. All state-imposed classifications that rearrange burdens and benefits on the basis of race are likely to be viewed with deep resentment by the individuals burdened.[45]

Of course, the Equal Protection Clause isn't framed in terms of "compelling state interest," either, or even in terms of "treating someone as an individual," Justice Powell's favorite touchstone. No less than "stigma" and "caste," these terms are extracted by inference from the words "equal protection of the laws." Moreover, in dismissing "stigma" as mere "subjective judgment," Justice Powell skirted dangerously close to the foolish pronouncement of Justice Brown in *Plessy* that if "the enforced separation of the two races stamps the colored race with a badge of inferiority . . . this is so . . . not by reason of anything found in the [legislative] act, but solely because the colored race chooses to put that construction upon it."[46] The stigma felt by blacks at forced segregation was no mere "subjective judgment." The dissenting Justice Harlan knew better; the Louisiana statute wore its message of hate and caste-maintenance on its sleeve. It imposed a badge of inferiority that was objective and inescapable.

Thus, Powell never fully addressed the merits of the anticaste interpretation of equal protection offered by Brennan. In similar fashion, Brennan rushed past the concerns troubling Powell, who worried that in letting any public agency, on its own initiative, set out to make up for "societal discrimination," courts would open a Pandora's box. Like Powell, Brennan nested his reply to this worry in a footnote, finding in the fact that the Board of Regents of the University of California is a creature of the California constitution all the authority it needed to make judgments about remedying societal discrimination. However, given his own recognition that racial classifications of any sort are dangerous tools, Brennan too blithely dismissed Powell's well-taken point: that the "mission [of the university] is education, not the formulation of any legislative policy or the adjudication of particular claims of illegality."[47]

Interestingly, Powell's point suggests a possibility neither he nor Brennan nor readers of *Bakke* ever seized upon. If the University of California was not a competent institution to formulate "legislative policy," the Assembly and Senate of California most certainly were. Instead of instructing universities on the intricacies of "diversity," Powell might have followed out the logic of his argument about authority. Conceding that California "has a legitimate and substantial interest in ameliorating, or eliminating where feasible, the disabling effects of identified discrimination,"[48] he could have explicitly put the burden back on the state legislature. If California wanted its universities to address discrimination in the way the medical school did, then the legislature could and should specifically direct them to adopt preferential policies, laying the basis for such a directive by extensive findings of past discrimination in California and a thorough enumeration of its present harmful effects. The University of California, whatever its constitutional authority, does not represent the people of California. The state's legislature does. If it—or any state's legislature—carefully lays the groundwork and instructs its public institutions of higher education to use affirmative action, nothing in the logic of Powell's argument precludes the constitutionality of its instruction.

Unfortunately, neither Powell nor Brennan, nor subsequent commentators, explored this democratic path to affirmative action that was gestating within Powell's opinion. Instead, Powell summoned the genie of "diversity." We will see in the next chapter what this genie wrought.

CODA: THE VAGARIES OF TITLE VI

Even as he was successfully pressing on the Court the view that the meaning of Title VI is coextensive with the Constitution's understanding of discrimination, Justice Brennan was casting a nervous sidelong glance at the mayhem he was about to unleash. Four years earlier, in *Lau v. Nichols*, the Court had decided that the San Francisco school system was in violation of Title VI because it did not provide enough instructional resources to eighteen hundred Chinese-speaking students. The Court relied on the regulations promulgated by the Department of Health, Education, and Welfare, charged in Title VI with enforcing its provisions. Those regulations included the disparate impact standard. Thus, the Court concluded, under Title VI "discrimination is barred which has that effect even though no purposeful design is present."[49]

Two years later, in 1976, the Court was faced with a case involving an employment test that blacks disproportionately failed. In its earlier *Griggs* decision, the Court had ratified the emerging construction of Title VII of the Civil Rights Act as including "unintended discrimination"—namely, practices that disproportionately excluded minorities but lacked "business necessity." (Government agencies charged with enforcing Title VI gave it a parallel construction.) However, in the 1976 case, *Washington v. Davis*, Title VII wasn't applicable. The test at issue was administered by the District of Columbia police department, and the District is a federal enclave. Consequently, the plaintiffs brought suit under the Due Process Clause of the Fifth Amendment (which "contains an equal protection component," observed the Court).[50] A Court of Appeals had found in favor of the plaintiffs, explicitly using the recently announced *Griggs* "disparate impact" standard to invalidate the police department's employment test. The Supreme Court reversed. "We have never held that the constitutional standard for adjudicating claims of invidious discrimination is identical to the standards applicable under Title VII, and we decline to do so today," wrote Justice White. The Court, he went on to say, has consistently required a "purpose to discriminate" as a basis for invalidating legislative or administrative rules under either the Fourteenth or Fifth Amendment.[51]

The Constitution limits the meaning of discrimination to purposeful acts of exclusion, while the Civil Rights Act broadens the meaning to encompass unintended disparate impact. The Constitution says one thing about discrimination and the statute books another.

Consider, then, the mischief unleashed when Justice Brennan assembled a majority in *Bakke* for the proposition that Title VI has no independent meaning, but forbids only what the Constitution forbids. Brennan saw the impending train wreck:

> We recognize that *Lau*, especially when read in light of . . . *Washington v. Davis* . . . may be read as predicated upon the view that . . . Title VI proscribes conduct which might not be prohibited by the Constitution. Since we are now of the opinion . . . that Title VI's standard . . . is no broader than the Constitution's,

we have serious doubts concerning the correctness of what appears to be the premise of that decision.[52]

Even so, Brennan plowed ahead. For him, a bird in the hand was worth two in the bush. The Constitution, Brennan thought, was generous toward *purposeful* discrimination done for a good cause; and the immediate case at hand had to do with a program of purposeful discrimination that Brennan wanted to save. Unfortunately, he ended up without the bird in hand; he didn't save the medical school program. In the meantime, what had he done to the two birds in the bush? After all, though the Constitution may arguably be more lax than legislation when it comes to purposeful discrimination done for a good cause, it is downright miserly when it comes to unintended discrimination; it doesn't recognize any such thing. Had Brennan, in trying to save the medical school's program, led the Court to eviscerate a powerful tool for reaching a vast array of educational practices that, without much justification, unduly burden minorities, though that is not their purpose? Had the Court undermined the Department of Health, Education, and Welfare's (HEW)(and later the Department of Education's) enforcement rules, which rely heavily on disparate impact theory? Quite obviously, *Lau*, *Davis*, and *Bakke* had to be reconciled somehow.

The reconciliation wasn't pretty. In 1983, the Court took up the apparent conflict it had created. In *Guardians Association v. Civil Service Commission*, Justice White tried to finesse the difficulty:

> I recognize that in *Bakke* five Justices, including myself, declared that Title VI on its own bottom reaches no further than the Constitution, which suggests that, in light of *Washington v. Davis* . . . Title VI does not of its own force proscribe unintentional racial discrimination. . . . [However, saying that Title VI allows intentional affirmative action if the Constitution allows it isn't the same thing as saying Title VI doesn't go beyond the Constitution to forbid unintentional discrimination.] It is sensible to construe Title VI, a statute intended to protect racial minorities, as not forbidding those intentional, but benign, racial classifications that are permitted by the Constitution, yet as proscribing burdensome, nonbenign discriminations of a kind not contrary to the Constitution. . . . [T]he holdings in Bakke and Lau are entirely consistent.[53]

Fearing, however, that the attentive reader might remember in *Bakke* that five justices called the meaning of discrimination in Title VI "absolutely coextensive" with the meaning in the Constitution, and call his bluff, Justice White took a second tack. "Even if I am wrong in concluding that *Bakke* did not overrule *Lau*, as so many of my colleagues believe," he wrote, still, the implementing regulations of Title VI incorporate disparate impact theory, and *they* remain "valid because not inconsistent with the purposes of Title VI."[54] There, then, was the resolution. The meaning of discrimination

in Title VI excluded the idea of disparate impact, but the government regulations enforcing Title VI included the idea of disparate impact; and the regulations were valid because consistent with the purposes of the Title, though
inconsistent with its meaning!

Title VI law remained in this odd "equilibrium" for another twenty years.
Subsequent litigation under Title VI involved courts using the disparate
impact analysis supplied by the implementing regulations to Title VI, not by
the title itself. The court in *Cureton*, discussed in the preceding chapter, is a
case in point. It reached the question of the discriminatory impact of the
SAT cut-off by reference to the government regulations.[55]

One further oddity. For a long time courts were uncertain whether any
individual could bring suit under Title VI. The other titles of the Civil Rights
Act explicitly allow individuals to initiate litigation and spell out in detail
how and where. Title VI, by contrast, is silent on this matter. As we've
already noted, it is very short and simple, forbidding discrimination in government-funded programs and instructing government agencies to enforce
this antidiscrimination mandate. In *Bakke* itself, while the other justices were
assuming Allan Bakke could bring a suit under Title VI and were debating
how to apply the title to his case, Justice White introduced a different concern: whether the Title provides for any private action at all. (He argued that
it did not.)[56] This matter never got clearly resolved, in *Bakke* or any other
case. However, in a decision the year after *Bakke*, the Supreme Court did
explicitly permit private suits under Title IX of the Education Amendments
of 1972, which was modeled on Title VI (adding gender to the prohibited
grounds of discrimination in government-funded programs).[57] Through this
indirect precedent, federal courts at all levels assumed the legitimacy of individual suits under Title VI.

The train wreck Brennan obliquely glimpsed as he fought in *Bakke* to
make Title VI into a tool that would save the medical school's program
rather than eviscerate it, though a long time coming, finally happened in
2001. Justice Scalia, in the majority opinion in *Alexander v. Sandoval*, sorted
out (to his satisfaction and that of four other justices) the tangle left in the
trail of *Bakke*. Scalia set out a list:

1. Private individuals *can* sue in court to enforce the antidiscrimination
   provision of Title VI. The Court's earlier decision about Title IX settled the matter.
2. *Bakke* established that the antidiscrimination provision of Title VI forbids only intentional discrimination.
3. *Guardians* established the legal anomaly that the government's regulations implementing Title VI forbid what the title permits.[58]

The Court must accept all three of these propositions, insisted Scalia, but
from these propositions the Court can only draw the inference that private

individuals can sue in court to enforce Title VI's prohibition of intentional discrimination, not that they can sue in court to enforce the government's implementing regulations. On the contrary, argued Scalia, "a private right of action to enforce . . . [the title] does not include a private right to enforce . . . [the regulations].[59]

In short, as matters now stand, there seems no longer a basis in law for the kind of suit Khadijah Sharif brought against New York and Tai Kwan Cureton brought against the NCAA. There is no basis in law for any private individual to challenge in court the SAT's disparate impact. The Office of Civil Rights in the Department of Education may administratively challenge the use of the SAT because its regulations, which include disparate impact theory, remain on the books. But no longer can an aggrieved individual shop for a judge willing to substitute his judgment for that of educators about the validity of SAT cut-offs or about the evidence sufficient to establish "logical break points" among SAT scores.

10

Justifying Affirmative Action

In the decision that Justice Powell announced for the Supreme Court in *Bakke*, colleges and universities saw a green light to continue—or expand—their affirmative action policies. These policies could henceforth be couched in terms of diversity, an idea rooted in the very idea of liberal learning that underpins much of higher education. Although Justice Powell didn't quote him, John Stuart Mill, one of the philosophical giants, could easily have been enlisted as an ally. "The only way in which a human being can make some approach to learning the whole of a subject," wrote Mill in *On Liberty*, "is by hearing what can be said about it by persons of every variety of opinion, and studying all modes in which it can be looked at by every character of mind. No wise man ever acquired his wisdom in any mode but this; nor is it in the nature of human intellect to become wise in any other manner."[1] When Powell paid tribute to the "atmosphere of speculation, experiment, and creation" so vital to good education, he could have been paraphrasing Mill (although in fact he was quoting Justice Felix Frankfurter). When he praised the "Harvard plan," he delivered the perfect bouquet of aspirations, one every other selective university could claim for itself.

In 1996, as storm clouds began gathering over affirmative action, Neil Rudenstine, Harvard's president, offered up the Harvard plan once again as a guiding model, describing how

> after the Civil War, Charles W. Eliot, president of Harvard from 1896 to 1909, expanded the conception of diversity, which he saw as a defining feature of American democratic society. He wanted students from a variety of "nations, states, families, sects, and conditions of life" at Harvard, so that they could experience "the wholesome influence that comes from observation of and contact with" people different from themselves. He wanted students who were children of the "rich and poor" and of the "educated and uneducated," students

"from North and South, from East and West," students belonging to "every religious communion, from Roman Catholic to the Jew and the Japanese Buddhist."

In Mill-like tones, Rudenstine continued:

> Students benefit in countless ways from the opportunity to live and learn among peers whose perspectives and experiences differ from their own. . . . A diverse educational environment challenges them to explore ideas and arguments at a deeper level—to see issues from various sides, to rethink their own premises, to achieve a kind of understanding that comes only from testing their own hypotheses against those of people with other views.[2]

Rudenstine was writing on the heels of *Hopwood v. Texas*, a court decision calling into question diversity's constitutional bona fides. Two years earlier, a federal district court had invalidated the admissions program at the University of Texas law school. The program didn't fit within the four corners of Justice Powell's theory of diversity in *Bakke*, said the court.[3] Now, in 1996, on appeal, the Court of Appeals for the Fifth Circuit went further and said that Powell's theory was no longer law. Achieving diversity was *not* a compelling state interest.[4]

What had happened between 1978 and 1996? Why was "diversity" suspect as a legal basis for affirmative action? Could it be rehabilitated in the face of the *Hopwood* court's adverse decision and more recent threats from yet other quarters?

BLIND UNIVERSITIES

As institutions of higher education, colleges and universities are supposed to teach their students how to read carefully and think logically. However, when it came to *Bakke* and affirmative action, colleges and universities themselves didn't read carefully, and they became spellbound by their own equivocations. Consider the casual effrontery of a law school that in 1992—the year Cheryl Hopwood, an aggrieved white applicant, began her legal proceedings against the University of Texas—had in place an admissions scheme hardly distinguishable from the two-track University of California–Davis medical school's system found unconstitutional in *Bakke* fourteen years earlier! At the Texas law school, a "minority subcommittee" evaluated "minority" applications (applications from blacks and Mexican Americans) while all other applications were assessed separately.[5] In addition, the law school used a double standard. The index scores it set for "presumptive admits" and "presumptive denials" (based on undergraduate grades and LSAT results) were higher for nonminority than for minority applicants.[6]

The law school pleaded that using a dual system was more efficient than commingling all the applications together, and besides, it was only doing what most other selective law schools did.[7] Its plea failed. The district court judge held that the law school could continue giving a "plus" to applicants because of their race, consistently with the holding in *Bakke*, but was constitutionally off-base in failing "to afford each individual applicant a comparison with the entire pool of applicants, not just those of the applicant's own race."[8] The case went forward on appeal, but even before the district court's decision the law school abandoned its dual system as obviously indefensible.

Awaiting the law school at the appeals level was a rude shock. The Court of Appeals for the Fifth Circuit ruled that Justice Powell's singular view in *Bakke* was "no longer binding precedent" and that diversity did *not* constitute "a compelling justification for governmental race-based discrimination."[9] The law school, it asserted, couldn't even use race as a "plus" in its admissions program.

Here was a seismic event that shook the pillars of affirmative action everywhere. Soon affirmative action plans at the University of Washington, the University of Georgia, and the University of Michigan landed in court.[10] Colleges and universities protested that they had relied on *Bakke* for two decades and that, despite *Hopwood*, it remained good law until the Supreme Court itself said otherwise. Federal courts differed on this question, some following *Hopwood*, some not.[11]

Was the reliance by institutions of higher education on *Bakke* perceptive and appropriate? This question arises because of the equivocation so common in current academic use of the word "diversity." In *Bakke*, Justice Powell was clear that the diversity in which a college or university has an interest cannot be reduced to racial and ethnic diversity. The diversity encompassed by the Harvard plan, as updated by Neil Rudenstine, includes an extensive range of personal attributes and qualities that might spark learning by one student from another. Race and ethnicity are but two items on a very long list. Consider some of the talents, experiences, viewpoints, and backgrounds of applicants that might enliven the intellectual climate on campus:

- *Age.* How we look at the world varies considerably by age. Older students on campus might help diminish some of the self-absorption common to eighteen- to twenty-two-year-olds.
- *Region.* Though more so earlier in our history, even now people from different regions of the country possess somewhat different values and perspectives.
- *Political affiliation.* People divide deeply and sharply on matters of politics. Political views play an important identity-defining role in individual lives.

- *Nation.* This was one of the items mentioned in Charles W. Eliot's "expanded conception" of diversity at Harvard in the nineteenth century. Differences in national background underlie strikingly different outlooks on the world. An American student body with a fair representation of Pakistanis, Germans, Brazilians, Iranians, Kenyans, Australians, and Chinese will have many of its standard preconceptions and stereotypes unsettled.
- *Occupation.* Whether we labor with our hands or minds, use tools or concepts, work on teams or individually, occupation affects our values and outlooks. People with prior work experience bring something important to a pool of students just out of high school.
- *Historical experience.* People who have lived through economic collapse, war, natural disaster, or mass migration are deeply marked by their experiences and often possess different outlooks on life than people who have had more fortunate lives.
- *Religion.* People's religious (and philosophical) views shape their attitudes toward politics, education, community, justice, war, family, work, and the like. The college campus is an especially fertile venue for testing one's religious ideas.
- *Military service.* The experience of being a soldier shapes people's outlooks in both predictable and unpredictable ways.
- *Special aptitudes and skills.* Being an accomplished pianist, painter, cook, chess master, competition swimmer, or skydiver counts as a valuable addition to "diversity" because each of these exemplifies an excellence and models a vocation that can inform and inspire others.

In short, to foster the "atmosphere of speculation, experiment, and creation" praised by Justice Powell, a great variety of traits, circumstances, and kinds of people are relevant.

Yet today when colleges and universities point to their offices of diversity affairs, write reports on their progress in achieving diversity, or set out to defend diversity against hostile courts, they are not talking about the items on this list. Their reports are not about the number of Japanese Buddhists on campus, or the number of rugby players, Young Socialists, Mormons, bluegrass fiddlers, award-winning pianists, military veterans, refugees from Bosnia, former 4-H members, dedicated mountain climbers, or ex-newspaper columnists. When they defend their programs, their focus is on *race and ethnicity.*

When the chancellor of UCLA remarked, after the Board of Regents of the University of California voted to abolish affirmative action, that his university "would not have achieved its current level of diversity without affirmative action," he was referring to the presence of ethnic and racial minorities on campus.[12] When the American Association for Higher Education, alarmed at the *Hopwood* decision, issued a "Statement on Diversity" urging its members to defend diversity as a core ideal of higher education, it was urging them to help preserve the use of "race, ethnicity, and gender in admissions and scholarship decisions."[13] When Herma Hill Kay, then dean of the law school at the University of California, Berkeley, spoke of the "diverse educational experience" to which her institution was committed, she meant achieving entering classes with a "critical mass of blacks and Hispanics."[14]

In these and countless other examples, "diversity" is identified with "racial and ethnic diversity," a conflation Justice Powell explicitly warned against. Thus, although colleges and universities appealed to *Bakke* as the grounds for their affirmative action policies, they were not attentive to Justice Powell's actual conclusions. They equivocated in exactly the way Justice Powell decried.

Had the University of Texas law school truly been interested in diversity as defined by Justice Powell, it might have found Cheryl Hopwood a more attractive applicant. Despite her very high undergraduate grades and LSAT scores, the law school placed her on a wait-list, holding against her the fact that she had pursued her undergraduate education at "inferior" institutions (a junior college and California State University at Sacramento). Here are some "diversity items" the law school apparently had no interest in: Cheryl Hopwood was an older applicant with a work history as a certified public accountant; an academically accomplished student despite working twenty to thirty hours a week throughout college; active in Big Brothers and Big Sisters in California; a mother of a child with cerebral palsy; and married to a member of the Armed Forces.[15]

A COMPELLING INTEREST:
THE ANSWER SUPPLIED

In 1997, two rejected applicants, Jennifer Gratz and Barbara Grutter, brought suit against the University of Michigan—Gratz against the university's undergraduate College of Literature, Science, and the Arts, and Grutter against the law school. The two cases, *Gratz v. Bollinger* and *Grutter v. Bollinger*,[16] finally prompted the Supreme Court in 2003 to revisit the issue of affirmative action in the university.

The complaint in each case was the same: the university's affirmative action policies violated the Constitution. The university, mounting a vigorous defense, sought to locate its policies within the *Bakke* framework. Part of its initial strategy was to provide empirical confirmation that diversity—and by this it meant "racial and ethnic diversity"—is indeed a compelling university interest.

One of the university's expert witnesses was Patricia Gurin, a professor of psychology on its own faculty. Professor Gurin had done extensive surveys on racial and ethnic diversity and at trial she reported her findings and summarized other work along similar lines. "Racial diversity in a college or university student body," she argued, "provides the very features that research has determined are central to producing the conscious mode of thought educators demand from their students." Her surveys found that "students who had experienced the most diversity in classroom settings and in informal interactions with peers showed the greatest engagement in active thinking processes, growth in intellectual engagement and motivation, and growth in intellectual and academic skills."[17] She testified that "diversity is a critically important factor in creating the richly varied educational experience that helps students learn and prepares them for participation in a democracy."[18]

The university's law school likewise sought empirical confirmation of the educational benefits of diversity. A study by Richard Lempert and colleagues showed that the law school's graduates valued racial and ethnic diversity in the classroom.[19] In oral argument before the Appeals Court in *Grutter*, the law school's counsel went further, intimating that "ethnic diversity was *essential* to the achievement of . . . [the law school's] mission."[20]

The university was not alone in making such strong claims. Statements and studies by the American Council of Education, the American Association of University Professors, and the Association of American Universities echoed the same theme: a college without racial diversity in the classroom is considerably diminished in its ability to carry out its mission. "In determining their diversity policies . . . universities . . . must grapple with the following question: To what extent can students receive a meaningful education that prepares them to participate in an increasingly diverse society if the student body and faculty are not diverse?"[21] The question was rhetorical: *without* racial and ethnic diversity, the writers believed, students will receive an education significantly less meaningful.

These propositions won out in the Supreme Court. In *Grutter v. Bollinger*, one of two opinions handed down by the Supreme Court in June 2003, Justice Sandra Day O'Connor accepted the University of Michigan law school's diversity argument without qualification. Joined by the votes of four other justices, O'Connor lifted the cloud about the binding force of Justice Powell's *Bakke* opinion and eliminated its singularity. Although "some language" in prior Court decisions "might be read to suggest that remedying past discrimination is the only permissible justification for race-based governmental action," she wrote, "today we endorse Justice Powell's view that student body diversity is a compelling state interest that can justify the use of race in university admissions."[22]

O'Connor fully embraced Powell's tribute to educational diversity: "Nothing less than the nation's future [he had maintained] depends upon leaders trained through wide exposure to the ideas and mores of students as diverse as this Nation of many peoples." O'Connor went on to note, quoting further from Powell, that "in seeking the right to select those students who will contribute to the most 'robust exchange of ideas,' a university seeks to achieve a goal that is of paramount importance in the fulfillment of its mission."[23] The University of Michigan had premised its affirmative action programs squarely on diversity, and, at least in the case of the law school, it had in O'Connor's judgment used a sufficiently subtle thumb on the racial scales to meet all constitutional demands.

For twenty-five years, *Bakke* had stirred controversy. For nearly a decade, the legality of university affirmative action plans had fallen under a darkening shadow. *Grutter* (with its companion case, *Gratz v. Bollinger*,[24] discussed below) should have set matters aright, one way or the other. In one sense it did: there is now no question about the legal justification of certain forms of racial preferences in higher education. Nevertheless, those who read Justice O'Connor's opinion not only for legal closure but for intellectual clarity on the vexed question of racial preferences are bound to be disappointed. The coherence of the diversity argument as a defense of racial preferences is, if anything, more rather than less dubious after O'Connor's treatment of it.

Future commentators, we believe, will discern in O'Connor's opinion three different strands of argument. The first two are blurred together. The third makes a brief, unexpected appearance and then quickly disappears, but leaves behind critical implications. Here we set out the three strands as separable arguments.

The first strand in O'Connor's opinion accepts the University of Michigan's diversity defense on its face, without probing its merits.

> The Law School's educational judgment that . . . diversity is essential to its educational mission is one to which we *defer* . . . [she writes]. Our scrutiny of the interest asserted by the Law School is no less strict for taking into account complex educational judgments in an area that lies primarily within the expertise of the university. Our holding today is in keeping with our tradition of giving a degree of deference to a university's academic decisions, within constitutionally prescribed limits.[25]

In other words, the Court simply accepts the university's claim that it needs a "diverse" student body to carry out its educational mission, presuming the university's "good faith" in making the claim.[26]

However unsatisfying this argument might be to the opponents of affirmative action, it at least has the merits of clarity and coherence. This virtue hardly attaches to Justice O'Connor's second argument, which endorses the university's diversity claims as sound and persuasive on their own terms.

This second argument, based on the university's various contentions about its "diversity" aims, is puzzling if not outright self-contradictory.

On the one hand, O'Connor hews to the conventional line about diversity. The law school, she writes, aims at a diversity that will "enrich everyone's education." There are many dimensions to diversity, to be sure, but the law school is especially committed to one of those dimensions, namely "racial and ethnic diversity with special reference to the inclusion of students from groups which have been historically discriminated against, like African-Americans, Hispanics, and Native Americans. . . . By enrolling a 'critical mass' of . . . [these students] the Law School seeks to 'ensur[e] their ability to make unique contributions to the character of the Law School.' "27 The students thus admitted will supply "a perspective different from that of members of groups which have not been victims of such discrimination." They will make classroom discussion "livelier, more spirited, and simply more enlightening and interesting" in light of their backgrounds. "By virtue of our Nation's struggle with racial inequality," O'Connor concludes, black and Hispanic students "are . . . likely to have experiences of particular importance to the Law School's mission."28

On the other hand, O'Connor also endorses the proposition that there *is* no "minority perspective." According to one of the law school's trial witnesses whom O'Connor paraphrases approvingly, "when a critical mass of underrepresented minority students is present [in the classroom], racial stereotypes lose their force because nonminority students learn that there is no 'minority viewpoint' but rather a variety of viewpoints among minority students."29

Can we have it both ways? Do the experiences of minority students with "racial inequality" give them a special viewpoint that would otherwise be missing from the law school classroom? If minority students exhibit a "variety of viewpoints" just as do white students, why on grounds of viewpoint diversity must a "critical mass" of them be enrolled?

O'Connor appears not to see how these two sides of her case for diversity stand in tension with one another. Indeed, she yokes them together in one final summation of the law school's position:

> The Law School does not premise its need for critical mass on "any belief that minority students always (or even consistently) express some characteristic minority viewpoint on *any* issue." . . . To the contrary, diminishing the force of such stereotypes is both a crucial part of the Law School's mission, and one that it cannot accomplish with only token numbers of minority students. Just as growing up in a particular region or having a particular professional experience is likely to affect an individual's views, so too is one's own, unique experience of being a racial minority in a society, like our own, in which unfortunately, race still matters. The Law School has determined, based on its

experience and expertise, that a "critical mass" of underrepresented minorities is necessary to further its compelling interest in securing the educational benefits of a diverse student body.[30]

This passage hardly explains how diversity requires affirmative action. If the experience of being a racial minority in a society where race still matters "is likely to affect an individual's views," then minority students are likely to have viewpoints at some variance with those who lack this experience. Yet the law school "does not premise" its affirmative action on "any belief" about viewpoint predictability. In fact, the only asserted educational benefit of diversity described in this paragraph is a rather narrow and limited one: to confound any belief at the law school that there is a distinctive minority viewpoint! Otherwise, the absence of substantial numbers of blacks and Hispanics in the classroom would seem to shortchange no important dimension of any student's legal education.

Suppose we set aside these apparent contradictions and assume that minority students do bring perspectives to the study of the law that would otherwise be missing. Does this supposition support the University of Michigan's diversity defense of affirmative action? Would the absence of these minority perspectives seriously degrade the law school's education? The university insisted, and O'Connor seems to agree, that racial and ethnic diversity are essential to the law school supplying a good education. Yet if a legal education in a racially homogeneous setting is bound to be inadequate, it follows that the law schools at Southern University, Howard, and Florida A&M began to provide adequate legal education only after they began admitting white students. This is a rather stunning implication.

We will return to discuss further the relation of racial diversity to educational outcomes, but here we leave off describing Justice O'Connor's second argument to take up her third. The first two strands of O'Connor's defense of racial preference at the University of Michigan law school fall squarely within the bounds laid out by Justice Powell in *Bakke* twenty-five years ago. Toward the end of her opinion, however, a new argument appears. Impressed by the contention in the amici curiae brief by several former military officers that the "military cannot achieve an officer corps that is both highly qualified *and* racially diverse unless the service academies and ROTC . . . [use] limited race-conscious recruiting and admissions policies," and persuaded that a military with an officer corps entirely white, or nearly so, is now unacceptable in America, O'Connor concludes that all selective educational institutions should take measures to "remain both diverse and selective"—that is, selective *and* racially integrated.[31]

Selective universities, and law schools in particular, produce America's future leaders. "In order to cultivate a set of leaders with legitimacy in the eyes of the citizenry," O'Connor writes, "it is necessary that the path to leadership be visibly open to talented and qualified individuals of every race and ethnicity. All members of our heterogeneous society must have confidence in the openness and integrity of the educational institutions that provide this training."[32] An officer corps with only a smattering of racial and ethnic minorities would lack legitimacy. A state or national leadership stratum with only a smattering of racial and ethnic minorities would lack legitimacy. Thus, the institutions that develop leaders—military and civilian—must achieve racial and ethnic integration. If it takes racial and ethnic preferences to achieve integration, then such preferences are justified.

This legitimacy rationale bursts into the middle of O'Connor's argument and then quickly disappears as O'Connor returns to the standard diversity defense of affirmative action. But the two rationales are fundamentally different. The legitimacy argument provides a reason for institutions that feed America's leadership class to be integrated *even if* no student's education is thereby enriched, *even if* the "robust exchange of ideas" on campus is not affected one way or another. We return to this issue shortly.

In any event, O'Connor draws her defense of affirmative action in the university to a close with a surprise. Unbidden by any party to the university litigation, or any amici, she sets a time limit on university affirmative action. "[M]indful . . . that [a] core purpose of the Fourteenth Amendment was to do away with all governmentally imposed discrimination based on race," she writes, "race-conscious admissions policies must be limited in time."[33]

> The requirement that all race-conscious admissions programs have a termination point "assure[s] all citizens that the deviation from the norm of equal treatment of all racial and ethnic groups is a temporary matter, a measure taken in the service of the goal of equality itself." . . . We take the Law School at its word that it would "like nothing better than to find a race-neutral admissions formula" and will terminate its race-conscious admissions program as soon as practicable. . . . We expect that 25 years from now, the use of racial preferences will no longer be necessary to further the interest approved today.[34]

O'Connor's "expectation" looks less like anticipation than decree. It puts universities on notice: get rid of racial preferences by 2028.

One further conclusion follows from the *Grutter* and *Gratz* decisions. Universities must use preferences in subtle and discreet ways. While in *Grutter* O'Connor joined four justices in upholding the affirmative action program at the University of Michigan's law school, in *Gratz* she joined four other justices in striking down the university's undergraduate affirmative action program.

The undergraduate admissions office used a mechanical system similar to the one used by the University of Georgia, described in chapter 7. The office assigned numbers to various academic and nonacademic factors in an applicant's file, and for the most part admitted all those applicants whose total scores were above a certain number while rejecting all those whose totals were below a certain number. In its system—which allowed a maximum of 150 points—"underrepresented minorities" were automatically given 20 points. By contrast, Michigan residency counted 10 points, legacy counted 4 points, an outstanding personal essay could count up to 3 points, and a stellar record of leadership could garner 5 points. The automatic assignment of 20 points for race or ethnicity meant that almost every minimally qualified minority applicant got admitted to a university very difficult for other applicants to get into.[35]

Writing in concurrence in *Gratz*, O'Connor found this mechanical point system badly tailored to promote the university's legitimate interest in educational diversity broadly understood. The point system stood in "sharp contrast to the Law School's admission plan," wrote O'Connor, "which enables admissions officers to make nuanced judgments with respect to the contributions each applicant is likely to make to the diversity of the incoming class."[36] The law school, O'Connor had already noted in *Grutter*, uses "a highly individualized, holistic review of each applicant's file, giving serious consideration to all the ways an applicant might contribute to a diverse educational environment."[37] Race might count as a "plus," but the magnitude of the "plus" would vary from case to case, as other diversity considerations were taken into account. (Of course, the law school's admissions director was keeping tabs on the "daily reports" of admissions, with an eye on the racial and ethnic profile they displayed; and the number of minorities enrolled consistently fell within a well-defined range, 13 to 20 percent of each class.)

In defense of its undergraduate admissions system, the University of Michigan, like the University of Georgia, pleaded the impracticality of closely reading and individually assessing every application it got, but the defense was unavailing. Wrote Chief Justice Rehnquist for the Court: "The fact that the implementation of a program capable of providing individualized consideration might present administrative challenges does not render constitutional an otherwise problematic system."[38]

The bottom line is that *Gratz* and *Grutter* together let universities and colleges continue giving racial and ethnic preferences, but only if the procedures they use are not crude and mechanical. And Justice O'Connor's "expectation" of a definite termination date puts higher education on notice that it had better find other ways to secure places for underrepresented minorities in the nation's selective institutions.

THE LINK BETWEEN ENDS AND MEANS

Universities defend their use of racial and ethnic preferences by appeal to an educational goal—attaining the benefits of diversity. However, the connec-

tion between racial and ethnic preferences (the means) and the benefits of
diversity broadly understood (the end) is quite loose. Nor is this slackness
overcome by many of the extravagant claims universities make.

Consider again the University of Michigan's defense of its affirmative
action programs. Its expert witness, Patricia Gurin, testified that racial and
ethnic diversity is "a critically important factor in creating . . . [a] varied educational experience"; in another forum, she insisted that "racially and ethnically diverse student bodies [are] essential to providing the best possible
educational environment for students, white and minority alike."[39] This is
simply not a credible claim. There are too many possible settings and combi-
nations of diversity that can lead to effective intellectual growth. Students
benefit from a setting that is richly diverse, but not necessarily diverse in any
particular way. Students at Wellesley, Dillard, Berea, Princeton, and Calvin
College develop their ability to think critically and creatively and become
more cosmopolitan in their outlooks. Yet these campuses do without some
of the items on the Harvard plan's long list of "diversities." Calvin College
does without atheists, Wellesley without males, Dillard without whites,
Berea without upper-class urbanites, and Princeton without the children of
the "uneducated"—one of Charles W. Eliot's desiderata. No one or two
items on the long list of "diversities" is indispensable, and this is as true for
race or ethnicity as for any other item.

Gurin's own theory and findings support this contention. Her theory
holds that undergraduates just out of high school are especially susceptible
to being provoked into "active thinking processes."[40] What she means is this.
An eighteen-year-old, fresh from the comfortable bosom of family and
neighborhood, comes to college with a set of unreflective prejudices and
automatic cognitive responses. College confronts her with unsettling and
discordant experiences. People and ideas don't fit within her neat categories.
She is forced to *think* her way to views she previously took for granted,
think her way in terms that seem persuasive to others of a different cast of
mind—or abandon her old ideas and develop new ones.[41]

Of course, unsettling and discordant experiences by themselves don't
guarantee desirable learning outcomes. The experiences must be managed in
a way that makes intellectual discomfort tolerable and opens students to new
ideas. Otherwise, such experiences may prompt students to retreat further
into their comfortable prejudices.

Racial and ethnic diversity can serve growth in "active thinking" if managed properly. Gurin notes that 92 percent of the University of Michigan's
white students and 52 percent of its African American students come from
racially segregated backgrounds. Thus, the racially integrated campus setting
confronts many students with "new and unfamiliar" classmates who are a
"source of multiple and different perspectives" that generate "contradictory
expectations."[42] Moreover, if we take Gurin's empirical findings at face value

(and some critics do not[43]), racial and ethnic diversity at the University of Michigan not only *can* but *has* produced positive educational outcomes.[44]

Such findings, however, do not establish that racial diversity is *essential* to a good educational experience. The linkage between racial and ethnic diversity, on the one hand, and students' cognitive growth, on the other, is not tight.

In her study, Gurin not only looks for "educational outcomes" but "democracy outcomes" as well. "One goal embraced by most colleges and universities, and certainly by the University of Michigan," she observes, "is to prepare people for active participation in our democratic society, which is an increasingly diverse society."[45] Now, racial and ethnic diversity on campus seem more closely connected to civic learning outcomes than to cognitive development in general. Even so, it would be a conceit for Gurin to insist the University of Michigan turns out better citizens than St. Anselm College,[46] the College of Wooster,[47] Spelman College,[48] or Florida A&M University.[49] Colleges and universities treat race and ethnicity differently than other items on the long list of "diversities" that might enrich the educational and civic experience of students. Yet, in the story they tell about this differential treatment, the relation between means and ends is quite loose.

One way to tighten the connection between racial preferences and institutional mission is to incorporate racial representation directly into the mission. Thus, in 1987 the "Michigan Mandate," adopted by the University of Michigan, committed the school to becoming "a national and world leader in the racial and ethnic diversity of its faculty, students, and staff."[50] Racial and ethnic "inclusiveness is not merely a policy . . . [for the university], it is an integral part of . . . [its] mission and . . . vision for the future."[51]

Of course, unless this goal of "inclusiveness" itself serves some further goal, the university would be guilty of what Justice Powell and Justice O'Connor called "discrimination for its own sake."[52] What independent goal, then, does this subgoal of "inclusiveness" serve? The Michigan Mandate offers a number of candidates. The university wants to serve "as a model for higher education and a model for society-at-large. We are convinced that our capacity to serve our state, our nation, and our world . . . [depends] on our capacity to reflect the strengths, perspectives, talents, and experiences of all peoples—all of America's rich diversity of races, cultures, and nationalities—in everything we do." [53]

Unfortunately, here the equivocations we have noted concerning "diversity" are back. *All* of America's rich diversity of races, cultures, and nationalities are not reflected in the university's narrowly focused affirmative action policy. The imprecision in the mandate—and in the University of Michigan's more recent efforts to defend itself in court—are revealed in the statement of resolve offered by Lee Bollinger, president of the university when Jennifer Gratz and Barbara Grutter filed suit:

We believe these lawsuits threaten the ability of the University to bring together students from a wide array of backgrounds to create the richest possible environment for education and learning. We cannot let the University of Michigan be thwarted from playing a leadership role—as we believe a leading public university must—in building a tolerant and integrated society.[54]

The two sentences point in quite different directions. The first indicates diversity in the broader sense we have discussed at length. The second gestures toward something else. Consider two phrases from the second sentence: "public university" and "integrated society." They suggest a version of the legitimacy argument that Justice O'Connor briefly rehearsed in *Grutter*. Since the university is the flagship public campus of Michigan, and since, from Michigan's point of view, it is important that its future leadership class be more racially and ethnically integrated, the university plays its role by assuring that its graduates include racially and ethnically underrepresented populations. The university does so by using racial and ethnic preferences (when necessary).

There is no anomaly in building a "representational" dimension directly into the university's mission. That is to say, there is no anomaly in the university's building into its mission a commitment to educating specific populations. The university already does so. Like all state universities, it gives preference to applicants from its own state.[55] The university exists to benefit the citizens of Michigan and to educate their children. It benefits the state by training those who will occupy future roles in Michigan as teachers, business managers, civic leaders, municipal and state officials, political representatives, directors of cultural institutions, and suppliers of professional expertise (medical, legal, engineering, and the like). If this civic stratum, in Justice O'Connor's words, would lack "legitimacy" without including a reasonable proportion of racial and ethnic minorities, then the university must ensure their inclusion by assuring a reasonable integration of its student body.

Call this the *integration argument*. It justifies universities in using racial and ethnic preferences much more straightforwardly than the diversity argument. There is no slack between means and ends. For the good of the state, the university must graduate integrated classes. To achieve integrated classes, it must employ racial and ethnic preferences. Therefore, it is justified in giving such preferences.

In the midst of her recitation of the standard diversity shibboleths in *Grutter*, Justice O'Connor draws back the curtain on a much more convincing rationale for affirmative action, one that elicits a moment of passion in her opinion before disappearing among the debris of "distinctive minority viewpoints" and "no distinctive minority viewpoints," diversity "pluses" whose weights vary unpredictably and diversity "pluses" whose weights uncannily display a standing pattern.

In the integration argument, means and ends go hand in hand.[56] Moreover, the means are not hostage to fickle social science findings. If Patricia Gurin had *not* found that racial diversity enhanced the development of complex thinking in students, would the University of Michigan have been prepared to shut down its affirmative action program? Surely not.

MORAL PRINCIPLES

It might be thought that we have labored too long at narrow and arcane legal matters when the real issues have to do with the moral standing of affirmative action. It is certainly true that molding arguments so they fit into legal formulas such as "compelling interest" is limiting; and there is no reason why a defender of affirmative action should feel satisfied with the heavy reliance on precedent adopted by the courts. Nevertheless, behind the legal formulas lie more substantive issues. For example, it is commonplace to point out that universities give all sorts of preferences—for example, preferences for athletes and for the children of alumni. Why, then, should people make such a big deal when universities give modest preferences to blacks? The answer: *race is different*. When the Supreme Court insists that racial classifications must be given "strict scrutiny" and measured against a test of "compelling state interest," this is its formulaic way of making that point. Even the Brennan bloc in *Bakke* emphatically joined this view. Putting into the hands of any public authority the power to make distinctions on the basis of race is dangerous business given our country's history of racial oppression. That power cannot be casually deferred to, and it cannot be justified in the same way we would justify a public department's power to set the age for driver's licenses or a public university's power to set criteria of academic eligibility.

This unique history of racial oppression necessarily hovers over any argument for or against affirmative action. Even those who invoke lofty principles implicitly summon a story of cause and effect tied to our past. Justice Clarence Thomas provides an instructive example, as he tried but failed in *Adarand v. Pena*, a 1995 case, to show racial preferences to be wrong as a matter of principle alone, irrespective of context. He declared:

> I believe there is a "moral [and] constitutional equivalence" . . . between laws designed to subjugate a race and those that distribute benefits on the basis of race in order to foster some current notion of equality. . . . That these programs may have been motivated, in part, by good intentions cannot provide refuge from the principle that under our Constitution, the government may not make distinctions on the basis of race.[57]

The "principle" in our Constitution, however, says nothing about making distinctions on the basis of race. Rather, it commands the states to extend to all within their jurisdictions the "equal protection of the laws." How does Justice Thomas get from *this* principle to the colorblind principle? He gets there by appealing to a set of assumptions about social and psychological processes:

> There can be no doubt that racial paternalism and its unintended consequences can be as poisonous and pernicious as any other form of discrimination. So-called "benign" discrimination teaches many that because of chronic and apparently immutable handicaps, minorities cannot compete with them without their patronizing indulgence. Inevitably, such programs engender attitudes of superiority or, alternatively, provoke resentment among those who believe that they have been wronged by the government's use of race. These programs stamp minorities with the badge of inferiority and may cause them to develop dependencies or to adopt an attitude that they are "entitled" to preferences.[58]

It is alleged *facts*, not principle, that dominate this passage, as Thomas appeals to unintended consequences, inevitable resentments, and unfortunate dependencies. It is the same set of purported facts that dominates his scathing dissent in *Grutter*.[59] In place of principle, Thomas substitutes speculative sociology (made plausible, of course, by both the remote and recent histories of race in our country). But speculative sociology is just that: speculative. There might well be adverse unintended consequences of affirmative action programs, such as attitudes of superiority and resentment among whites or feelings of stigma among blacks. Would such effects add up to a case against affirmative action? Not unless they swamped its many positive effects. There is convincing evidence that affirmative action is, on the whole, a positive good both for campuses and for its beneficiaries. For example, the careful study done by William Bowen and Derek Bok, *The Shape of the River: Long-Term Consequences of Considering Race in College and University Admissions*, provides an important glimpse at how the positives and negatives add up in a number of selective colleges—and the balance favors affirmative action.[60] We describe these findings at the end of this chapter.

Carl Cohen, a professor at the University of Michigan and a long-time critic of affirmative action, also appeals to principle. "Worthy aims cannot justify racially discriminatory devices. Racial discrimination is wrong; it always was and it always will be wrong." But *why* is racial discrimination always wrong regardless of its purpose? Cohen follows in Justice Thomas's footsteps by quickly shifting ground: the "advantages given [in affirmative action] to persons of some races but not others do great damage—to the University as a whole, but especially to those who were supposed to have been helped."[61] Once again the real issue for Cohen is one of purported fact. How is the university damaged and how is it improved by affirmative action?

How are those persons affirmative action is supposed to benefit really hurt and how are they helped? How do the benefits stack up against the costs? These questions can't be answered from the armchair.

Jennifer Gratz felt aggrieved because she was denied a place at Ann Arbor while affirmative action recipients with less stellar academic records were admitted. However, suppose the university had granted affirmative action preferences on the basis of class, not race. Suppose Jennifer Gratz had been displaced not by a black from Detroit but a poor white from Saginaw. The material injury to Jennifer Gratz's interests would have been exactly the same: she would have had to settle for attending the University of Michigan at Dearborn. Yet neither Carl Cohen nor Justice Thomas would have mounted the barricades for Jennifer Gratz in that case. Nor would she even get her foot in the courthouse door to voice her grievance. There is no principle of law, constitutional or otherwise, that prevents a public authority from classifying some people as "economically disadvantaged" and extending them special benefits. If it wanted to, the University of Michigan could explicitly reserve 5 percent of its freshman class to students whose parents make less than $20,000 a year. It wouldn't even have to compare the applicants in this group with all other applicants; it could openly run a two-track system.

The difference between the two scenarios is race. Race is special. Not because of principle, however, but because of history—American history. Race opens wounds and raises suspicions. Race is dangerous, inflammatory, subject to abuse. This is why the Supreme Court says, reasonably, that it must subject every racial classification made by public authority to a "searching scrutiny."

The point of this searching scrutiny, according to Justice O'Connor, is "to 'smoke out' illegitimate uses of race by assuring that [government] is pursuing a goal important enough to warrant use of a highly suspect tool."[62] On this account, contrary to the animadversions of Justice Thomas and Carl Cohen, good intentions and worthy ends *do* count. What disables a racial classification is that its real motive is to promote an illegitimate prejudice or stereotype.[63] Courts must make sure by very close scrutiny that the good intentions and worthy aims racial preferences avowedly serve aren't masks for something sordid and impermissible. One way courts exercise this scrutiny is to see how closely the design of a preferential program actually fits its purported intentions or aims.

Does affirmative action serve good purposes and produce net good effects? That is a central question. Still, it can't be the only one, readers may insist. Affirmative action demands a principled basis, not just a utilitarian calculation. But what is the relevant principle?

"TREAT PERSONS AS INDIVIDUALS"

A critical part of Justice Powell's opinion in *Bakke* focused on the proper interpretation of the principle of equality expressed in the Fourteenth Amendment. The right to equal protection of the laws conferred in that amendment is an *individual right*, declared Powell. It belongs to each person regardless of her color. From this principle of individualism Powell inferred another in the context of college admissions: the *right to be treated as an individual.* The virtue of the Harvard plan, in his mind, was that it treated each applicant as an individual, whereas the medical school's policy simply excluded Bakke and other white applicants from competing for certain slots.

This same idea runs throughout the Court's opinions in *Gratz* and *Grutter*. The system of racial preferences used in *Grutter* survived because it still allowed for the individualized assessment of all applicants, while the system in *Gratz* failed because its mechanical assignments undercut individualized assessment.

To be treated as an individual: this principle surely resonates favorably in most readers of this book. But what does it mean? What does it imply about law and public policy?

These questions aren't easily answered. Take a commonplace example. When the state classifies people under the age of sixteen as ineligible for driver's licenses, it does not treat them as individuals. Plenty of fifteen-year-olds have physical skills and driving judgment as good as any sixteen-year-old. But they are treated simply as members of a class and denied the opportunity to prove their worthiness to drive. The social utility of classifications such as this one justifies their ubiquity.

In some contexts, however, social usefulness isn't good enough; it cannot justify being treated merely as a member of some class. What special features mark out these contexts? Two suggest themselves: where a person's most basic interests are involved, and where her standing as a citizen, and, more crucially, as a person, are at stake. A precocious fifteen-year-old is inconvenienced by having to wait a few months to apply for a driver's license. A person accused of a crime and facing loss of her freedom faces an entirely different set of costs. In such cases most people would agree that social utility must give way to individualized assessment. Even if it were socially beneficial to round up and jail certain kinds of people (vagrants and drifters, say, or people with certain psychological profiles), our law and morality require that no individual be deprived of her liberty except for a crime she has actually committed.

Similarly, one's standing as a citizen and as a person cannot to be traded off for some social gain. Were basic civic and social standing not inviolate, a political majority might happily disenfranchise a hated minority, or legally segregate it into a ghetto that marks its members as inferior human beings.

The burden on a man who has to walk an extra twenty feet in the courthouse to a restroom designated "men" is negligible; the burden on a man who has to walk an extra twenty feet to a restroom designated "colored" is crushing and cruel. It is *meant* to be—it is meant as a public endorsement of the proposition that the colored man is less of a person than the noncolored, not fit to urinate in the other's proximity.

Thus, in some contexts, "to be treated as an individual" is a moral imperative. However, although the recent *Grutter* and *Gratz* holdings made "individualized treatment" an apparent touchstone principle, in fact it has no independent force in those cases. Suppose the University of Michigan's undergraduate college *never* assigned any points for race or ethnicity. It would never have been hailed into court. It would be legally free to continue using its mechanical point system, even if it assigned nonacademic points in ways that gave a considerable leg up to some groups of students (for example, to residents of Michigan's upper peninsula or to children of alumni). What makes "individualized treatment" seem salient in these cases is the presence of race. And not just the mere presence of race. There must be some danger of stigma, social exclusion, official hostility, or other assault on basic dignity or civic standing, not as side-effect but as intended outcome. Contemporary affirmative action, we submit, poses no such danger.

These remarks require many qualifications and elaborations. Even so, they sketch the contours likely to be found in any plausible, fully worked out account of the principle "Treat persons as individuals." Any account will have to allow for many classifications of "convenience," where people are treated as members of legally established categories and no more. Such classifications overstep their limits when they infringe on individuals' fundamental interests or have as their purpose the disenfranchising of citizens or the humiliation of classes of persons. In short, any attractive account will track portions of the argument Justice Brennan offered in *Bakke*. Purpose, as Justice O'Connor allows, will be central to legitimating suspect classifications. And, as Justice Harlan forcefully underlined in *Plessy*, discerning a vicious and hateful purpose behind racial classifications is not a taxing assignment.

"DO NOT DISCRIMINATE"

Another principle at stake in the affirmative action debate is the principle of nondiscrimination. It is a widespread American belief that the operations of public institutions should honor this principle. But what does the principle mean? Some insist that affirmative action itself directly contravenes the principle, while others say that the refusal to use affirmative action is what violates it. We can't begin to decide who is right until we know what discrimination is.

In the *Gratz* litigation, the district court allowed several University of Michigan minority undergraduates to become parties to the case as student-intervenors. The student-intervenors argued separately in defense of the university's affirmative policy. They eschewed *Bakke*'s diversity rationale, arguing instead that the university's affirmative action program served its "compelling interest in remedying . . . [its own] past and current discrimination against minorities."[64] What constituted the current discrimination? The student-intervenors pointed to a "hostile racial environment" on campus and to university admissions policies that have an adverse impact on minorities.[65]

One reason the student-intervenors in *Gratz* proffered a remedial defense of the University of Michigan's affirmative action policy is that they see discrimination everywhere. Discrimination's story, they feel, has to be told again and again.

It is not hard to see the force of this view if we share the concept of discrimination used by the student-intervenors (and by a great many others who support affirmative action). Practices that transmit patterns of inequality, they believe, constitute discrimination. Given how deeply legally enforced racial segregation was embedded in our social system, and how long it lasted, the inequalities it produced continue to be reproduced every day by almost everything we do as a society. It could not be otherwise. The student-intervenors and their allies have plenty of evidence on their side.

But something is missing in the student-intervenors' concept (or, anyway, the concept we are imputing to them for expository purposes). Recall the statutory notion of discrimination we discussed in chapter 8. In 1971, the Supreme Court construed Title VII of the Civil Rights Act to forbid any practice or policy of a firm producing adverse impact and not justified by "business necessity." We can generalize this concept as a broad moral understanding of discrimination. It has two parts. The first part recognizes how facially neutral practices constantly reproduce racial inequality. The second part condemns those practices unsupported by "necessity" of some sort, where "necessity" is understood as "reasons of a very strong sort." What's missing in the student-intervenors' view of discrimination is the second part, which lets some reasons justify practices that reproduce racial inequality and thereby renders them not discriminatory. To the student-intervenors, social practices that reproduce racial inequality are discriminatory, period.[66] *No* justifying reasons are sufficient to balance the scales. Thus, the student-intervenors and others sympathetic to their view see discrimination everywhere and are baffled that other people of good will do not.

This account may not do justice to the student-intervenors' view, so let us offer a slightly altered version. The broad moral concept of discrimination we introduced counts all practices that adversely affect blacks as discriminatory unless the practices are supported by *strong enough reasons*. The idea of "strong enough reasons" is vague. It defines a continuum. Individuals at one end are extremely parsimonious in what they count as strong enough reasons and individuals at the other end are more generous. We can then say that the student-intervenors' view lies at the very parsimonious end of the continuum. While some people, for example, count the use of SAT and AP scores in admissions decisions as sufficiently related to legitimate university objectives, others do not. According to the latter, if using these screens adversely affects minorities (and they do), then don't use them. If the screens are closely related to what universities view as academic merit, then change the notion of merit. If the screens predict academic success, then change the idea of success.[67] And if universities don't change, this is further proof that discrimination is everywhere, pervasive and enduring.

By extreme contrast to the view of the student-intervenors, some people don't locate themselves on any part of the continuum determined by our broad moral concept of discrimination because they reject the very idea of "nonintentional discrimination."[68] To them, "discrimination" means purposefully giving to or withholding from a group defined by race or ethnicity some good or benefit. Thus, affirmative action preferences count as discrimination, in their view, because such preferences explicitly and purposefully use a racial or ethnic classification. Yet these people would not see university practices that, as an unintended by-product, weigh more heavily against minority groups as discriminatory, no matter how easy it would be to substitute less burdensome practices.[69]

In short, the parties in the affirmative action debate are separated by wide gulfs. According to the concept of discrimination we have described, institutional practices that adversely affect minorities are discriminatory unless supported by strong reasons. But even people who accept this general view may disagree sharply about how strong the reasons have to be to justify adverse effects; the degree of adversity matters too. Further, some people reject this concept altogether, believing that a discriminatory practice must be intentional. Thus, invoking the "principle of nondiscrimination" won't move the debate forward when people can't even agree on its meaning or scope of application.

The affirmative action argument involves principles, to be sure. But appealing to principles isn't, and can't be, a substitute for detailed and thorough argument because the meaning of the principles at stake is as contested as the policies they are meant to subsume.

A LAST WORD ON AFFIRMATIVE ACTION

If highly selective colleges want to enroll a decent percentage of African American students, putting the racial thumb on the admissions scale is an *efficient* means to that end. It allows these colleges to "cream" the college applicant pool, admitting those black students most likely to succeed.

Why do very selective colleges need to put the thumb on the scale? We saw what happened at UCLA and Berkeley when state law and Regents' policy barred color-conscious admissions. In *The Shape of the River*, their study of affirmative action, William Bowen and Derek Bok show with great clarity the causes and effects glimpsed only dimly in the bare data from the two California universities. One figure from their book, reproduced here, graphically illustrates the problem.

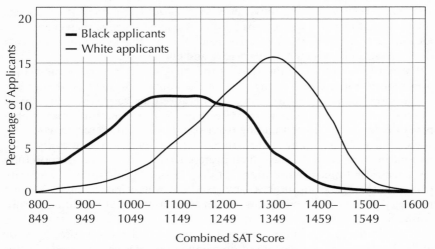

Bowen, William G., and Derek Bok; *The Shape of the River: Long-Term Consequences of Considering Race in College and University Admissions.* Copyright © 1998 by Princeton University Press. Reprinted by permission of Princeton University Press.

The two lines in this figure represent the distribution of SAT scores of applicants at five selective schools.[70] The darker line shows the scores of black applicants, the lighter line those of white applicants. The two lines together illustrate in dramatic fashion the problem of the "right tail." When a Stanford or a Williams chooses a freshman class, the farther to the right it moves along the SAT scoreline, the fewer black students there are to select from, until they vanish altogether. Moreover, this figure could stand in for other credentials as well. Whether it is SAT scores, grades, strength of high school curriculum, or special academic and artistic achievements, when colleges look for "super credentials," black students almost disappear from the pool. To get significant numbers of them into the freshman class, these schools must take race into account. In 1989, at the five schools reflected in the figure above, about 25 percent of the white applicants and 42 percent of the black applicants were admitted. The white students who matriculated had average SAT scores 170 points higher than the black matriculants.[71]

The differences in scores (and other credentials) among the 1989 cohort studied by Bowen and Bok showed up in performance. On average, the black students did not attain college class rankings, grades, or graduation rates on a par with the white students. Nevertheless, they graduated at very high rates (more than double the rate of black college students in general);[72] went on to professional or graduate schools in very substantial numbers;[73] succeeded in the work world, earning incomes that would make most of us sick with envy;[74] and subsequently reported high satisfaction with their lives.[75] Both black and white students valued their interracial experience on campus, counting it a "plus" in their schooling.[76]

Bowen and Bok were able to estimate for all twenty-eight institutions they studied the effect of using a race-blind policy in admitting the 1976 cohort: 700 black matriculants would have been replaced by 700 white matriculants. Of those 700 black students who gained admission via the thumb on the scale, 225 went on to attain professional or doctorate degrees; 70 are now doctors, 60 lawyers; over 300 are leaders of civic activities; their average earnings in the mid-1990s exceeded $71,000 a year; two-thirds were very satisfied with their undergraduate experience.[77]

Now, it would be a fallacy to infer that without affirmative action this cohort of 700 successful and civic-minded individuals would have followed substantially less rewarding paths. Graduating from one of the twenty-eight institutions studied in *The Shape of the River* is not a sine qua non of becoming a successful professional and a civic leader. Nevertheless, the Yales, Amhersts, Oberlins, and Stanfords of this country do feed a substantial segment of the American elite. As David Wilkins has found, 47 percent of black partners in the major law firms around the country are graduates of Harvard or Yale law school, and fully 77 percent are from eleven elite law schools.[78] The matriculants at these laws schools are more likely to come with baccalaureates from Yale, Amherst, Oberlin, or Stanford than from Kansas State, LSU, Ohio University, Montclair State, or the University of Akron. Highly selective colleges and universities propel students into segments of the American elite they are less likely to enter otherwise.

Flagship campuses and state law schools play a similar role. To enter the top legal and political ranks in Kentucky, there is no substitute for graduating from the University of Kentucky law school; to enter the same ranks in Tennessee, you had best come from the University of Tennessee or Vanderbilt. Graduating from the University of Michigan law school facilitates entry into Michigan's leadership community with an ease not duplicated by degrees from other institutions.[79] Boalt Hall (Berkeley) and UCLA law school are vital sources of members of California's best law firms. Something important is lost to Kentucky, Tennessee, Michigan, and California if these schools graduate virtually no blacks.

The social good produced by affirmative action is the creation of highly trained, very competent black (and other minority) graduates with entrée into the circles of leadership that set the cultural, moral, and legal tone in our country and its various communities. We are persuaded that this social good is real and not merely conjectural, and that it clearly outweighs the small diminution of chances of admissions that whites suffer as a consequence of affirmative action.

Of course, affirmative action may come with costs. One cost is a slight decline in a white applicant's chance of being admitted to a selective school. Bowen and Bok estimate that in five selective institutions for which they have particularly good data, race-blind admissions would have reduced blacks as a portion of the 1989 entering class from 7.1 percent to 2.1 percent; and it would have increased the likelihood of any white applicant's getting admitted from 25 percent to 26.5 percent.[80] Affirmative action at the five institutions, then, reduced the chance of acceptance for white applicants by 1.5 percentage points. Although any decrease in chances of acceptance is a cost, individually and collectively a reduction of this size is not an onerous burden. Because affirmative action across the board—and not only in especially selective schools—is a relatively modest affair, white students as a whole are not shouldering a large cost.

Affirmative action could conceivably have other costs as well. It might roil campuses in racial acrimony; it might produce in its beneficiaries an illegitimate sense of entitlement, as Justice Thomas feared, or encourage in whites a sense of resentment or superiority, or stigmatize its beneficiaries in some way.[81] So it might. We must weigh affirmative action on the scales of good and bad consequences. Against some of Justice Thomas's fears, we juxtapose those several hundred black partners at the nation's very best law firms, who undoubtedly help to undermine any complacent sense of superiority in the whites with whom they interact. Similarly, the presence of blacks in a state's elite circles surely serves to remind whites that their communities are racially diverse and that constituencies other than their own matter. Still, circumstances on some college campuses could render affirmative action toxic. If so, the campuses ought to fix their affirmative action policies or abandon them.

Bowen and Bok's rosy picture might not hold true for institutions significantly different from the very select ones they studied, but one piece of impressionistic evidence stands out. We never hear of minority students tearing up and rejecting the admissions letters they get from outstanding schools. Of course, they all may labor under a delusion, believing that affirmative action had nothing to do with their acceptances and that therefore they have no reason to fear the stigma or other baleful effects predicted for its beneficiaries. (Nor do we hear of legacies refusing the leg up because of such fears.) More likely, they consider the benefits of going to a selective college to outweigh any cost from being—or being perceived as—an "affirmative action baby."[82]

11

Sowing the Seeds of Higher Education

Even if it is on the whole beneficial, affirmative action in higher education is by now—two and a half decades after *Bakke*—a somewhat shopworn routine that does nothing directly to address the causes of the credentials gap between minority and white students that prompts its use in the first place.[1] Although the Supreme Court has lifted the constitutional cloud over affirmative action, racial preferences still remain forbidden in California and Washington, and future political mobilization may bring more states into alignment with them. If universities in such states desire to retain their racial and ethnic diversity, they will have to find other ways to make the numbers. In this chapter we explore some of their options.

CLASS PREFERENCES AND
"X PERCENT SOLUTIONS"

Many critics of the racial preferences used in affirmative action urge colleges and universities to move to a class-based scheme of preferences. This proposal sounds from all political quarters, left as well as right.[2] In a nation committed to equal opportunity, what could be fairer than giving a leg up to students from lower-income backgrounds? And because black students are more likely to come from such backgrounds than white students, class-based affirmative action will disproportionately favor the former, supplying the racial diversity campuses currently seek through their use of racial preferences. So runs the argument.[3]

But the argument is flawed. At the highly selective schools studied by William Bowen and Derek Bok, class-based instead of race-based affirmative action would result in admission of far fewer black students. The problem is that the black–white achievement gap manifests itself at every socioeconomic level.[4] Moreover, there are very few students, white or black, from the lowest economic strata who can succeed in a high-powered academic environment. As Bowen and Bok put it, "the problem is not that poor but qualified candidates go undiscovered [by admissions committees], but that there are simply very few of these candidates in the first place."[5] At the twenty-eight colleges and universities Bowen and Bok studied, 86 percent of the African American students on campus and 98 percent of the white students were from middle and upper-middle class backgrounds—even though all these institutions look intently for disadvantaged applicants to admit (and fully subsidize).[6]

High school graduates whose annual family income is below $25,000 are far less prepared to go to *any* four-year college, much less a selective college, than other students; fully 47 percent of the 1992 cohort fell below minimal college qualifications as measured by the National Center for Education Statistics.[7] Only 21 percent had academic credentials that matched or exceeded those of average students at a good state university. Most colleges and universities already give extra consideration to applicants who are first-time college-goers and come from low-income families, so class-based affirmative action of a sort is already in place. It doesn't much alter campus profiles anywhere.

A second alternative to affirmative action has been introduced in Texas, Florida, and California—the "X percent solution." In Texas, after *Hopwood* put race-conscious admissions policies under a cloud, the legislature passed a law requiring automatic admission to a state university of any in-state applicant who ranked in the top 10 percent of her high school class.[8] The primary impact of this law falls on the University of Texas at Austin and Texas A&M University at College Station, the two most selective public institutions in the state, where previous affirmative action policies were abandoned after *Hopwood*. The law exploits the extensive racial segregation in Texas high schools to propel blacks and Hispanics into these two universities, because in many of Texas's high schools the top 10 percent will be entirely black or Hispanic. Now in operation for six years, the Top Ten Percent policy seems to have restored racial and ethnic diversity at the University of Texas and Texas A&M to pre-*Hopwood* levels. For example, the freshmen class enrolled at the University of Texas in 1996, when it used affirmative action, was 4 percent black and 14 percent Hispanic.[9] The class enrolled in 2001 displayed the same pattern. The percentage of whites entering the university fell four points between 1996 and 2001, and the percentage of Asian Americans rose by the same amount.[10]

Although the population of Texas is over 32 percent Hispanic and 11 percent black, the percentages admitted to the University of Texas are far smaller, reflecting the very limited pool of students from these two groups eligible even under the automatic admission law. To be automatically admitted, a student must graduate from high school with grades putting her in the top 10 percent of her class; must have taken a college preparatory curriculum; and must have taken and reported scores from the SAT or ACT. In 1999, only 901 black students and 2,465 Hispanic students in the entire state met these conditions.[11] In that year, the university's Top Ten Percent admits included 268 blacks and 911 Hispanics.[12]

The Top Ten Percent policy has modestly increased the number of high schools in Texas that send students to the University at Austin. It has benefited large urban schools in Dallas and Houston and small rural schools spread throughout the state—the former mostly black, the latter mostly white.[13] Indeed, of the Top Ten Percent students admitted to Austin in 2001, thirty-two hundred were white.[14]

According to the university's reports, the automatic admission law has not adversely affected the academic preparation of its students, although the mean SAT scores of the top 10 percent have fallen steadily. Even so, the Top Ten Percent matriculants attain average freshman-year grades higher than their non–Top Ten Percent counterparts within every SAT score-band.[15] The rosy picture provided by the university's reports makes it hard to pin down precisely the extent to which the Top Ten Percenters arrive on campus with academic deficiencies. However, its own prior study of Houston and Dallas–Fort Worth high schools suggested that some of the new matriculants would struggle to meet its academic expectations. The study found that while the top 5 percent from these schools possessed high school grades in the 90s, the next segment, 6 to 10 percent, had grades in the 80s and even 70s.[16] If these findings hold true throughout the state, then a great many of the "top 10 percent" entering the university will possess academic records inferior to—in some cases far inferior to—those of students in the top 20 or 30 percent of their classes at the highly competitive high schools that traditionally send large numbers of students to Austin. (These findings are consistent with national data. According to a 1994 report, in mathematics, A students in high-poverty secondary schools most closely resemble D students in the most affluent schools; in English, A students in high-poverty schools "got the same reading scores as . . . C and D students in the most affluent schools."[17])

The university points to a low overall remediation rate for all students, including Top Ten Percenters, but it doesn't disaggregate the rate by race and ethnicity. However, according to the Texas Higher Education Coordinating Board, in the academic year 1999–2000, 6.6 percent of the students at the university needed remediation—4.2 percent of white students, 22.5 percent of black students, and 11.1 percent of Hispanic students. Certainly, the legislation establishing the Top Ten Percent policy anticipated some difficulties, explicitly permitting universities to require automatically admitted students who need remediation to take summer classes before fall enrollment. At least in the early stages of the program, the university was scrambling to create special courses and add extra counselors to deal with the academic deficits it anticipated in the new students.[18]

Overall, the Top Ten Percenters are succeeding by the university's main standard, posting graduation rates better than the rest of the students. However, once these rates are disaggregated by race and ethnicity, the picture is not so uniformly positive. While 73 percent of the white Top Ten Percenters who entered school in 1996 graduated after five years, only 54 percent of the blacks and 57 percent of the Hispanics did. Although these latter rates were higher than the rates for black and Hispanic non–Top Ten Percenters they are approximately the same as the rate for white non–Top Ten Percenters.

The university has publicly claimed satisfaction with the Top Ten Percent program. However, now that the Supreme Court has effectively nullified the *Hopwood* ruling that spawned the Top Ten Percent policy, the university may return to using racial preferences.

The Florida plan, "One Florida," eliminated affirmative action at Florida's public universities and guarantees admission into one of them to students who graduate in the top 20 percent of their class, as long as they complete the 19 credits of college preparatory work mandated by the State Board of Education and take the SAT or ACT. According to the state, roughly 20,000 students each year should meet these criteria.[19] However, particular campuses in the state system can require additional, more rigorous admissions standards. Thus, unlike in the Texas automatic admission plan, Florida high school students are not assured a place at one of the state's flagship campuses if they meet the One Florida conditions. Moreover, most of the 20,000 are already eligible under older criteria, which require students to possess a minimum 3.0 HSGPA. In the year 2001, only 118 students graduated in the top 20 percent of their classes with grades lower than 3.0. Twenty-three of them entered the state system.[20]

In the freshman class that enrolled at the University of Florida in the fall of 2000, most of whom had been selected before One Florida took effect, 11 percent were black. In the fall of 2001, after the elimination of affirmative action, the number fell to 5 percent. Estimates for the fall of 2002 see a rise to 8 percent. The decline in 2001 for Hispanics was less dramatic, and they are expected to constitute 12.5 percent of the freshman class of 2002.[21]

California's Top Four Percent Plan, initiated after the Regents abolished affirmative action, has as its primary aim increasing the pool of UC eligible students. Under the plan, students whose sophomore and junior year grades in university-approved high school courses put them in the top 4 percent of their classes are notified at the beginning of their senior year by the university system that they may apply as "Eligible in the Local Context" (ELC). If they complete their remaining required coursework and take all the examinations demanded by the university system,[22] they are guaranteed admission to a UC campus. This route to eligibility contrasts with "Eligibility in a

Statewide Context," in which applicants must likewise satisfy all of the course and testing requirements and then acquire eligibility through a complex formula matching grades and test scores on a sliding scale. For example, an otherwise qualified student with a HSGPA of 2.8 needs a total test score of 4640 to become UC eligible; a student with a HSGPA of 3.35 needs a total test score of only 3192.[23] The "4 percent path," which went into effect for the class admitted in 2001, means that a student with outstanding grades can gain admission even if ineligible by the statewide eligibility formula.

In 2001, the university designated over 11,000 students ELC and in 2002 over 13,000. A very high proportion of students identified as ELC would have been eligible under alternative criteria, but because they now apply under ELC, if is difficult to estimate how many new and different kinds of applicants the Top Four Percent Program is adding to the UC mix. High schools—both urban and rural—that had sent very few students to the university in the past seem most positively affected, although the increase in rural applications through ELC last year was offset by a decline in rural applications from students not in the top 4 percent of their classes. ELC seems to be picking up applications from blacks and Hispanics at a higher-than-average rate, so the Top Four Percent path may help increase the racial and ethnic diversity on the university's campuses, especially the most competitive campuses, because these schools now give priority to ELC applications. For example, last year Berkeley admitted 74 percent of its ELC applicants and only 26 percent of other California applicants.[24]

Each of the "percent plans" is very different from the others, and each takes place in a very different context. The fruits of the Texas plan are discernible by now; the effects of the Florida and California plans remain to be seen, though there is already some basis for speculation.

PRE-COLLEGE INTERVENTIONS

One thing is clear, however. Increasing minority representation on selective campuses requires vigorous interventions of several sorts. After One Florida went into effect, the University of Florida became much more active in reaching out to minority high school students. Among other things, it formed partnerships with three low-performing high schools in Jacksonville and Miami, supplying encouragement, advice, and mentoring to students and teachers both, and supplying cash as well: $12,500 scholarships to the top five graduates of each school.[25]

After the Top Ten Percent plan went into effect in Texas, both the University of Texas and Texas A&M revamped their recruiting procedures. In the first year, the University of Texas bought the name-list of all Top Ten Percenters in the state who took the ACT or SAT and notified them that they were candidates for admission, making frequent follow-up contacts to see that those who wanted to apply to Austin completed their paperwork. In subsequent years the university expanded publicity and outreach events designed to alert Top Ten Percenters across the state of the opportunities available to them.[26] In addition, like the University of Florida, it put up cash, establishing and publicizing its "Longhorn Scholarships" for students from "under-represented schools."

These interventions only scratch the surface, however. Even before *Hopwood* and HB 588, the University of Texas and Texas A&M had in place jointly run "Outreach Centers" in Austin, Dallas, Houston, Corpus Christi, San Antonio, and the Rio Grande Valley—staffed centers offering a range of services designed to give middle and high school students the idea that college is for them. Once students have picked up on the idea of college, the centers facilitate translation of the idea into reality. The Outreach Centers give tutorial assistance, conduct parent information workshops, arrange college campus visits, assist in college entrance exam preparations, and offer summer enrichment programs.[27] The work of these Outreach Centers has intensified since the creation of the Top Ten Percent Plan.

The Texas Longhorn PREP program by the University of Texas—of post–HB 588 origin—is a university–public school collaborative active in Dallas, Houston, Beaumont, Port Arthur, San Antonio, and Wilmer Hutchens school districts, providing "pre-college preparation" resources for high school juniors and seniors. The focus of this program is strengthening students' academic skills, especially skills in English.[28]

The Charles Dana Center at the university runs its own intervention system throughout Texas—Advancement Via Individual Determination (AVID), a twenty-year-old, nationwide, privately supported program that recruits promising students in middle and high school and supports their aspirations for college. In its own words, AVID "provides what first generation college students usually lack, what advantaged students receive from their parents and community: high expectations, encouragement, day to day help, a vision of college as attainable, an advocate, and guidance on how to negotiate the system."[29] Students who join AVID make a contract to stick with the program, study two hours a day and complete all school assignments, participate in AVID tutorials, take an academically rigorous curriculum, and enroll in a for-credit, high school elective AVID class that meets daily. Parents have to sign a contract too. Through the work of the Dana Center, AVID programs run in seventy-five middle and high schools throughout the state.

Intervention of the sort we've described—especially the kind captured in the AVID programs—reflects a consensus formed in the last twenty years about the prerequisites for college success. This consensus, given voice in the influential 1983 report *A Nation at Risk*,[30] is reflected in the requirement by selective colleges and universities—discussed at some length in chapter 7—that applicants complete an academically solid curriculum in high school. The implications for intervention? Kids have to be set on a solid academic track by the seventh or eighth grade, otherwise it may be too late for them to have a shot at academically demanding colleges.

In previous chapters we have referred to the work of Clifford Adelman, Senior Research Analyst at the U.S. Department of Education. His study, *Answers in the Tool Box: Academic Intensity, Attendance Patterns, and Bachelor's Degree Attainment*, represents core aspects of the consensus view (a view his own researches over the years have helped shape).[31] Adelman's study, which is based on high school graduating classes of 1972, 1982, and 1992, examines "what contributes most to long-term bachelor's degree completion of students who attend 4-year colleges."[32] His research points to two important variables as predictors of bachelor's degree completion: "academic resources" and continuous enrollment once a student has made a "true start" in college.

Here we focus on academic resources. Its three components are (i) the quality of students' high school curriculum, (ii) their high school grades, and (iii) their scores on SAT-like tests. Adelman divided the subjects of his studies into quintiles, high to low in possession of these components. On one calculation, 70 percent who entered college with a strong high school curriculum completed their degree, as did 64 percent with strong test scores[33] and 59 percent with strong HSGPAs. By contrast to these students in the top quintile, only 19 percent of students who entered college from the third quintile, trailing a mediocre curriculum behind them, completed their degree, as did only 16 percent with mediocre test scores, and only 19 percent with mediocre grades. Not surprisingly, students in the lowest quintile, with very weak high school course work, low test scores, and low grades, chalked up abysmal graduation rates.[34]

Writes Adelman: "No matter how one cuts the population, roughly the same proportions earn bachelor's degrees by quintile of the three component resource measures. Furthermore, academic intensity of high school curriculum emerges as the strongest of the three."[35] Moreover, of all the aspects of curriculum intensity, "none has such an obvious and powerful relationship to ultimate completion of degrees as the highest level of mathematics one studies in high school."[36] Students who had completed calculus in high school graduated college at a rate of 81.6 percent, students who had completed precalculus graduated at 75.7 percent, students who had completed trigonometry graduated at 65.1 percent, and students who had completed only algebra II graduated at 44.4 percent.[37]

It is no accident, then, that the institutions we discussed in chapter 7—Brown, Tennessee, Lewis and Clark, Johns Hopkins, Nebraska, Claremont McKenna, to name a few—require a demanding course of studies in high school, including at least three years of college preparatory math, several years of a foreign language, multiple lab courses in the natural sciences, three years of history and social studies, and four years of English. It is no accident that the University of Florida, the University of Texas, and the University of California impose similarly demanding high school coursework requirements.

Students who miss the math train in particular are ruled out of competition years before college admission time. That is why aggressive intervention programs that aim to broaden opportunities for underrepresented groups increasingly focus on middle school as the pivot point. If seventh and eighth graders aren't taking pre-algebra and algebra as preludes to algebra II, trigonometry, and precalculus in high school, they won't be in the pool that California, Texas, and Florida choose from, even if they end up in the top 4, 10, or 20 percent of their high school classes.

Likewise, as AVID emphasizes, middle school is the time to direct students into the other important preparatory pathways toward an academically rigorous high school curriculum—foreign language classes, intensive writing workshops, history and geography courses, and the like. Successful intervention at the middle school level promises long-term payoffs. As Adelman's research shows, a strong math background trumps social and economic disadvantage. In the cohort of students he studied, each quintile rise in a student's socioeconomic background increased his odds of graduating from college by 1.68 to 1, but each quintile rise in math accomplishment increased his odds by 2.59 to 1.[38]

This finding is consistent with the work that underlies Equity 2000, the College Board's decade-old initiative to "close the gap in college-going and success rates between minority and nonminority, advantaged and disadvantaged students."[39] According to a study commissioned for the College Board, when low income and minority students take advanced math courses in high school and aspire to go to college, "they not only go to college at about the same rate as whites, they also succeed at about the same rate."[40] Moreover, the same study indicates that SAT I Math scores approach parity when blacks and Hispanics take the same math courses as their white counterparts.[41]

Using "mathematics at the middle grade as its initial leverage for reform," Equity 2000 itself leveraged $20 million from major foundations to pilot its program in 700 schools across the country beginning in the early 1990s. Its avowed aim was 100 percent enrollment in algebra by ninth grade. At its pilot sites it provided extensive professional development for teachers starting two years before program implementation; academic support for students through the use of Saturday Academies, a Summer Scholars Program, Academic Enrichment Laboratories, and SAT prep activities; and encouragement of parental support by means of Parent Academies that helped parents understand the importance of math literacy.[42] It also brokered partnerships between high schools and a range of other community organizations.

Studies reported by the American Youth Policy Forum showed significant increases in the number of ninth graders taking algebra in the Equity 2000 sites. The proportion of African Americans taking algebra increased from 45 to 72 percent, the proportion of Hispanics from 40 to 72 percent.[43] These figures don't automatically spell success, however. It is one thing to encourage and support kids prepared to handle algebra, quite another to force every ninth grader into algebra class. In the Milwaukee school system, for example, the percentage of ninth graders taking algebra under Equity 2000 rose from 31 to 99 percent, but nearly half the ninth graders failed. The daily absentee rate in algebra courses was 25 percent, 30 to 40 percent of the classes consisted of repeaters, and some teachers had "watered down" their presentations.[44]

Strong math achievement—plus strong foreign language preparation, good English reading and writing skills, and a solid background in the natural sciences and history—translate into better chances of getting into, and completing, a competitive college program. In middle school, the pathways toward and away from college preparation diverge. Consequently, colleges and universities seeking long-term fixes to the problem of racial, ethnic, and socioeconomic diversity do well to focus upon middle school as the place to begin.

GEAR UP AND COLLEGE NOW

Intervening in middle school is the strategy behind a new federal program that may add substantially to the resources already directed at preparing minority youth for college. The idea of providing special encouragement and assistance to minority students goes back forty years, to the Great Society programs initiated under Lyndon Johnson. TRIO—a set of initiatives directed largely at youth from families earning under $24,000 a year—serves more than 700,000 students across the country. Two of the best known TRIO endeavors are Talent Search, which tries to identify and assist students between the sixth and twelfth grades who show college potential, and Upward Bound, which instructs middle and high school students in math, literature, composition, and science on college campus during the summer and on Saturdays during the school year.[45] Other TRIO programs focus on students already in college, helping them over hurdles to successful completion.

The new federal program directed toward middle schools, GEAR UP (Gaining Early Awareness and Readiness for Undergraduate Programs), is only four years old. It funds states, universities, school systems, and community groups on a matching basis to create partnerships that bring the idea and reality of college to middle and high school students. GEAR UP's self-declared mission "is to significantly increase the number of low-income students who are prepared to enter and succeed in postsecondary education."[46] GEAR UP projects pursue this mission on a number of fronts: by improving the quality of teachers, by aligning curricula at all levels (K–16) for greater coherence, and by educating parents and supporting their efforts.

As we saw in chapter 4, the City University of New York faces a considerable challenge in making its remediation reforms work without diverting large numbers of college-aspirants away from its senior colleges. It has been able to fold GEAR UP programs directly into one of its already-existing initiatives, College Now. College Now links New York City high schools with CUNY campuses to stimulate college awareness and preparation. Qualified students can take college courses while still in high school. Other students who want to go to college but lack the needed skills can take special preparatory courses and workshops. Students get special help preparing for the Regents exams and the SATs. The aim is to get students with academic promise to understand early in high school what it takes to succeed in college and to arrive at the college gates ready to go, not needing remediation. Just as in the AVID program, students have day-to-day help from the high schools and partner colleges in following a pathway to successful college admission—and graduation.[47]

GEAR UP supplements College Now and extends it into the middle school grades. For example, Bronx Educational Alliance (BEA) GEAR UP links together Lehman College with seven middle or intermediate schools in the Bronx. It enrolls sixteen hundred students in the sixth grade. Each of the students participates in one of six "cohorts," each led by a full-time coordinator. In addition, Lehman College faculty harmonize guidance counseling in the schools, oversee extensive mentoring, administer the overall program, and maintain a website in English and Spanish. Finally, if a student's parents are willing to pay fifteen dollars a month for an Internet connection and take a no-cost computer course, BEA GEAR UP gives the student a free Macintosh computer as well.

These mentoring and counseling activities aim to sow the seeds of college in the Bronx sixth graders and encourage their best performance in the classroom. BEA GEAR UP works closely with parents to make the supportive seed grow in them as well.[48] Combined with College Now, which kicks in at the high school level, Bronx sixth graders who aspire to college will have six years of counseling, mentoring, and academic enrichment to prepare them for what lies ahead.

GEAR UP and College Now undoubtedly make a real difference in college aspirations and college readiness among New York City students, but the accomplishments of these programs are inevitably pretty modest. BEA

GEAR UP, for example, spreads its seeds on stony soil, as a cursory look at the seven Bronx middle schools shows. At only two of them does the rate of students eligible for free lunch fall below 90 percent. At Paul Robeson School, only 12 percent of the mostly black and Hispanic students meet the city and state standards in English proficiency and only 4 percent meet math standards. More significantly, 34 percent of the students are *far below* the English standards and 65 percent are *far below* the math standards. A story nearly as dismal holds true at four of the other schools. Slightly better is the Henry Hudson School, where 26 and 18 percent of the students meet the city and state standards in English and math, while 30 and 48 percent fall far below. Academically the best school in the group is Daniel Hale Williams, where 45 percent of the students meet the English standards and 32 percent meet the math standards. From this soil, even with the earnest interventionist endeavors of GEAR UP, College Now, and many other programs working in concert, the harvest of successful senior college entrants will not be abundant.

Intervention and college–middle school partnerships are not new ideas, and many of the Bronx schools already have in place other linkages beside those provided by GEAR UP. Columbia, Fordham, Manhattan College, and City College of New York, along with Bronx Community College, Hostos Community College, New York University, New York College of Podiatry, Montefiore Hospital, and Lincoln Center, among others, have working arrangements with the Bronx schools, in addition to Lehman College's intense investment through GEAR UP.

The dreary picture of academic achievement among the largely black and Hispanic fifth through eighth graders in the Bronx schools makes plain that intervention needs to start much earlier. Indeed, it needs to start before children enter kindergarten, where kids from poor families start off with cognitive deficits that are rarely fully made up in school.

THE PERSISTENCE OF THE BLACK–WHITE ACHIEVEMENT GAP

According to Ronald Ferguson, writing in a volume of essays on the black–white test score gap, "the average black child arrives at kindergarten with fewer academic skills than the average white child."[49] This gap increases over time. "All else equal," write Meredith Phillips and her colleagues in the same volume,

> white students who start school with test scores at the population mean can be expected to finish high school with test scores that are still at the mean. Black students who start elementary school with . . . test scores at the population

mean can be expected to finish high school with math scores that lie 0.34 standard deviations below the mean and reading scores that lie 0.39 standard deviations below the mean. These gaps are equivalent to a decline of about 35 or 40 SAT points.[50]

Why does this happen? Ferguson explores one common answer: blacks and whites are treated differently in schools. Teachers have lower expectations of black students than white students, and these lower expectations have a dampening effect on black achievement. Ferguson believes there may be some truth to this view, although the magnitude of the effects is uncertain and any conclusions "currently hang by thin threads of evidence."[51] The problem arises not so much because teachers—white or black—judge students through distorting preconceptions but because the teachers form conclusions based on observable performance.[52] Since black students start out on average performing less well, teachers may form diminished expectations of their future achievements. Unfortunately, these lowered expectations may in turn produce self-fulfilling effects.

There are many other explanations offered for black student underperformance. One well-known theory put forward by Signithia Fordham and John Ogbu postulates a "cultural orientation" among black youth, "which defines academic learning in school as 'acting white,' and academic success as the prerogative of white Americans. This orientation embodies both social pressures against striving for academic success and fear of striving for academic success."[53] For African Americans to excel in school, they have to separate themselves from their peers and "give up aspects of their identities," a high price to pay.[54] This account of student motivations fits with observations by Claude Steele, who describes the "psychic alienation—the act of not caring" about school that enables some black children to maintain their self-esteem. Steele reports a study of fifth-graders in an Illinois school district by Bruce Hare, who found that

> although the black boys had considerably lower achievement-test scores than their white classmates, their overall self-esteem was just as high. This stunning imperviousness to poor academic performance was accomplished . . . [Hare] found, by their de-emphasizing school achievement as a basis of self-esteem and giving preference to peer-group relations—a domain in which their esteem prospects were better.[55]

Steele is well-known for his work on "stereotype threat." In a study first published in 1995, Steele and a colleague, Joshua Aronson, randomly assigned 114 Stanford University undergraduates, half white and half black, to three experimental groups. All three groups were given a test based on Graduate Record Exam questions. The first group was told that the test was diagnostic of individual intelligence, the second group that it was a simple laboratory problem-solving exercise, and the third that it was a challenge task. The black participants performed worse on the first test than the others, and performed worse on it than the whites.[56] According to Steele and Aronson, telling the first group they were undertaking an "intelligence" test activated "stereotype threat" among the black students. The black students showed "significantly greater activation of African American stereotypes, greater activation of concerns about their own ability, a greater tendency to avoid racially stereotypic preferences, a greater tendency to make excuses for their performance, and a greater reluctance to make their racial identity known."[57]

Although suggestive, this experiment and a great many recent ones like it (some of whose findings are fairly modestly supported and much of it yet unpublished) provide a rather slim basis upon which to generalize about the black–white gap from prekindergarten through high school.[58] "Stereotype threat" in one manifestation, at least, is a form of test anxiety, a much-studied phenomenon over the years, and one for which the literature is inconclusive about cause-and-effect relationships.[59]

Ferguson points to some test-score studies of sixth graders in Maryland that might indicate the presence of "stereotype threat" *if* the sixth graders, like the Stanford college students, perceived their tests as "diagnostic of intelligence"—a big "if." In any case, for Ferguson, "stereotype threat" is just one piece of the larger picture, including the Fordham–Ogbu thesis and yet other evidence, in support of the view that black students disengage from academic achievement.[60]

However, although the "black disengagement" thesis has wide currency, Phillip Cook and Jens Ludwig, using National Education Longitudinal data, have found the thesis falling wide of the mark.

> Black high school students are not particularly alienated from school. They are as likely as whites to expect to enter and complete college, and their actual rate of high school completion is as high as that among whites from the same socioeconomic background. Also, black and white students report that they spend about the same amount of time on homework and have similar rates of absenteeism. . . . Moreover, black and white tenth-graders who excel in school are no more likely to be unpopular than other students.[61]

Ferguson himself has recently completed a detailed study of the Shaker Heights, Ohio school system that fits more closely with the Cook–Ludwig findings. Shaker Heights is an affluent, racially integrated suburb of Cleveland (about 34 percent of its residents are African American) with only one middle school and one high school, so that black and white students attend the same schools. The black students, seventh through eleventh grade, possess an average GPA (C+) one letter grade below the average GPA (B+)

possessed by whites. The grade difference, writes Ferguson, appears related "most directly to academic skill and social background advantages, as opposed to effort, interest, or behavior." The black students do not put out less effort than whites nor is "their peer culture . . . more opposed to achievement." [62]

> [B]lack teenagers in Shaker Heights complete less homework on average, participate less in class discussions, and are more inclined than white students to act tough and get into fights. Black students also enroll in honors and AP courses at a much lower rate, and it is well known in Shaker Heights that peers sometimes accuse blacks who enroll in such courses of acting white. While these patterns seem consistent with the oppositional culture explanation for black-white achievement disparities . . . [the Shaker Heights data reveal] a more complicated story. First, some things that appear to be elements of black youth culture are best understood nonracially, in terms of socioeconomic background. For example, blacks' lower self-reported propensity to participate in class discussion disappears once I control for parental education and other nonracial measures of family background. Holding family backgrounds constant, black males report more interest in their studies than white males and there is no black-white difference among females. Second, black students report spending as much (or more) time doing their homework each day as white students who take the same classes. This and related findings suggest that the reason blacks complete less homework than whites may be that they have fewer skills and get less help from home, not that they care less or exert less effort. [63]

The difference in home backgrounds is striking. "Mothers and fathers together," writes Ferguson, "average at least four years of college in roughly 90 percent of white households, compared to 45 percent of black households. Parents in one quarter of black households have only twelve or fewer years of schooling." [64] These differences translate into differences in performance and aspirations at school.

Parents with high levels of education, writes Ferguson, are better able to prepare their children "to concentrate, to be curious, to enjoy the exchange of ideas [and] to have high academic aspirations." [65] What is true of Shaker Heights is true generally. The problem is not that well-educated parents care more about education for their children than less-educated ones. Some evidence testifies to a strong belief among black parents that education is a route to success for their children and to a strong desire on their part that their children take challenging courses. [66] The problem is that less well-educated parents (whether black or white) are less efficient in turning these beliefs into high performance by their children. [67]

If social and economic class significantly affect school achievement in Shaker Heights, where most residents don't drop below the lower-middle classes (only 15 percent of fifth and sixth graders are eligible for free lunches),[68] it plays a much larger role in those Bronx communities served by GEAR UP, and in numerous other school districts across the country. One set of data on income notes that "57 percent of black children born between 1978 and 1980 lived in census tracks where a fifth or more of their neighbors were poor compared with only 7 percent of white children."[69] Thus, large numbers of minority children grow up in neighborhoods where the limitations in their own families are compounded by the drag exerted by their peers and neighbors.

At the beginning of this section we asked why the black–white achievement gap persists through school. Differences in teacher expectations might be a small contributory factor. The peer costs that some black students have to pay to excel academically may play a small role. Test anxiety induced by "stereotype threat" may generate a small negative effect. But all these seem to pale next to socioeconomic class. This fact holds true for Hispanics as well as blacks. In studies of white and Mexican American mothers reported by Scott Miller, differences in education played a critical role in the way families prepared their children for school. When the educational level of white and Mexican American families was held constant, the parenting practices of white and Mexican American mothers converged. "The teaching strategies used by the more highly educated mothers, white or Mexican American," writes Miller, "were quite consistent with those typically used in school."[70]

Whatever the cause of the gap and its persistence, the medicine favored by school reformers is *further intervention*. Intervention already begins early, as we've noted, with Head Start and other preschool programs designed to help both parent and child get ready for school. In the last two decades, many additional intervention reforms have been tested and used widely across the country. Some focus on the early school years exclusively and tackle students at highest risk of failure. One such program, Success for All, incubated at Johns Hopkins University and now used in hundreds of schools across the country, was nominated by the U.S. Department of Education as one of a dozen highly effective "comprehensive school reform" models.[71] Ferguson singles it out for special attention in a companion to his article on teacher expectations. Success for All concentrates on teaching children in the first few grades to become good readers. It uses a highly scripted format that teachers must follow closely, involves frequent assessment, utilizes tutors for one-on-one instruction, involves students working together in teams, and employs a full-time facilitator to make all the parts work in harmony. More important, perhaps, than the pedagogical and support tools deployed by Success for All is the spirit that animates its programs. Ferguson quotes Robert Slavin, the creator of Success for All, who avows that "there is one factor we try to make consistent in all schools: a relentless focus on the success of every child."[72]

Success for All's impact on students has been measured using control groups of similar children in schools not using the program. Ferguson is impressed with the gains in reading skills Success for All students show over their control counterparts, and concludes, "Success for All shows that it is possible to produce sustained improvement in students' achievement test scores when schools and communities make the commitment to do so."[73]

The school and community commitment in Success for All programs is indeed significant in terms of financial cost, teacher zeal, and family commitment. However, the effect sizes are significant, too. In a multistate assessment reported by Slavin and Nancy Madden, Success for All cohorts showed effect sizes of about half a standard deviation for each grade, one through five.[74] This means that about 70 percent of control group students were not reading as well as the average student in Success for All.

Yet since Success for All students are drawn from populations of children who enter first grade already deficient in their reading skills, the improvements wrought by Success for All's "relentless focus" do not necessarily bring the students even to grade-level reading ability. Indeed, one study of Baltimore schools, where Success for All began, concluded that after five years in the program, only 13 percent of students were reading at grade level.[75]

If even relentlessly focused and well-financed school reform leaves low-income and minority children struggling to catch up, intensive school intervention will not by itself significantly change current patterns of achievement for a long time. The elementary schools that feed the seven BEA GEAR UP middle schools in the Bronx deliver to their doors many students well behind in math and reading scores at grade five. BEA GEAR UP schools, in turn, deliver to the Bronx's high schools students not yet ready for an intense, college preparatory curriculum.

Intervention at any level that makes any positive difference is to be welcomed and embraced; and GEAR UP, Equity 2000, and their cousins do alter the trajectory for many promising students who would otherwise drift without encouragement and focus when they reach the middle school level. These programs can add to the pool of qualified minority students in the college admissions competition—but they won't add big numbers in the short run, and they won't make the black–white achievement gap disappear soon.

12

Summing Up, Looking Ahead

The routines and rituals surrounding college admissions in the United States have attracted growing attention and controversy over the last several decades. Affirmative action; the use of standardized tests such as the SAT, and with it the growth of the coaching and test prep industry; admissions advantages for athletes; legacy preference; early admission policies; merit- versus need-based financial aid; open admissions; the burgeoning of college rankings guides begun by *U.S. News & World Report* and now produced by various other publications—all have come under scrutiny, subject to heated attacks and equally impassioned defenses by politicians, pundits, policymakers, professors, parents, students, and university administrators.

In this book we have offered analyses of these and other issues, underpinned by a picture of the missions of contemporary American colleges and universities. We begin this concluding chapter by describing our general outlook and approach. We go on to recapitulate our arguments, conclusions, and recommendations concerning the primary ethical issues surrounding college admissions today.

THEORY AND PRACTICE

The view we have set out might be called "egalitarianism with a pragmatic face." We began with the principle that educational opportunities should be enhanced for those who have traditionally been shortchanged. There is no dearth of rationales for the principle. Considered in itself, prudence, ethics, and aesthetics all provide support for it. A society deeply divided into haves and have-nots is insecure, wasteful, and ugly. That some people have the opportunity to develop their talents while others, through no fault of their own, do not is unseemly as well as unfair.

We stipulated another principle as well: that individuals should be neither helped nor hindered in their efforts at educational advancement by factors irrelevant to the legitimate goals of educational institutions. This principle underlies the popular sense that there is something wrong when those already blessed with educational advantages that enhance their qualifications, such as better learning environments, also benefit from perks such as legacy preference that do not make them superior students. Although this principle is less transparent than the first, we believe that both command widespread acceptance in our society when considered in themselves. The hesitation we may have in embracing them wholeheartedly comes about because, although the principles are attractive in theory, the question remains how they fare in practice, where they bump up against other principles and values and the constraints of the real world.[1] Because the crux of the matter is not foundational but practical, we have focused our efforts not on defending the principles themselves but instead on exploring the tensions between them and the other principles, values, and practical constraints that stand in the way of realizing them.

The devil, we said, was in the details. We don't pretend that by attending to the details we have resolved all the important questions about justice and college admissions. The devil still lurks around the place. But the details are not all of a piece (suggesting a plurality of devils). Some have to do with uncertainty about facts: the consequences of affirmative action for campus climate, for example, the efficacy of expensive test-prep courses, or the causes of the minority–white test-score gap. Despite the wealth of studies on such issues, much is still unknown, and various empirical questions remain disputed.

Sometimes our uncertainty is of a different kind, however. Recall the discussion in chapter 10 of the irreconcilable beliefs held by some opposing parties to the affirmative action debate. Some people see racial discrimination as requiring *intentional* action: the purposeful giving or withholding of a benefit or burden on account of race. Others, by contrast, think of discrimination in terms of *effects*. On this view, discrimination consists of practices that reproduce inequality.[2] Since racial segregation persisted in the United States for centuries, its effects endure and inequality is reproduced in all major social institutions. Those who believe discrimination is necessarily intentional, by contrast, see it as circumscribed even if pernicious. Although they may regret the racial inequality that persists in our society, they don't regard it as discrimination, and they believe its claims on us are less pressing than the claims of discrimination.

Clearly those who hold views about discrimination at the either end of this spectrum will find it virtually impossible to come to agreement with those at the other end—which helps to explain the intractability of the affirmative action debate and other aspects of the politics of race. Even for those who occupy positions away from the ends of the spectrum, however, a good deal of irresolution and indeterminacy remains. We have endorsed a concept of discrimination that counts practices that adversely affect blacks as discriminatory unless those practices are supported by *strong enough reasons*.[3] This formulation reflects the prevailing legal standard, according to which policies and practices with a disparate impact on minorities are discriminatory unless they can be justified by "business necessity."[4] The indeterminacy here is evident: terms such as "strong enough reasons" and "business necessity" are not, and cannot be, well-defined; they leave some wiggle room. As a result, people with different proclivities and values—varying tolerances for the costs and benefits of alternative policies and practices—will differ in their judgments about which reasons are strong enough to justify discrimination and which business practices are necessary.

To acknowledge this indeterminacy and uncertainty is not to capitulate to a vicious relativism in which all perspectives are equally valid. It is simply to point out what common sense makes abundantly clear: complex policy issues involve questions of fact and questions of value, not all of which can be settled once and for all. We hope to have mapped the conceptual, moral, and practical terrain in a useful way and to have made headway in answering some of the most important questions about admissions policies in higher education.

AFFIRMATIVE ACTION AND THE MISSIONS OF AMERICAN UNIVERSITIES

One thing that's clear is that the missions of colleges and universities in American society are broad and wide-ranging—much more so than the concept of merit hailed by traditionalists as *the* correct criterion of admissions would suggest. Selective colleges rightly prize academic talent, and at every kind of institution of higher education academic ability matters. Yet colleges and universities train and shape students in preparation for a multiplicity of roles in the world, and pure academic ability is only one of a number of relevant markers for these roles. Obviously it matters more for some positions than for others, even for some elite positions more than for others. The successful politician, we know, need not be an academic powerhouse; likewise the entrepreneur or trial lawyer. This is not news to colleges and universities, who have long considered many criteria—academic skills, extra-academic talents, character, drive, and other characteristics—in order to decide which students to admit. It's obvious too from the mission statements of colleges and universities that their own conceptions of their role are broader and more deeply connected to the larger society than casual attention to the subject might suggest. Vocational preparation, research, and liberal education—including what we have called education for work, for citizenship, and for living—are all integral to the modern university's mission, and all play a part in what universities commonly call "service." The University of Michigan, for example, takes as part of its mission "helping to define and assist in the solution of the problems of society" and "contributing to the growth of citizens, especially of future leaders."[5] Williams College is "dedicated to the welfare of the great common life of the State."[6] Such statements are typical of many public and private American colleges and universities.

It follows that merit is a more complex notion than is often thought, comprising more than strictly academic considerations. Preparing students for life in society, nurturing the leaders of tomorrow—these are goals that require a broad range of skills and talents. Equally important, they allow consideration of factors that are no part of a student's skills or talents—such as her race, ethnicity, socioeconomic status, or geographic origin. If we agree that the goals articulated by institutions such as Michigan and Williams are legitimate, we should also agree that the aim to produce a racially integrated and socioeconomically diverse student body is not merely a piece of politically correct ideology universities tack on to their core missions, but may be integral to them. In light of the roles universities play in society in distributing basic goods and the missions they have set for themselves, nothing could be more appropriate. Naturally, such goals must be weighed against the other functions universities serve. In making decisions, then, the contemporary college admissions office continually engages in a balancing act, weighing its various aims against each other and carefully choosing a mix of students accordingly.

We have argued that these larger social roles universities play provide the best defense of affirmative action, one that may satisfy the constitutional requirement that racial preferences must serve a compelling state interest. Reference to these roles provides a defense of affirmative action that, unlike the standard diversity argument, maintains a tight fit between the means employed and the end to be achieved. The production of an integrated society in which minorities are represented at every level including the highest is a morally compelling interest. Justice O'Connor alluded to this argument in her opinion in the *Grutter* case, although, like most of those who have written recently about affirmative action, she focused primary on the diversity rationale for it.

But the diversity rationale is inadequate. First, it hinges on a fatal equivocation within the idea of diversity. A student body can be diverse in myriad ways. Although defenders of affirmative action are interested only in one kind of diversity—racial diversity—their arguments often depend on a broader conception that does not single out racial diversity as special and that rests, moreover, on the thin reed of academic freedom articulated by

Justice Powell in the 1978 *Bakke* case. Second, when proponents of the diversity argument do appeal to the unique features of racial diversity, they are forced to rely on empirical studies of the benefits of racial diversity on college campuses, and these studies are not as persuasive as one might hope. In addition, they suggest that colleges that are not racially diverse—such as historically black colleges—must for that reason provide their students with an inferior education.

Nor should we favor affirmative action because it puts students into places they are personally entitled to be, or because it works any kind of microjustice. For reasons discussed in chapters 2 and 3, we reject the personal entitlement model of college admissions. White students who lose out because of affirmative action policies cannot complain that their rights have been violated, that they have suffered an injustice or have been deprived of something to which they are entitled. But beneficiaries of affirmative action should likewise see these matters in more impersonal terms. Affirmative action should be defended because it works a vital social good at a reasonable cost.[7]

The only persuasive rationale for affirmative action that may satisfy constitutional requirements is the one Justice O'Connor alluded to briefly in *Grutter* and that the service academies (not known for their radical views) advanced in an amicus brief in the Michigan cases: a society integrated at all levels and an elite that is not virtually all white is a compelling social interest, one that cannot be achieved today without affirmative action. Affirmative action may not be without its costs, and it will not solve the deeper problems that impede true integration. Moreover, in the *Grutter* decision, Justice O'Connor announced a life span for affirmative action of twenty-five years. Addressing these deeper problems, then, can wait no longer.

THE USE OF STANDARDIZED
TESTS IN ADMISSIONS

Despite widespread criticism of standardized tests such as the SAT as racially and class-biased, the gap in academic performance between white and affluent students and minority and low-income students remains no matter which academic yardsticks are employed—grades, other tests, class rank, academic intensity of courses taken. Unless one insists that every such measure is biased against minorities and the poor, this charge against the SAT does not survive. It doesn't follow that such tests are not seriously flawed, however. Recent critics have made a plausible case that because the SAT is not tied to specific subject matter (and perhaps for other reasons as well) it distorts learning and creates perverse incentives for students and schools.

Few people suggest, however, that we can do without standardized tests in college admissions altogether. Richard Atkinson, president of the University of California system, attracted a great deal of attention a few years ago when he sharply criticized the SAT on educational and equity grounds. Some who welcomed the attack from such a high place must have been disappointed to learn that Atkinson was suggesting that the UC system replace the SAT—formally known as the SAT I—with something like the SAT II, the achievement tests in particular subjects that many students now take in addition to the SAT I. Although achievement tests such as the SAT II may prove superior on educational grounds to the SAT I, it's clear that they have virtually the same exclusionary effects on minority and low-income students as the maligned SAT I. From an equity point of view, neither the SAT II nor other standardized tests differ significantly from the SAT I.

Students' scores on tests like the SAT I, the SAT II, and the ACT are said to be predictors of how they will perform in the first year of college, which in turn correlates (although less strongly) with how they do in college overall. The predictions are highly imperfect—as are predictions based on grades and on every other criterion colleges employ in deciding which students to admit. Students with high test scores can bomb in college, and students with low test scores can flourish; there is, to say the least, no necessary correlation between test scores and future academic success. These facts are clear. Nevertheless, when used judiciously and in conjunction with a variety of other measures, test scores give colleges useful information; at the very least, they provide a common yardstick to set against the enormous variability of grades from different teachers, courses, and schools.

Critics such as Lani Guinier and Susan Sturm argue that we should abandon the "predictive" model inherent in the use of standardized tests and move to a "performance-based" approach to admissions instead.[8] We have argued that in some respects this idea is impractical, and in others it is already in place. On the one hand, a lottery of the sort Guinier and Sturm suggest would not work unless rigged in such a way as to reproduce much the same results we find now. Moreover, open admissions at large state universities (which was virtually in effect at one time) or at other colleges would be enormously inefficient. Large numbers of students would soon flunk out, with costs not only to the institutions but also to the students' self-esteem and their desire to continue their education. On the other hand, community colleges and some four-year colleges already provide opportunities for students to enter selective institutions by showing what they can do—a performance-based approach—despite their poor high school records.

The flourishing test prep industry seems on its face unfair—just another example of how academically rich students get richer—because courses and tutors are often expensive, and thus affluent students are their primary beneficiaries. The better-designed empirical studies on the subject show quite modest gains from coaching—much smaller gains than the test-prep companies claim and than hearsay in the circles where coaching abounds suggests.

The studies only describe average gains, of course, and it's clear that coaching produces large score increases for some. Thus, ambitious students for whom money (usually their parents' money!) is not much of an object may be rational to judge that the possible benefits of coaching far outweigh the costs. On the other hand, we don't know whether or to what extent expensive test-prep courses produce better results than much cheaper alternatives, such as buying a few test-prep books and studying on one's own.

The issues surrounding the gains from test-prep are complex, and there remains interesting work to be done in this area.

CLOSING THE GAPS

The deeper problems that underlie the achievement gap between white and affluent students on the one hand and poor and minority students on the other are recalcitrant and only serious efforts will ameliorate them. Although the divide between minority and white students remains even when we control for socioeconomic factors, much of the gap is explained by these factors. Since the other elements that contribute to the gap are much more difficult to identify and address, the best way to reduce the achievement divide between minority and white students is also the way to close the gap between higher-income and lower-income students. The latter is, of course, an extremely important goal in its own right.

Money

More money for lower-income students is one part of the answer—theoretically simple even if practically difficult. The costs of college have risen steadily for thirty years and the relative contribution of state and local governments has declined. Between 1980 and 2000, government's share of the operating expenses of public colleges declined by almost 10 percent and the proportion contributed by tuition rose from 16 to 24 percent. During that period, at both private and public colleges, tuition and fees, accounting for inflation, approximately doubled.[9] New federal rules imposed in 2003 are expected to reduce government's contribution even further, in the process diminishing by several hundred million dollars the coffers of the Pell Grant, which serves low-income students.[10] To enhance the educational opportunities of lower-income students, these trends must be reversed. Contributions by government to assist students in need are investments that can be expected to increase productivity, decrease expenditures for social services and the criminal justice system, and generally improve human well-being.

Universities should also reverse recent trends by redirecting their financial aid away from merit-based scholarships, which often go to more affluent students for whom money is not a primary consideration, toward more need-based aid. A catalyst for the trend in recent years by public universities to a larger proportion of merit-based aid and a smaller proportion of need-based aid is the rankings game, fostered by *U.S. News & World Report* and other organizations. The heightened competition encouraged by the rankings is one important reason colleges feel pressed to award merit scholarships, thereby raising the average SAT scores and other academic indicators of their student bodies and improving their position in the rankings. If merit scholarships didn't exist, students wouldn't be drawn to one rather than another college on this basis, students in need would get more aid, and the relative position of universities would remain unchanged. Yet any hope of reversing the trend away from need-based aid would require universities to adopt similar policies. Colleges face a collective action problem because those that attempted to go the course alone would find themselves seriously disadvantaged in the competition for good students. On the other hand, cooperation among colleges could run afoul of antitrust considerations. The Ivy League schools ran into trouble with the Justice Department a decade ago for price-fixing when they attempted to agree on financial aid packages.[11]

Community College Reforms

Prospects for lower-income students would also be improved by introducing reforms that pertain to community colleges, where many such students begin their college education. As we explained in chapter 4, community college students are less likely to succeed in getting bachelor's degrees than those who begin at four-year colleges, holding other factors constant. They face various impediments that should be addressed. First, they receive less financial aid than students at four-year colleges. Second, they often face hurdles at transfer time. Some states have articulation agreements between their two- and four-year colleges, making transferring from one school to another and getting credits accepted easier, but other states do not. Finally, students who transfer from community colleges often find the work more difficult and the academic standards higher than they have come to expect. Increasing the numbers and improving the quality of full-time faculty with PhDs at community colleges, and reducing their heavy teaching loads, could improve the quality of liberal arts learning and reduce one of the hurdles to students' making a successful transition to four-year colleges.

Early interventions

Last but not least, to close the achievement gap between lower- and higher-income students—and thereby create a society less sharply divided into rich and poor—requires serious educational interventions long before students apply to college. The central reason low-income and minority students are underrepresented in higher education, especially at selective colleges, is that they possess inferior credentials to those who now attend. It's clear that the earlier we intervene to set students on the right track, the more likely they are to succeed academically; and evidence shows that students must begin taking solid academic courses by seventh or eighth grade if they are to have a chance of getting admitted to demanding colleges. We described in chapter 11 a variety of efforts along these lines: government programs such as Upward Bound, GEAR UP, and College Now that offer middle and high schools and their students a variety of services to make college a real option for students who might otherwise take a different path; university programs, often undertaken in partnership with middle and high schools, that provide similar services; and the College Board's Equity 2000 program, which aims at enrolling all students in algebra by the ninth grade. The importance of such programs cannot be overemphasized. But they cannot make up all the deficits that poor children experience from the start. To alleviate those deficits, interventions must begin even earlier; to remedy them would require more radical changes that are not on the political horizon.

REFORMS AT SELECTIVE COLLEGES

The proposals we have just described—more financial aid for low-income students, improvements in community college education and articulation with four-year schools, and interventions in middle and high school to promote college-going—address the problem of diminished opportunities for students (or would-be students) at the low end of the socioeconomic spectrum. These students, it seems clear, have the most pressing claims to our attention because their opportunities for higher education are most limited and, in the absence of reform, the development of their capabilities goes most to waste. Yet injustices exist elsewhere in the system as well, which, even if not as serious, deserve public attention. In particular, two policies in place at many selective colleges and universities—legacy preference and early decision—disproportionately benefit affluent and well-connected students who are already at an advantage in the college admissions process in almost every way.[12]

As we noted in chapter 5, those who lose out as a result of legacy and early decision policies are rarely those at the bottom of the socioeconomic ladder, for such students are rarely in a position to attend highly selective colleges in any case. The losers are more likely to be middle or lower-middle class kids with the credentials to compete at highly selective schools but without either legacy connections or the freedom to ignore the cost of a college education that committing to a college early entails. To be sure, the injustice here is not dire: by global standards these students are not disadvantaged, and they will probably do well enough even if forced to drop down a notch in the quality or prestige of the colleges they attend.

Still, something rankles when a society that prides itself on its mobility and its openness to talent and hard work retains vestiges of inherited privilege. No conceivable reforms, of course, will erase all or even most of the advantages possessed by the rich and well-connected. And despite the rhetoric of equal opportunity, despite even the reality that ours is a country more open and mobile than most, no one could labor under the illusion that we live in a classless society. Nonetheless, preferences for the children of alumni and early decision policies add insult to injury because they result from discrete policies by colleges rather than from broad features of the social landscape that would be very difficult to eliminate or reduce without introducing major—and politically impossible—changes in the economic system. By contrast, ending legacy and early decision is a relatively small step that colleges could take to level the playing field at least somewhat.

Whether it is realistic to abolish legacy depends on one's judgment about the extent to which it contributes to the financial well-being of universities, a subject we addressed in chapter 5. As for early decision, although it clearly delivers benefits to colleges, it is not unreasonable to think that they could forego these benefits as long as other colleges did likewise. A college that abolished early decision while its peer institutions did not would be disadvantaged because students it wanted to attract would have strong reason to go elsewhere. Early decision, then, like the decision between merit- and need-based aid, presents colleges with a collective action problem: no college would be seriously disadvantaged if all abolished it, but an institution that abolished it without the similar behavior of its peer institutions would take a big risk.

Much the same can be said about preferences for athletes. Although athletes benefit from large admissions advantages at the big sports powerhouses, which are often in the spotlight, at these schools athletic scholarships and preferences go to a tiny fraction of the student body. It's the small liberal arts colleges in Division III and the Ivy League schools that especially display a distorted conception of the missions of universities and an exaggerated emphasis on sports over many other talents.[13] As in the case of early decision and perhaps also legacy preference, however, a college that reduced admissions advantages for athletes would suffer unless its peer institutions took the same steps.

In this respect, policies regarding early decision, preferences for athletes, and legacy resemble the decision between merit- and need-based aid discussed in the previous section. Enhancing the educational opportunities of lower-income and minority students suggests abolishing early decision and legacy and emphasizing need-based rather than merit-based aid. Contrary to popular opinion, preferences for athletes do little to enhance the opportunities of such students and suffer from other defects as well. Yet perhaps the strongest impediment to reforming these policies is competition among colleges. Unless institutions of higher education adopt similar practices, there is little hope that the necessary steps will be taken.

Notes

CHAPTER 1

1. Bill Paul, *Getting In: Inside the College Admissions Process* (Reading, Mass.: Addison-Wesley, 1995), p. 10; Liz Seymour, "The Old College Try Gets a New Sales Pitch," *Washington Post*, November 27, 1999, A1.

2. Paul estimated almost ten years ago that Americans spend $250 million a year to gain "a competitive edge" in college admissions. The numbers are no doubt higher today. Paul, *Getting In*, p. 10.

3. Jean H. Fetter, *Questions and Admissions: Reflections on 100,000 Admissions Decisions at Stanford* (Stanford: Stanford University Press, 1995), pp. 10, 23–24. Stanford ranks each applicant along two scales—for academic achievement and for extracurricular achievement—so every student receives two numbers. Fetter is a former dean of undergraduate admissions at Stanford.

4. Amy Argetsinger, "Virginia Tech Gains Allure," *Washington Post*, April 24, 2000, B1.

5. Information found on the University of Texas website, www.utexas.edu/student/admissions/spring2001.html (accessed November 4, 2003).

6. For the class that entered the University of Maryland in 2002, 75 percent of admitted freshmen had high school GPAs over 3.5, and 25 percent were over 4.0 (these GPAs are weighted for honors and Advanced Placement courses); the middle 50 percent of admitted freshmen had combined SAT scores between 1230 and 1380. See www.uga.umd.edu/apply/profile.html (accessed October 27, 2003).

7. Patrick T. Terenzini, Alberto F. Cabrera, and Elena M. Bernal, *Swimming against the Tide: The Poor in American Higher Education*, College Board Research Report No. 2001-1 (New York: College Board, 2001), p. 18. In addition to family income, socioeconomic status depends on parental education, parental occupation, and the possession of cultural items in the home such as books and magazines.

8. Robert M. Shireman, "Enrolling Economic Diversity," *New York Times*, May 4, 2002, A25.

9. Terenzini et al., p. 22. Similar figures obtain for preparedness in science, social studies, and "general academic ability" as measured by SAT and ACT scores.

10. When we speak of "minority" students, we generally mean black, Hispanic, and Native American students (also known as "underrepresented minorities") but not Asian students, whose credentials are equal or superior to those of white students.

11. See Patricia Gandara with Julie Maxwell-Jolly, *Priming the Pump: Strategies for Increasing the Achievement of Underrepresented Minority Undergraduates*, College Board, 1999, at www.collegeboard.com/repository/primingthep_3949.pdf (accessed October 27, 2003), pp. 7–13.

12. In June 2003, the Supreme Court confronted affirmative action in higher education for the first time since its ruling in the *Bakke* decision in 1978. See *Gratz v. Bollinger*, 123 S. Ct. 2411 (2003) and *Grutter v. Bollinger*, 123 S. Ct. 232. We discuss these cases in chapters 9 and 10.

13. Bureau of the Census, National Population Projections, NP-T3-B and NP-T3-C, "Projection of Total Population by Five-Year Age Groups . . . 2001–2005," and "Projection . . . 2006–2010."

14. Paul, *Getting In*, p. ix.

15. Jennifer Cheeseman Day and Eric Newberger, "The Big Payoff: Educational Attainment and Synthetic Estimates of Work-Life Earnings," U.S. Census Bureau, Current Population Reports, July 2002, at www.census.gov/prod/2002pubs/p23-210.pdf (accessed October 31, 2003).

16. See Michael A. Fletcher, "Degrees of Separation: Gender Gap among College Graduates Has Educators Wondering Where the Men Are," *Washington Post*, June 25, 2002, A1.

17. Many women's colleges have also gone co-ed, although among the small, highly selective liberal arts colleges a few (such as Wellesley, Smith, Mount Holyoke, and Bryn Mawr) have remained single-sex, while none of the formerly men's colleges have.

18. For references, see chapter 3, notes 9 and 10.

19. There are more than 500 of these. All numbers have been rounded; they total just under 4,500. Figures are drawn from Table 1 of "Postsecondary Institutions in the United States: 1997–98," National Center for Education Statistics, U.S. Department of Education (NCES 1999-174, July 1999).

20. Cited in Richard W. Moll and Ann Wright, "What College Selectivity Looks Like to the Public," *Journal of College Admissions* 161 (Fall 1998).

21. Table 1 of "Postsecondary Institutions in the United States: 1997–98," National Center for Education Statistics, U.S. Department of Education (NCES 1999-174, July 1999), pp. 1–2. The preponderance of enrollment in public institutions stands in sharp contrast to the pattern of a century ago, when four-fifths of students were enrolled in private colleges. Gary Wolfram, "The Threat to Independent Education: Public Subsidies and Private Colleges," Cato Policy Analysis No. 278 (Washington, D.C.: Cato Institute, August 15, 1997).

22. Information gathered from *U.S. News and World Report*'s online college ranking site, at www.usnews.com/usnews/edu/college/rankings/rankindex.php (accessed October 31, 2003).

23. These numbers come from *U.S. News & World Report*'s 2004 rankings (see note 22 for URL). They change yearly and we cite the rounded figures for illustrative

purposes only. The statistics can be misleading for several reasons. Some colleges fudge and manipulate them; even absent malice aforethought, the numbers by themselves reveal nothing about the nature of the applicant pool and nothing, therefore, about the stringency of an institution's admissions criteria. For example, if 90 percent of a college's applicants score 600 (verbal and math combined) on their SATs—out of a possible total of 1600—the fact that the college rejects 75 percent of them does not show it to be highly selective.

24. This figure is extrapolated from the data in Wolfram, "The Threat to Independent Education."

25. Angela Browne-Mills, *Shameful Admissions: The Losing Battle to Serve Everyone in Our Universities* (San Francisco: Jossey-Bass, 1996), p. 17.

26. Erik Lords, "Community Colleges Turn to Consultants to Help Them Recruit and Retain Students," *Chronicle of Higher Education*, May 12, 2000.

27. For example, the University of California at Berkeley offered 8,300 students admission (out of 33,100) to fill its fall 2000 freshman class of 3,700. *Berkeleyan*, April 5, 2000, at www.berkeley.edu/news/berkleyan/2003/04/23_fresh.shtml (accessed October 31, 2003).

28. Karen W. Arenson, "Tackling Student Debt, Princeton to Replace Loans with Scholarships," *New York Times*, January 28, 2001, p. 19. Arthur Levine, president of Columbia Teachers College, remarked: "Every Ivy League university is going to have to try to match this if they want to compete for the best of the middle-class students."

29. Jacques Steinberg, "College Ratings by *U.S. News* Drops Factor in Admissions," *New York Times*, July 10, 2003, A14.

30. J. S. Mill, *Utilitarianism* (originally published 1861), in John Stuart Mill, *On Liberty and Other Essays* (Oxford: Oxford University Press, 1991), p. 140.

31. Michael Heise, "Choosing Equal Educational Opportunity," *University of Chicago Law Review* 68 (Summer 2001), p. 1135.

32. R. H. Tawney, *Equality* (London: George Allen & Unwin, 1931), p. 142.

33. John Schaar, "Equality of Opportunity and Beyond," in J. R. Pennock and J. Chapman, eds., *Equality* (New York: Atherton Press, 1967), pp. 239, 236.

34. Sandra Harding, "Is the Equality of Opportunity Principle Democratic?" *Philosophical Forum* 10 (Winter-Summer 1978–1979), p. 221.

35. Marlene Gerber Fried, "The Invisibility of Oppression," *Philosophical Forum* 11 (Fall 1979), p. 23.

36. Friedrich von Hayek, *Law, Legislation, and Liberty*, vol. 2, *The Mirage of Social Justice* (Chicago: University of Chicago Press, 1978), p. 84–85.

37. David A Strauss, "The Illusory Distinction between Equality of Opportunity and Equality of Result," in N. Devins and D. M. Douglas, eds., *Redefining Equality* (New York: Oxford University Press, 1997), p. 53. See also James Fishkin, *Justice, Equal Opportunity, and the Family* (New Haven, Conn.: Yale University Press, 1983).

38. Bernadette D. Proctor and Joseph Dalaker, "Poverty in the United States: 200l," U.S. Census Bureau Current Population Reports, at www.census.gov/prod/2002pubs/p60-219.pdf (accessed October 31, 2003).

39. Data available at www.whitehouse.gov/fsbr/income.html (accessed October 31, 2003).

CHAPTER 2

1. Richard Berke, "The Ad Campaign: Pete Wilson's 'Courage,'" *New York Times*, August 25, 1995.

2. Justice William Brennan in the famous *Bakke* case referred to "our deep belief that . . . advancement sanctioned, sponsored, or approved by the State should ideally be based on individual merit or achievement, or at least on factors within the control of an individual." *Regents of the University of California v. Bakke*, 438 U.S. 265 (1978), at 361. Political theorists as different as Michael Walzer and Friedrich A. Hayek endorse some version of "careers open to talents" as a distributive principle. See Michael Walzer, *Spheres of Justice: A Defense of Pluralism and Equality* (New York: Basic Books, 1983), chapter 5, and Friedrich A. Hayek, "Equality, Value, and Merit," in Michael Sandel, ed., *Liberalism and Its Critics* (New York: New York University Press, 1984), p. 87.

3. "We Shall Overcome—But Only through Merit," *Wall Street Journal*, September 16, 1999.

4. Ernest W. Lefever, "Bill Gates' Diversity Subverts Merit," *Los Angeles Times*, November 1, 1999.

5. Patrick Healy, "Harvard Asks Faculty to Justify Grading Methods," *Boston Globe*, October 23, 2001.

6. Robert H. Frank and Philip J. Cook, *The Winner-Take-All Society* (New York: Free Press, 1995), p. 148.

7. For discussion, other examples, and references, see Deborah Rhode, *Justice and Gender* (Cambridge, Mass.: Harvard University Press, 1989), pp. 169–72, 373–75.

8. Michael Fix and Raymond J. Struyk, eds., *Clear and Convincing Evidence: Measurement of Discrimination in America* (Washington, D.C.: Urban Institute Press, 1993), pp. 173–74.

9. Frank and Cook, *The Winner-Take-All Society* (New York: Free Press, 1995).

10. Admission Criteria for the University of Maryland, College Park, Fall 2001, on file with authors.

11. From a Stanford publication entitled "Criteria for Undergraduate Admissions," quoted in Jean H. Fetter, *Questions and Admissions: Reflections on 100,000 Admissions Decisions at Stanford* (Stanford: Stanford University Press, 1995), pp. 9–10. Stanford is much more selective than Maryland or indeed any public university, and we present both to illustrate different locations on the spectrum of selectivity. Nevertheless, the criteria themselves are quite similar.

12. See the discussion in chapter 7 of the complex University of California formula and the formula used until recently at the University of Georgia. Books about the admissions processes of selective colleges have become a cottage industry. See, e.g., Bill Paul, *Getting In: Inside the College Admissions Process* (Perseus, 1997); Michele Hernandez, *A Is for Admission: The Insider's Guide to Getting Into the Ivy League and Other Top Colleges* (New York: Warner Books, 1999); Rachel Toor, *Admissions Confidential: An Insider's Account of the Elite College Selection Process* (New York: St. Martin's Press, 2001); Jacques Steinberg, *The Gatekeepers: Inside the Admissions Process at a Premier College* (New York: Viking, 2002). Jean Fetter's *Questions and*

Admissions is a more reflective account by a former director of admissions and lacks the "how to" focus of many of the others.

13. James Morgan Hart, *German Universities: A Narrative of Personal Experience* (New York: 1874), excerpted in Richard Hofstadter and Wilson Smith, eds., *American Higher Education: A Documentary History*, vol. 2 (Chicago: University of Chicago Press, 1961), p. 577.

14. For further discussion of the assumptions underlying legacy preference, see chapter 5. To the extent that admissions advantages for athletes are rooted in the argument that good sports teams enrich colleges, the same point can be made. For more on this and other arguments about preferences for athletes, see the last section of this chapter.

15. But the latter can be interpreted in a way that does reflect merit, as we argue in the following section.

16. See, e.g., Immanuel Kant, *Critique of Practical Reason* (Indianapolis: Bobbs-Merrill, 1956), trans. Lewis White Beck, p. 4.

17. Many philosophers who find the logic of determinism compelling compromise by distinguishing between "hard" and "soft" determinism, also known as compatibilism. Soft determinists accepts the basic deterministic claim that all actions (yes, all) are caused or determined by prior actions and states, but they believe this thesis is compatible with free will, and that we do in fact have free will. In this way they preserve our commonsense notions of merit and desert. See, e.g., P. F. Strawson's classic essay "Freedom and Resentment," originally published in 1962, reprinted in Strawson, *Freedom and Resentment* (London: Methuen, 1974).

18. This view is related to the Kantian idea that the only thing that is good "without qualification" is a "good will." Immanuel Kant, *Foundations of the Metaphysics of Morals* (Indianapolis: Bobbs-Merrill, 1959), trans. Lewis White Beck, p. 9.

19. The question is relevant to the debate in admissions circles about whether to admit well-rounded students (the old view) or instead a well-rounded class that may consist of "spiky" students who possess special talents but are not necessarily well-rounded (and are perhaps necessarily not well-rounded). Shulman and Bowen (reference below) describe some mathematics professors at one college who objected when students with very high math scores but otherwise undistinguished records were rejected (p. 282).

20. Stanford ranks students' extracurricular achievements on a scale from 1 to 5. The top ranking is reserved for students who have "earned recognition at a national level," such as by writing a published novel, winning a Westinghouse (now Intel) science prize, or earning an Olympic Medal—all real examples, according to Jean Fetter. See Fetter, *Questions and Admissions*, p. 24.

21. Princeton, N.J.: Princeton University Press, 2001. Shulman and Bowen work at the Mellon Foundation (Bowen is a former president of Princeton), which built the College and Beyond database on which the analysis of this book is based. With Derek Bok, Bowen earlier coauthored *The Shape of the River: Long-Term Consequences of Affirmative Action* (Princeton, N.J.: Princeton University Press, 1998), which relied on the same database. (See chapter 10 for discussion of *The Shape of the River*.) Bowen and Sarah Levin have since published a sequel to *The Game of Life*, *Reclaiming the Game: College Sports and Educational Values* (Princeton, N.J.: Princeton University Press, 2003).

22. The schools in the database include 16 private and public Division I universities, and 14 Division III private colleges and universities. Division III schools, as well as those in the Ivy League, do not offer athletic scholarships. (The Ivy League schools compete in Division I-AA, while other large private universities and the large state universities represented in the study are in Division I-A.) Overall, 318 institutions play in Division I, 290 in Division II, and 422 in Division III.

23. Shulman and Bowen, *The Game of Life*, pp. 40–42.

24. Quoted in Edward B. Fiske, "Gaining Admission: Athletes Win Preference," *New York Times*, Education Life (January 7, 2001), p. 22.

In 1999–2000, the Amherst College student newspaper ran a series of articles on athletics and admissions. Amherst sorts students into five categories according to the strength of their record. Among students in the top category, athletes enjoyed a slight advantage over nonathletes. In category 2, athletes were admitted 71 percent of the time, nonathletes 41 percent; in category 3, athletes were admitted 48 percent of the time, nonathletes 10 percent; in category 4, athletes got in 33 percent of the time, nonathletes 5 percent. See *The Amherst Student Online* at www.amherst.edu/~astudent/1999-2000/issue002/news/charts.html (accessed October 31, 2003).

25. Fiske, "Gaining Admission," p. 22. In late 2001, about half of the eleven colleges in the New England Small College Athletic Conference (NESCAC), including Williams and Amherst, agreed to reduce the admissions advantage for athletes. Williams said it would reduce the number of recruited athletes by at least 10 percent. See Pamela Ferdinand, "Good Sports—and Maybe Not: Colleges That Once Promoted Athletics Take a Second Look," *Washington Post*, December 28, 2001, A3. According to the article, the changes were prompted in part by Shulman and Bowen's findings.

26. Shulman and Bowen, *The Game of Life*, pp. 43–45.

27. Shulman and Bowen, *The Game of Life*, p. 50.

28. Shulman and Bowen, *The Game of Life*, p. 52. As Shulman and Bowen point out, although we associate sports especially with large state universities, at such schools athletes constitute a very small fraction of the total student body. At Michigan, 3 percent of the students play intercollegiate sports, at Williams 40 percent do. Shulman and Bowen, *The Game of Life*, pp. 32–33.

29. Shulman and Bowen, *The Game of Life*, p. 54.

30. Shulman and Bowen, *The Game of Life*, p. 55.

31. Shulman and Bowen, *The Game of Life*, p. 225. One group, High Profile athletes at Division I-A schools, is "*much* less likely than others to be contributors" (p. 266). Shulman and Bowen surmise that these athletes are more focused on their athletic careers and that they do not see themselves as part of the academic community "and may even disidentify with it."

32. Shulman and Bowen, *The Game of Life*, p. 266.

33. Shulman and Bowen, *The Game of Life*, p. 201.

34. Shulman and Bowen, *The Game of Life*, pp. 223, 266.

35. Shulman and Bowen, *The Game of Life*, p. 224.

36. Shulman and Bowen, *The Game of Life*, p. 267.

37. Shulman and Bowen, *The Game of Life*, p. 260.

38. Shulman and Bowen, *The Game of Life*, p. 82.

39. Shulman and Bowen, *The Game of Life*.

40. Shulman and Bowen, *The Game of Life*, pp. 92–97. Female athletes in the 1989 cohort earned advanced degrees at the same rate as nonathletes (whereas in the 1976 group they earned them at a higher rate) and did not make more money.

41. Shulman and Bowen, *The Game of Life*, pp. 99–101.

42. Shulman and Bowen, *The Game of Life*, p. 185.

43. Shulman and Bowen, *The Game of Life*, p. 192. Shulman and Bowen note that, by contrast, one finding of Bowen and Bok's *The Shape of the River* was that the 1976 and 1989 black graduates of these same institutions (drawn from the same database) were much more likely to be civic leaders than their white classmates. See Bowen and Bok, *The Shape of the River*, pp. 168–74.

44. Shulman and Bowen, *The Game of Life*, p. 187.

45. Shulman and Bowen, *The Game of Life*, pp. 188–90.

46. Shulman and Bowen, *The Game of Life*, p. 36–37.

47. Jere Longman, "No More Football, Lots of Questions at Swarthmore," *New York Times*, December 5, 2000. See also "Brief Summary of the Report from Athletics Review Committee to the Board of Managers," at http://athleticsreview.swarthmore.edu/summary.html (accessed October 31, 2003). This was not the first time Swarthmore faced a difficult dilemma concerning athletics. In 1907 a Quaker heiress offered the college between $1 and $3 million on the condition that it abolish intercollegiate sports; Swarthmore declined the gift. See Ronald Smith, *Sports and Freedom: The Rise of Big-Time College Athletics* (New York: Oxford, 1988), pp. 209–12.

48. "Brief Summary of the Report from Athletics Review Committee."

49. Longman, "No More Football."

CHAPTER 3

1. See Elizabeth A. Duffy and Idana Goldberg, *Crafting a Class: College Admissions and Financial Aid, 1955–1994* (Princeton, N.J.: Princeton University Press, 1998).

2. Calvin College website, www.calvin.edu/about (accessed November 6, 2003).

3. Berea College website, www.berea.edu/Publications/Great-Commitments .html (accessed November 6, 2003).

4. Juilliard School website, www.juilliard.edu/about/about.html (accessed November 6, 2003).

5. Morehouse College website, www.morehouse.edu/aboutmc/mission/index. html (accessed November 6, 2003).

6. U.S. Military Academy website, www.usma.edu/admissions (accessed November 6, 2003).

7. Digest of Education Statistics, 2000. Table 174: Total fall enrollment in degree-granting institutions, by control and type of institution, 1965–1998 (National Center for Education Statistics, at www.nces.ed.gov).

8. Jennifer Cheeseman Day and Eric Newberger, "The Big Payoff: Educational Attainment and Synthetic Estimates of Work-Life Earnings, U.S. Census Bureau, Current Population Reports, July 2002, at www.census.gov/prod/2002pubs/

p23-210.pdf (accessed October 31, 2003). Women's economic gains from education are smaller than men's.

9. Ernest T. Pascarella and Patrick T. Terenzini, *How College Affects Students: Findings and Insights from Twenty Years of Research* (San Francisco: Jossey-Bass, 1991), pp. 508–11. See also Ronald G. Ehrenberg, "Does It Pay to Attend an Elite Private College? Cross Cohort Evidence of the Effect of College Type on Earnings," *Journal of Human Resources* 34 (Winter 1999), pp. 104–23. For a challenge to this view, see Stacey Berg Dale and Alan Krueger, "Estimating the Payoff to Attending a More Selective College: An Application of Selection on Observables and Unobservables," Working Paper No. 409, Princeton University, Industrial Relations Section, December 1998. Virtually all the studies we have seen measure the value of a college degree in economic terms.

10. Susan Caminiti, "Where the CEOs Went to College," *Fortune*, June 18, 1990, pp. 120–22. Cited in Robert Frank and Philip Cook, *The Winner-Take-All Society* (New York: Free Press, 1995), p. 152.

11. William Bowen and Derek Bok, *The Shape of the River: Long-Term Consequences of Affirmative Action* (Princeton, N.J.: Princeton University Press, 1998), pp. 122–28.

12. We develop this point further in chapter 5.

13. For an excellent history, see Laurence Veysey, *The Emergence of the American University* (Chicago: University of Chicago Press, 1965), p. 267. We are indebted to Veysey's book for the discussion that follows.

14. Veysey, *The Emergence of the American University*, p. 21.

15. Veysey, *The Emergence of the American University*, p. 25.

16. T. J. Backus, "The Philosophy of the College Curriculum," University of the State of New York, *Annual Report of the Regents*, 1884, p. 239, quoted in Veysey, *The Emergence of the American University*, p. 24.

17. Veysey, *The Emergence of the American University*, p. 36.

18. Veysey, *The Emergence of the American University*, p. 6.

19. Veysey, *The Emergence of the American University*, p. 12.

20. Veysey, *The Emergence of the American University*, p. 61. According to Veysey, the advocates of utility in higher education owed little in the way of direct inspiration to the philosophical utilitarians Jeremy Bentham and John Stuart Mill, although Mill was active at the same time (and Bentham a generation earlier).

21. Veysey, *The Emergence of the American University*, p. 15.

22. Thorstein Veblen, *The Higher Learning in America* (New York: Sagamore Press, 1957), p. 13. Most of the work was written before 1905.

23. James Morgan Hart, *German Universities: A Narrative of Personal Experience* (New York:, 1874), excerpted in Richard Hofstadter and Wilson Smith, eds., *American Higher Education: A Documentary History*, vol. 2 (Chicago: University of Chicago Press, 1961), p. 577. Hart taught English and modern languages at the University of Cincinnati and at Cornell. In the nineteenth century almost 9,000 Americans studied in German universities (Louis Menand, *The Metaphysical Club: A Story of Ideas in America* [New York: Farrar Straus Giroux, 2001]), p. 256.

24. Veysey, *The Emergence of the American University*, p. 184. A professor at Trinity College in North Carolina set out five elements, the first of which was

"instinctive correct appreciation of the sound-sequence, both vowel and consonantal"; the other four were equally precise. C. F. Johnson, "The Development of Literary Taste in College Students," American Institute of Instruction Proceedings, 1892, pp. 81-3; quoted in Veysey, *The Emergence of the American University*, p. 185.

25. J. J. Lewis (professor at Madison University), "Culture and Limitation," University of the State of New York, *Annual Report of the Regents*, 1878, p. 429 (quoted in Veysey, *The Emergence of the American University*, p. 186).

26. Veysey, *The Emergence of the American University*, pp. 188–89.

27. Letter to C. F. Adams, 1907, quoted in Veysey, *The Emergence of the American University*, p. 90. In fact, Eliot was responsible for eliminating almost all requirements at Harvard and introducing an elective system for undergraduates. As a result, more than half the graduates took only introductory courses during their entire college career (Menand, *The Metaphysical Club*, p. 256).

28. Veysey, *The Emergence of the American University*, p. 180.

29. Veysey, *The Emergence of the American University*, p. 202.

30. Irving Babbit, *Literature and the American College* (Boston, 1908), pp. 118–19 (quoted in Veysey, p. 217).

31. Tom Stoppard, *Invention of Love* (New York: Grove Press, 1997), p. 37.

32. Stoppard, *Invention of Love*, p. 71.

33. Brian Barry, *Culture and Equality* (Cambridge, Mass.: Harvard University Press, 2001), p. 221.

34. Quoted in Veysey, *The Emergence of the American University*, p. 68.

35. See J. S. Mill, *Utilitarianism* (originally published 1861). See *On Liberty and Other Essays* (New York: Oxford University Press, 1991), pp. 137–38.

36. W. A. Merrill (professor of Latin at Miami Univerity, Ohio), "The Practical Value of a Liberal Education," *Education* 10 (1890), p. 441, quoted in Veysey, *The Emergence of the American University*, p. 198.

37. Quoted in Veysey, *The Emergence of the American University*, p. 211.

38. Alexander Meiklejohn, "What the Liberal College Is," *The Liberal College* (Boston, 1920), excerpted in Hofstadter and Smith, *American Higher Education*, p. 903.

39. Duke University website, www.planning.duke.edu/mission.html (accessed November 6, 2003).

40. University of Texas at Austin website, www.utexas.edu/welcome (accessed November 6, 2003).

41. Williams College website, www.williams.edu/admin-depts/registrar/geninfo/mission.html (accessed November 6, 2003).

42. University of Michigan website, www.umich.edu/%7Eprovost/slfstudy/ir/criteria/index.html (accessed November 6, 2003).

43. See Amy Gutmann, *Democratic Education* (Princeton, N.J.: Princeton University Press, 1987), chapter 6, and Martha Nussbaum, *Cultivating Humanity: A Classical Defense of Reform in Liberal Education* (Cambridge, Mass.: Harvard University Press, 1997).

44. This statement can be found at www.umich.edu/%7Eprovost/slfstudy/ir/criteria (accessed November 6, 2003).

45. Also found at www.umich.edu/%7Eprovost/slfstudy/ir/criteria.

46. Swarthmore College website, www.swarthmore.edu/admissions/academic_program.html (accessed November 6, 2003).

47. See Shulman and Bowen, *The Game of Life*, pp. 201–2. In surveys of college alumni, "faculty research" tops the list of activities they would like to see less of.

48. And both individual teachers and departments have an interest in not giving low grades, which can mean lower evaluations for the teacher and smaller enrollments for the department.

49. *Time*, November 17, 1958. According to Shulman and Bowen, Kerr was mistaken about the alumni, who (except for former athletes) want to see less, not more, emphasis on sports (*The Game of Life*, pp. 199–204).

50. See Judith Lichtenberg, "Foundations and Limits of Freedom of the Press," *Philosophy & Public Affairs* 16 (1987).

51. Wellesley College website, www.wellesley.edu/welcome/college.html (accessed November 6, 2003).

52. Sometimes being extremely smart can be a disadvantage. See Malcolm Gladwell, "The Talent Myth," *The New Yorker*, July 22, 2002, about the premium placed by companies like Enron on hiring the very best students from the very best business schools, and the pitfalls of this approach, which assumes "that people make organizations smart. More often than not, it's the other way around" (p. 32).

53. For evidence, see W. Michael Byrd and Linda A. Clayton, *An American Health Dilemma: Race, Medicine, and Health Care in the United States, 1900–2000* (New York: Routledge, 2002), especially the tables in chapters 2 and 4.

54. See Bowen and Bok, *The Shape of the River*, pp. 155–74, and Richard O. Lempert et al., "Michigan's Minority Graduates in Practice: The River Runs through Law School," *Law and Social Inquiry* 25 (2000). For further discussion, see chapter 10.

55. A recent survey of law students at Harvard and Michigan found that 69 percent of the Harvard students and 73 percent of those at Michigan thought that racial diversity in the classroom affected how they thought about problems as well as their ability to work with people from other racial groups. See Gary Orfield and Dean Whitla, "Diversity and Legal Education: Students' Experiences in Leading Law Schools" (1999), at www.civilrightsproject.harvard.edu/research/lawmichigan/law survey.php (accessed November 5, 2003). For further discussion of the diversity rationale and other arguments for affirmative action sometimes confused with it, see chapter 10.

56. Bowen and Bok, *The Shape of the River*, p. 280.

57. For a good summary see Michael S. McPherson and Morton Owen Schapiro, *The Student Aid Game: Meeting Need and Rewarding Talent in American Higher Education* (Princeton, N.J.: Princeton University Press, 1998), pp. 112–14.

CHAPTER 4

1. Speech by Horace Webster at the Academy's opening ceremony, quoted in James Traub, *City on a Hill: Testing the American Dream at City College* (Reading, Mass.: Addison-Wesley, 1994), p. 25.

2. Traub, *City on a Hill*, pp. 9–10.

3. Traub, *City on a Hill*, p. 321.

4. David E. Lavin and David Hyllegard, *Changing the Odds: Open Admissions and the Life Chances of the Disadvantaged* (New Haven, Conn.: Yale University Press, 1996), pp. 6–7. In 1961, the city's disparate campuses were organized into a single system, the City University of New York–CUNY.

5. David E. Lavin, Richard D. Alba, and Richard A. Silberstein, *Right versus Privilege: The Open-Admissions Experiment at the City University of New York* (New York: Free Press, 1981), p. 5.

6. Traub, *City on a Hill*, pp. 49–52.

7. Traub, *City on a Hill*, p. 66; Lavin and Hyllegard, *Changing the Odds*, p. 15; Lavin et al., *Right versus Privilege*, p. 18.

8. Lavin et al., *Right versus Privilege*, p. 15.

9. Lavin and Hyllegard, *Changing the Odds*, p. 32.

10. Lavin et al., *Right versus Privilege*, p. 64; Lavin and Hyllegard, *Changing the Odds*, pp. 38–39.

11. Traub, *City on a Hill*, p. 71.

12. Theodore L. Gross, *Academic Turmoil: The Reality and Promise of Open Education* (Garden City, N.Y.: Anchor Press/Doubleday, 1980), pp. 1–68.

13. Lavin and Hyllegard, *Changing the Odds*, pp. 225, 228, 229.

14. Lavin and Hyllegard, *Changing the Odds*, p. 216.

15. Traub, *City on a Hill*, p. 13.

16. William Trombley, "Remedial Education under Attack," *National Crosstalk* 6 (July 1998), p. 15.

17. Karen W. Arenson, "Plan to Exclude Remedial Students Approved at CUNY," *New York Times*, November 23, 1999, A1.

18. Minutes of Board of Trustees, May 26, 1998; Minutes of the University Faculty Senate, January 26, 1999.

19. Heather MacDonald, "Downward Mobility: The Failure of Open Admissions at City University," *City Journal* (Summer 1994), p. 17.

20. Clifford Adelman, "The Kiss of Death? An Alternative View of College Remediation," *National Crosstalk* 6 (July 1998), p. 11. Adelman's views are discussed further later in this chapter and in chapter 11.

21. See comments of Kathleen Pesile, CUNY Trustee, Minutes of the University Faculty, January 26, 1999.

22. Resolution 9, Board of Trustees Meeting January 25, 1999; see also Minutes of the Meeting of the Board of Trustees, May 26, 1998.

23. Traub, *City on a Hill*, p. 204. At the end of his book, however, Traub seems to have some reservations about channeling remediation into community colleges (see pp. 345–47).

24. Gross, *Academic Turmoil*, p. 25.

25. Lavin and Hyllegard, *Changing the Odds*, p. 52.

26. Kevin J. Dougherty, *The Contradictory College: The Conflicting Origins, Impacts, and Futures of the Community College* (Albany: State University of New York Press, 1994), p. 53.

27. Dougherty, *The Contradictory College*, pp. 86–88.

28. Dougherty, *The Contradictory College*, pp. 88–90.

29. Dougherty, *The Contradictory College*, pp. 92ff.

30. Dougherty, *The Contradictory College*, pp. 97–101.

31. Lavin and Hyllegard, *Changing the Odds*, pp. 54–55.

32. Lavin et al., *Right versus Privilege*, p. 217.

33. Robert Marshak, President of City College, quoted by Gross, *Academic Turmoil*, pp. 88–89.

34. Adelman, "The Kiss of Death?" p. 11.

35. Report of the Mayor's Advisory Task Force on the City University of New York, *The City University of New York: An Institution Adrift* (June 7, 1999), p. 22.

36. *An Institution Adrift*, p. 24. One of the Schmidt Report's criticisms focused on the lack of objective measures within CUNY to allow nationwide comparisons. The university required from a prospective entrant only his high school grades, class ranking, and scores on the skills tests. It did not require scores from the SAT or any comparable national exam. Nevertheless, about 30 percent of CUNY applicants take the SAT. Commissioned by the Task Force, the Rand Corporation matched existing SAT scores with student scores on the reading and math skills tests and extrapolated an SAT "average" profile for each CUNY institution. This is the basis for the Schmidt Report's comparison of CUNY senior colleges with others across the country.

37. *An Institution Adrift*, pp. 24, 37–38.

38. *An Institution Adrift*, pp. 36, 37–38.

39. *An Institution Adrift*, pp. 35–36.

40. *An Institution Adrift*, pp. 37–38.

41. Report of the Commission on the Future of CUNY, "Remediation and Access: To Educate the 'Children of the Whole of the People,'" New York: Association of the Bar of the City of New York, October 1999.

42. The Board's resolution of January 1999 was ambiguous in its language:

> Resolved, That all *remedial course instruction* shall be phased-out of all baccalaureate degree programs. . . . Following . . . discontinuation of *remediation*, no student who has not passed all three Freshman Skills Assessment Tests . . . shall be allowed to enroll. . . . Students . . . in need of *remediation* shall be able to obtain such *remediation services* at a CUNY community college [emphasis added].

Board of Trustees Meeting, January 25, 1999. As we note in the text, the policy eventually implemented distinguishes between *remedial courses* (which are eliminated from the senior colleges *in a manner of speaking*) and *remedial services* (which are not eliminated).

43. See CUNY Skills Assessment Program http://portal.cuny.edu/cms/id/cuny/documents/informationpage/002144.htm (accessed October 31, 2003).

44. Karen W. Arenson, "CUNY Plan to Bar Remedial Students from 4-Year Programs Faces Final Test," *The New York Times*, November 22, 1999, B3; testimony of David Caputo (President of Hunter College) to New York State Regents, September 9, 1999; Report of the Commission on the Future of CUNY.

45. Comments by Chancellor Goldstein, Minutes of CUNY Faculty Senate, September 14, 1999.

46. CUNY Master Plan 2000–2004. See, for example, the services offered by the Post Secondary Readiness Center at Medgar Evers College, available at www.mec.

cuny.edu/academic_affairs/academic_supp_servs/post_secondary_cntr.htm (accessed October 31, 2003) or the Academic Center for Excellence at Lehman College, at www.lehman.cuny.edu/programs/pdf/Section7.pdf (accessed November 5, 2003).

47. Comments by Chancellor Goldstein, Minutes of CUNY Faculty Senate, September 14, 1999.

48. "Good Summer News at CUNY," *The New York Post*, June 6, 1998, editorial page; Comments by Chancellor Goldstein, Minutes of CUNY Faculty Senate, March 20, 2000; CUNY Master Plan 2000–2004.

49. See www.collegenow.cuny.edu/teachers/goals/index.html (accessed November 3, 2003).

50. For further discussion of college partnerships with middle and high schools, see chapter 11.

51. However, there has been a significant decline in the number of ESL students in recent years. This may have to do with policy changes not discussed here. See Marc Ward, "Where Have All the Students Gone," *Clarion* (newspaper of the Professional Staff Congress/CUNY), October 2001, p. 8.

52. For further discussion, see Robert K. Fullinwider, "Open Admissions and Remedial Education at CUNY," *Report from the Institute for Philosophy and Public Policy* 19 (Winter 1999).

53. David W. Breneman and William N. Haarlow, "Remedial Education: Costs and Consequences," Washington, D.C.: Thomas B. Fordham Foundation, July 1998, p. 1.

54. Massachusetts Board of Higher Education, "Implementation Guidelines for Massachusetts Board of Higher Education Developmental Education Policy for the Commonwealth's Public Colleges and Universities," Boston, Massachusetts, 1996, at www.mass.edu/academic/deved.htm (accessed July 10, 2000); Sara Hebel, "Georgia Strives to Raise Standards without Leaving Students Behind," *Chronicle of Higher Education* 45 (April 9, 1999), A34; Richard J. Coley, *The American Community College Turns 100: A Look at Its Students, Programs, and Prospects* (Princeton, N.J.: Educational Testing Service, 2000), p. 4; Breneman and Haarlow, "Remedial Education," p. 8.

55. Articulation isn't perfect in the CUNY system, by any means, and is one of the areas receiving special attention in the new reform efforts.

56. Armando Trujillo and Eusebius Diaz, " 'Be a Name, Not a Number': The Role of Cultural and Social Capital in the Transfer Process," in Kathleen M. Shaw et al., eds., *Community Colleges As Cultural Texts: Qualitative Explorations of Organizational and Student Culture* (Albany: State University of New York Press, 1999), pp. 125–31.

57. Dougherty, *The Contradictory College*, pp. 93–96.

58. Coley, *The American Community College Turns 100*, p. 17, table 1.

59. This is true as a generalization but pairs of individual cases can show interesting variations. For example, a very low-income student might use a combination of Pell Grants, low-interest loans, and part-time work to finance two years at Prince George's Community College and two further years at nearby Bowie State University (tuition $3,500), acquiring a BA in computer science burdened by a debt of, say,

$15,000; while his middle-class neighbor, admitted to Johns Hopkins (tuition $26,000), uses low-interest loans and help from parents to finish a BA in computer science burdened by a debt of $45,000. Which faced the greater financial barrier? Of course, the BA from Hopkins may have greater monetary worth than the one from Bowie. The Hopkins graduate over a lifetime may earn far more than her counterpart, so that the return on her investment is substantially greater. Still, this is not invariably true, and the fact remains that the Hopkins student had to assume enormous financial burdens at the beginning of her career that the Prince George's CC/Bowie State student did not.

60. Section 403 of the 1998 Amendments to the Higher Education Act of 1965, at www.ed.gov/policy/highered/leg/hea98/sec403.html (accessed November 3, 2003).

61. See "Why GEAR UP is Important for America's Young People," U.S. Department of Education, May 2000, at www.ed.gov/gearup/whyGU.html (accessed January 24, 2002). See also Stephen Burd, "Rift Grows Over What Keeps Low-Income Students Out of College," *Chronicle of Higher Education* 48 (January 25, 2002), A18–19.

CHAPTER 5

1. Patrick T. Terenzini, Alberto F. Cabrera, and Elena M. Bernal, *Swimming against the Tide: The Poor in American Higher Education*, College Board Research Report No. 2001–1 (New York: College Board, 2001), p. 18.

2. Robert M. Shireman, "Enrolling Economic Diversity," *New York Times*, May 4, 2002, A25.

3. See the discussion at the end of chapter 3 and below, note 29 and text accompanying it.

4. According to a recent study by Michael McPherson and Morton Owen Schapiro. Quoted in Jacques Steinberg, "More Family Income Committed to College," *New York Times*, May 2, 2002.

5. Thomas Kane, "Rising Public College Tuition and College Entry: How Well Do Public Subsidies Promote Access to College?" National Bureau of Economic Research Working Paper No. 5164, July 1995, cited in McPherson and Schapiro, *The Student Aid Game: Meeting Need and Rewarding Talent in American Higher Education* (Princeton, N.J.: Princeton University Press, 1998), p. 40.

6. McPherson and Schapiro, *The Student Aid Game*, p. 49.

7. College Board, *Trends in Student Aid, 2001*, at www.collegeboard.com. On file with authors.

8. "Forum: As Tuitions Rise, What Will Happen to Quality and Access?" *Chronicle of Higher Education*, September 19, 2003, B7.

9. McPherson and Schapiro, *The Student Aid Game*, p. 27. For an extensive discussion of the reasons for rising costs, see Ronald G. Ehrenberg, *Tuition Rising: Why College Costs So Much* (Cambridge, Mass.: Harvard University Press, 2000).

10. McPherson and Schapiro, *The Student Aid Game*, p. 40, citing Kane study.

11. As of 1999. See the American Association of University Professors (AAUP) website at www.aaup.org/govrel/studentaid/pell.htm (accessed November 2, 2003).

12. McPherson and Schapiro, *The Student Aid Game*, p. 30.

13. AAUP website. "Increasing Pell Grants by $1000 in a given semester decreased the drop-out rates among African American students by 7 percent and among Hispanic American students by 8 percent." For more information see U.S. General Accounting Office, "Higher Education: Restructuring Student Aid Could Reduce Low-Income Student Dropout Rate," March 1995, at www.gao.gov (accessed November 2, 2003).

14. McPherson and Schapiro, *The Student Aid Game*, p. 33.

15. For the comparison between 1980 and today, see Christopher Shea, "Five Truths about Tuition," *New York Times Education Life*, November 9, 2003, p. 20.

16. College Board, *Trends in Student Aid*, p. 4.

17. Jacqueline E. King, "Student Aid: Who Benefits Now?," *Educational Record* (Winter 1996), p. 26.

18. College Board, *Trends in Student Aid*, figure 2: Estimated Student Aid by Source for Academic Year 2000–2001.

19. Stephen R. Lewis, "Ensuring Access, Strengthening Institutions," *College Board Review*, 175 (Spring 1995).

20. Both McPherson and Schapiro and Ehrenberg (all economists) make the airline analogy.

21. Elizabeth A. Duffy and Idana Goldberg, *Crafting a Class: College Admissions and Financial Aid, 1955–1994* (Princeton, N.J.: Princeton University Press, 1998), p. 198.

22. Ehrenberg, *Tuition Rising*, p. 84.

23. McPherson and Schapiro, *The Student Aid Game*, pp. 94–96. Another practice is "need-aware second review": the college considers ability to pay for students who are wait-listed or on some kind of delayed-admission list (p. 96).

24. This account derives from McPherson and Schapiro, *The Student Aid Game*, pp. 6–8, and Ehrenberg, *Tuition Rising*, pp. 76–78.

25. We give an example in the section on early decision policies.

26. The metaphor is from Fred Hirsch, *The Social Limits of Growth* (Cambridge, Mass.: Harvard University Press, 1976), p. 49.

27. According to McPherson and Schapiro, "merit competition is particularly intense among relatively prestigious universities of the 'second tier' and among liberal arts colleges in the Midwest that are facing enrollment declines and increasingly severe public-sector price competition" (*The Student Aid Game*, p. 105).

28. The distinction is drawn by McPherson and Schapiro, *The Student Aid Game*; see pp. 109–14.

29. We discussed this point at the end of chapter 3. See McPherson and Schapiro, *The Student Aid Game*, pp. 112–14. They argue that the scholarships given to the better students can be viewed as compensation for any decrease in the quality of *their* education.

30. The numbers increased slightly for men, from 20 percent in 1976 to 25 percent in 1999; in both 1976 and 1999 the advantage was 24 percent for women. See James Shulman and William Bowen, *The Game of Life: College Sports and Educational Values* (Princeton, N.J.: Princeton University Press, 2001), pp. 41, 131.

31. Cited in James Monks, "The Academic Performance of Legacies," *Economics Letters* 67 (2000), p. 99.

32. Fetter, pp. 75–76. But at Stanford, "an alumnus is defined as any holder of a Stanford degree, graduate or undergraduate."

33. Quoted in Daniel Golden, "Family Ties: Preference for Alumni Children in College Admission Draws Fire," *Wall Street Journal*, January 15, 2003, A1.

34. Fetter, *Questions and Admissions*, p. 72.

35. Quoted in Golden, "Family Ties." The article also describes the financial argument as the "chief reason" for legacy preference. Another reason for preferring legacies is that their families tend to get involved in interviewing applicants and other such tasks. We assimilate these reasons here to the material, "hard" argument for legacy.

36. David O. Levine, *The American College and the Culture of Aspiration, 1915–1940* (Ithaca, N.Y.: Cornell University Press, 1986), p. 139.

37. Fetter, *Questions and Admissions*, p. 72.

38. Letter from Hopkins to Morton C. Tuttle, August 15, 1930, cited in Levine, *The American College and the Culture of Aspiration*, p. 140.

39. Levine, *The American College and the Culture of Aspiration*, pp. 141–42. Italics in original.

40. Today Jewish students comprise about 23 percent of the students at Ivy League schools, even though they make up only 2 percent of the population of the U.S. According to a front-page *Wall Street Journal* article, some selective colleges now actively recruit Jewish students because of their reputation as high academic achievers. See Daniel Golden, "Colleges Court Jewish Students in Effort to Raise Rankings," *Wall Street Journal*, April 29, 2002, p. 1.

41. Levine, *The American College and the Culture of Aspiration*, p. 154.

42. See Elizabeth A. Duffy and Idana Goldberg, *Crafting a Class: College Admissions and Financial Aid, 1955–1994* (Princeton, N.J.: Princeton University Press, 1998), chapter 1. Duffy and Goldberg describe the period between 1955 and 1970 as the "tidal wave"; between the 1970s and the mid-1990s there was a decline in enrollments; beginning around the mid-1990s, when the children of the baby boomers reached college age, enrollments began to rise again.

43. Jane Gross, "Different Lives, One Goal: Finding the Key to College," *New York Times*, May 5, 2002.

44. See Daniel Golden, "Many Colleges Bend Rules to Admit Rich Applicants," *Wall Street Journal*, February 20, 2003, which focuses on the relaxation of academic standards in Duke University's efforts to woo "development admits."

45. See Michael Walzer, *Spheres of Justice* (New York: Basic Books, 1983), pp. 6–10, 197–99.

46. Duffy and Goldberg, *Crafting a Class*.

47. "Acceptance rate" is a distinct category in the *U.S. News* rankings. Until recently, "yield" has been one element among several in the composite category "student selectivity." The others are acceptance rate, SAT/ACT scores, and the percentage of students in the top 10 percent or top 25 percent of their high school class (10 percent if the institution is a doctoral or liberal arts college, 25 percent if it is a "comprehensive" institution that offers few doctoral programs). Both acceptance rate and selectivity contribute to an institution's overall score. See "Undergraduate Criteria Rankings and Weights" on the *U.S. News* website at www.usnews.com/

usnews/edu/college/rankings/about/_brief.php (accessed November 2, 2003). In July 2003, *U.S. News* announced that it would drop yield as a factor in its rankings because using it had drawn the editors "into the debate about early admissions" and because of concerns that colleges had an incentive to manipulate their yield to improve their ranking. Jacques Steinberg, "College Rating by *U.S. News* Drops Factor in Admissions," *New York Times*, July 10, 2003, A14.

48. Christopher Avery, Andrew Fairbanks, and Richard Zeckhauser, *The Early Admissions Game: Joining the Elite* (Cambridge, Mass.: Harvard University Press, 2003), ch. 5. The study did not count athletes, legacies, and minorities, groups that are generally given priority in their own right. The study's finding is perfectly consistent with the common claim that the pool of early-decision applicants is on the whole more qualified than the pool of regular-decision applicants. See also James Fallows, "The Early Decision Racket," *Atlantic Monthly*, September 2001, p. 39.

49. Avery et al., *The Early Admissions Game*, p. 58–62.

50. Wayne J. Camara and Dianne Schneider, "Testing with Extended Time on the SAT I: Effects for Students with Learning Disabilities," Research Notes RN-08, January 2000 (New York: College Board, 2000), p. 1.

51. See Tamar Lewin, "Disabled Student Is Suing Over Test-Score Labeling," *New York Times*, April 11, 2000, A14.

52. Camara and Schneider, "Testing with Extended Time," p. 1.

53. Camara and Schneider, "Testing with Extended Time," pp. 6–8.

54. Lewin, "Disabled Student Is Suing Over Test-Score Labeling."

55. Tamar Lewin, "Abuse Is Feared as SAT Test Changes Disability Policy," *New York Times*, July 15, 2002.

56. Kenneth R. Weiss, "Audit Confirms Disparities in SAT Testing: White, Affluent Students Are Granted Disproportionate Share of Time Extension Based on Learning Disabilities, State Report Finds," *Los Angeles Times*, December 1, 2000.

57. Jay Mathews, "Parents' Push Gives Students More SAT Time," *Washington Post*, May 8, 2000, B1.

58. National Center for Policy Analysis, at www.ncpa.org/pi/edu/pd011100a .html (accessed November 3, 2003).

59. Weiss, "Audit Confirms Disparities in SAT Testing."

60. Based on an informal survey of some Washington area high schools, and on Ken Gewertz, "COACHing the High-jump to Higher Education," *Harvard Gazette*, September 30, 1999.

61. Jane Gross, "Different Lives, One Goal."

62. Admissions Consultants' fees can be found at www.admissionsconsultants .com/college/payment.asp; College Admissions Consultants' fees can be found at www.iapplycollege.com/about_us.shtml#fee (both accessed November 3, 2003).

63. Terenzini et al., *Swimming against the Tide*, p. v.

64. See www.collegeboard.com/student/testing/sat/scores/sending/release.html (accessed November 3, 2003). For most tests (such as the SAT I) the College Board sends all scores, not just the best scores, to colleges. That will be the new policy governing the SAT II. But having the financial resources to repeat tests can also benefit students on the SAT I because, although the College Board sends all scores, colleges often count only the highest. Thus students have an incentive to pay the substantial fees to retake these tests.

65. Terenzini et al., *Swimming against the Tide*, pp. v, 7.

66. Jane Gross, "Different Lives, One Goal."

67. According to Fred Hargadon, director of admissions at Princeton. See "Applications With a Winning Edge: College Admissions Officials Tell What Catches Their Attention—and What Kinds of Responses Don't Impress Them," *Washington Post*, April 23, 2002, A9.

68. From the abstract of "Estimating the Payoff to Attending a More Selective College: An Application of Selection on Observables and Unobservables" (Working Paper #409, Princeton University, December 1998). If Dale and Krueger are right, it's not simply students who could have attended more selective schools but chose others instead who benefit; even those who are rejected get the halo effect. Yet it seems clear that it would not be wise to advise just any high school senior to apply to Princeton on the grounds that even rejection would improve her material prospects.

CHAPTER 6

1. Information gleaned from the websites of the College Board, which sponsors the SAT, and ACT, Inc. (until 1996 known as the American College Testing Program), which administers the ACT. The College Board refers to 1.3 million SAT test-takers entering college in the autumn of 2001 (www.collegeboard.com/press/senior01/html/082801.html [accessed November 4, 2003]) and ACT reports giving its exam to 1.1 million members of the class of 2002 (www.act.org/news/releases/2002/08-21-02.html [accessed November 4, 2003]). Since some SAT-takers may not have entered college and since ACT-takers could have taken it more than once during the year, the number of people who took the SAT in 2000–2001 may have been somewhat larger than 1.3 million and the number of students who took the ACT was surely somewhat less than 2 million. Moreover, some students took both tests during 2000–2001, so we have settled on the conservative estimate in the text. *Time* magazine reports (without attribution) that 2 million students took the SAT in 2000 and 1.8 million took the ACT. *Time*, March 12, 2001, p. 62.

2. In recent years, an extensive academic literature has developed on the LSAT as well. See William C. Kidder, "Portia Denied: Unmasking Gender Bias in the LSAT and Its Relationship to Racial Diversity in Legal Education," *Yale Journal of Law and Feminism* 12 (2000), pp. 1–42; William C. Kidder, "Does the LSAT Mirror or Magnify Racial and Ethnic Differences in Educational Attainment? A Study of Equally Achieving 'Elite' College Students," *California Law Review* 89 (July 2001), pp. 1055–1124.

3. Banesh Hoffmann, *The Tyranny of Testing* (New York: Crowell-Collier, 1962); Allan Nairn and associates, *The Reign of the ETS: The Corporation That Makes Up People's Minds* (The Ralph Nader Report, 1980); David Owen, *None of the Above: Behind the Myth of Scholastic Aptitude* (Boston: Houghton Mifflin, 1985; reissued, revised, and updated by Rowman & Littlefield, 1999). Banesh Hoffman's book had a judicial influence none of the others can claim. In 1974 the Supreme Court considered a case, *DeFunis v. Odegaard* (416 U.S. 312), charging the University of Washington Law School with using illegal racial preferences in its affirmative action program.

Since DeFunis had been admitted to the law school by an earlier court decision, a majority of the Supreme Court declared the case moot. Justice William O. Douglas wanted the Court to decide the case anyway, and wrote an impassioned dissent, one part a hymn to colorblind standards of admissions and the other part a screed against the LSAT, which Douglas took to be the real agent of injustice in this case. Douglas drew all his understanding of the LSAT from Banesh Hoffman.

4. Peter Sacks, *Standardized Minds: The High Price of America's Testing Culture and What We Can Do to Change It* (Cambridge: Perseus Press, 1999).

5. Guinier and Sturm, *Who's Qualified?* (Boston: Beacon Press, 2001).

6. Nicholas Lemann, *The Big Test: The Secret History of the American Meritocracy* (New York: Farrar, Straus and Giroux, 1999).

7. "N.A.A.C.P. Seeks to Limit Use of College Board Tests," *New York Times*, November 21, 1999, p. 39; Julie Blair, "NAACP Criticizes Colleges' Use of SAT, ACT," *Education Week*, December 1, 1999, p. 10.

8. *Cureton v. National Collegiate Athletic Association*, 37 F. Supp. 2d 687 (1999). For further discussion of this case see chapter 8.

9. Diana Jean Schemo, "Head of U. of California Seeks to End SAT Use in Admissions," *New York Times*, February 17, 2001, p. 1.

10. Schemo, "Head of U. of California Seeks to End SAT Use in Admissions."

11. Peter Sacks, "SAT—A Failing Test," *The Nation* 272 (April 2, 2001), p. 7.

12. Guinier and Sturm, *Who's Qualified?* p. 14.

13. Susan Sturm and Lani Guinier, "The Future of Affirmative Action: Reclaiming an Innovative Ideal," *California Law Review* 84 (July 1996), p. 988.

14. Julian Weissglass, "The SAT: Public Spirited or Preserving Privilege?" *Education Week* 17 (April 15, 1998), p. 60.

15. See data at www.crlt.umich.edu/A1.html (accessed May 24, 2002).

16. See data at www.emich.edu/aboutemu/fastfacts (accessed November 4, 2003). Other information provided by Patricia Pablo, Office of Public Information, Eastern Michigan University.

17. Data gathered from sources at www.csustan.edu/Inst_Research/ (accessed May 24, 2002).

18. Information derived from California County Data Book 2001, at www.childrennow.org (accessed May 5, 2003).

19. SES stands for "socioeconomic status."

20. See 2001 College-Bound Seniors: A Profile of SAT Program Test Takers, p. 6, at www.collegeboard.com/sat/cbsenior/yr2001/pdf/NATL.pdf (accessed November 4, 2003). "Combined average score" refers to the summing of scores for the SAT-V and SAT-M.

21. Richard Delgado, "Ten Arguments against Affirmative Action—How Valid? *Alabama Law Review* 50 (Fall 1998), pp. 1169–70; Steven Ramirez, "A General Theory of Cultural Diversity," *Michigan Journal of Race and Law* 33 (Fall 2001), p. 76; Julie Blair, "NAACP Criticizes Colleges Use of SAT, ACT," *Education Week*, December 1, 1999; John A. Powell and Marguerite L. Spencer, "Remaking the Urban University for the Urban Student: Talking About Race," *Connecticut Law Review* 30 (Summer 1998), p. 1285.

22. Stanley Fish, "Reverse Racism, or How the Pot Got to Call the Kettle Black,"

Atlantic Monthly (November 1993). His claim that the SAT was "devised by a racist" is a reference to Carl Campbell Brigham, one of the pioneers of intelligence testing in the 1920s. For a less ham-handed (and more honest) treatment of Brigham, see Lemann, *The Big Test*, pp. 29–41.

23. Delgado, "Ten Arguments," p. 143. Here is the question at issue: a *runner* is to a *marathon* as (a) an *envoy* is to an *embassy*, (b) a *martyr* is to a *massacre*, (c) an *oarsman* is to a *regatta*, (d) a *referee* is to a *tournament*, or (e) a *horse* is to a *stable*. The correct answer is (c). The regatta example is a favorite of Delgado's, showing up in "Rodrigo's Tenth Chronicle: Merit and Affirmative Action," *Georgetown Law Journal* 83 (April 1995), p. 1741; in "Why Universities Are Morally Obligated to Strive for Diversity: Restoring the Remedial Rationale for Affirmative Action," *University of Colorado Law Review* 68 (Fall 1997), p. 1170; and in "Official Elitism or Institutional Self Interest? 10 Reasons Why UC-Davis Should Abandon the LSAT (and Why Other Law Schools Should Follow Suit)," *University of California-Davis Law Review* 34 (Spring 2001), p. 600. See also Francis X. Dealy, Jr., *Win at Any Cost: The Sell Out of College Athletics* (New York: Birch Lane Press, 1990), pp. 116–17; Stanley Fish, "Affirmative Action and the SAT," *Journal of Blacks in Higher Education* (Winter 1993–94), p. 83; Laura Pentimone, "The National Collegiate Association's Quest to Educate the Student Athlete: Are the Academic Eligibility Requirements an Attempt to Foster Academic Integrity or Merely to Promote Racism?" *New York Law School Journal of Human Rights* 14 (1998), p. 473; Eli Denard Oates, "Cureton v. NCAA: The Recognition of Proposition 16's Misplaced Use of Standardized Tests in the Context of Collegiate Athletics as a Barrier to Educational Opportunities for Minorities," *Wake Forest Law Review* 35 (Summer 2000), p. 464. The regatta example first appeared in Owen, *None of the Above*, p. 222.

24. Carolyn Keene, *Making Waves* (New York: Pocket Books, 1993); Agatha Christie, *The Regatta Mystery* (New York: Dodd, Mead, 1939); William Makepeace Thackeray, *Vanity Fair* (New York: Modern Library, 1999) (originally published in 1847–1848). On this point, see Edmund Janko, "Overboard," *Teacher Magazine* 10 (November/December 1998), p. 50.

25. See Lemann, *The Big Test*, pp. 3–41, esp. 38.

26. On "cultural loading," see Richard R. Valencia and Lisa A. Suzuki, *Intelligence Testing and Minority Students: Foundations, Performance Factors, and Assessment Issues* (Thousand Oaks, Calif.: Sage Publications, 2001), pp. 113ff.

27. Lemann, *The Big Test*, p. 86.

28. Sturm and Guinier, "The Future of Affirmative Action," p. 971 (quoting David Owen, *None of the Above*, p. 207).

29. James Crouse and Dale Trusheim, *The Case against the SAT* (Chicago: University of Chicago Press, 1988), pp. 53, 62, 68.

30. W. M. Boyd II, "SATs and Minorities: The Dangers of Underprediction," *Change* 9 (November 1977), pp. 48–49.

31. Crouse and Trusheim, *The Case against the SAT*, p. 96. See also Kenneth D. Hopkins, Julian C. Stanley, and B. R. Hopkins, *Educational and Psychological Measurement*, 7th ed. (Englewood Cliffs, N.J.: Prentice-Hall, 1990), p. 375.

32. See tables at p. vii, 2001 Comprehensive Annual Report on Texas Public Schools (Texas Education Agency), at www.tea.state.tx.us/research/pdfs/2001comp.pdf (accessed November 4, 2003).

33. The scores are based on administration of the Stanford 9 Tests. Seventy-two percent of Asian Americans scored at or above the 50 national percentile rank (NPR), while the corresponding number for Hispanic/Latinos was 29 percent. See www.eddataonline.com/cst2002 (then click "State Report," then choose test and students from menus) (accessed November 4, 2003).

34. Similar black–white disparities showed up in lower grades and for other subjects. Sixty percent of Asian American students and seventeen percent of Hispanic students were advanced or proficient in math. See *Spring 2001 MCAS Tests: State Results by Race/Ethnicity and Student Status* (Malden, Mass.: Massachusetts Department of Education, October 2001), tables 8–11.

35. For decades the SAT was normed on a 1941 cohort of test-takers. In 1995, the test was renormed. The renorming resulted in a recentering of the actual median score to 500. For more about the mean score, see the discussion in the text later in chapter 6.

36. National Center for Education Statistics, *Science Highlights 2002: The Nation's Report Card* (Washington, D.C.: U.S. Department of Education, 2002), p. 8; see also p. 9 (62 percent of white, 59 percent of Asian American, 30 percent of Hispanic, and 22 percent of African American twelfth grade students were deemed "at or above basic" command of science); National Center for Education Statistics, *Civics Report Card for the Nation* (Washington, D.C.: U.S. Department of Education, 1999), p. 38; see also p. 51 (73 percent of white, 66 percent of Asian American, 44 percent of Hispanic, and 42 percent of African American twelfth-grade students were deemed "at or above basic" command of civics); National Center for Education Statistics, *Mathematics 2000: The Nation's Report Card* (Washington, D.C.: U.S. Department of Education, 2001), p. 59; see also pp. 64–65 (74 percent of white, 80 percent of Asian American, 44 percent of Hispanic, and 31 percent of African American twelfth-grade students were deemed "at or above basic" command of math); National Center for Education Statistics, *Writing: Report Card for the Nation and the States* (Washington, D.C.: U.S. Department of Education, 1998), p. 57; see also p. 71 (84 percent of white, 78 percent of Asian American, 65 percent of Hispanic, and 64 percent of African American twelfth-grade students were deemed "at or above basic" command of writing).

37. For further discussion, see Christopher Jencks and Meredith Phillips, "The Black–White Test Score Gap: An Introduction," in Christopher Jencks and Meredith Phillips, eds., *The Black–White Test Score Gap* (Washington, D.C.: Brookings Institution Press, 1998), pp. 1–51.

38. This statement is not quite accurate; a miniscule number of scores will fall beyond either value.

39. Hopkins et al., *Educational and Psychological Measurement*, pp. 42–58.

40. Hopkins et al., *Educational and Psychological Measurement*, p. 58.

41. SAT I Percentile Ranks, at www.collegeboard.com/prod_downloads/about/news_info/cbsenior/yr2003/pdf/ta ble_3a/pdf (accessed November 4, 2003).

42. SAT I Percentile Ranks.

43. See www.collegeboard.org/counselors/hs/sat/sat.html (accessed November 4, 2003).

44. As we noted in the text earlier, the student doesn't have to immerse herself in

Marcel Proust, James Joyce, and Arthur Schopenhauer to do well; Agatha Christie mysteries or *Nancy Drew* novels would have supplied the right clues to answer the "regatta" question!

45. "Overview: ETS Fairness Review" (Princeton, N.J.: Educational Testing Service, 1998), p. 2.

46. "Overview: ETS Fairness Review," p. 4.

47. For further discussion, see Rebecca Zwick, *Fair Game? The Use of Standardized Tests in Higher Education* (New York: Routledge Falmer, 2002), pp. 127–30. Because the selection of test items relies on a consistency between item answers and overall scores, a long-standing charge against standardized tests holds that choice of questions will unavoidably bias the tests against minority groups because item choosers will discard the questions minorities answer best as inconsistent with the questions most test-takers answer best. A recent version of this charge can be found in Charles Willie, "The Contextual Effects of Socioeconomic Status on Student Achievement Test Scores by Race," *Urban Education* 36 (September 2001), p. 471. For an empirical test (and disconfirmation) of the charge, see Xitao Fan and Victor L. Willson, "Ethnic Group Representation in Test Construction Samples and Test Bias: The Standardization Fallacy Revisited," *Educational & Psychological Measurement* 56 (June 1996), pp. 365–81.

48. "Academic Testing: Test Design and Construction," Penn State University Testing Services, p. 4, at www.uts.psu.edu/Test_construction_frame.htm (accessed November 4, 2003).

49. See Howard B. Lyman, *Test Scores and What They Mean*, 4th ed. (Englewood Cliffs, N.J.: Prentice-Hall, 1986), pp. 7, 32–36; Hopkins et al., *Educational and Psychological Measurement*, pp. 115–36.

50. See Hopkins et al., *Educational and Psychological Measurement*, p. 131; "Academic Testing: Test Design and Construction," p. 6.

51. Howard Wainer, "Comparing the Incomparable: An Essay on the Importance of Big Assumptions and Scant Evidence," *Educational Measurement: Issues and Practice* 18 (Winter 1999), pp. 10–11.

52. "SAT Program Information—Statistical Definitions," at www.collegeboard. com/about/news_info/cbsenior/yr2002/html/define.html (accessed November 4, 2003).

53. The equation used by a college to predict the grades on this year's applicants is based on the scores and grades of last year's students.

54. Hopkins et al., *Educational and Psychological Measurement*, p. 347. Of course, the populations of these schools may be skewed as well because students with high SATs are likely to be underrepresented. We thank Laura Hussey for this point.

55. Hopkins et al., *Educational and Psychological Measurement*, p. 347.

56. "Common Sense about SAT Score Differences and Test Validity," College Board Research Note RN-01, June 1997, p. 5 (table 5).

57. See Sturm and Guinier, note 28, above.

58. Lyman, *Test Scores and What They Mean*, pp. 57–58.

59. "Common Sense," p. 4.

60. Crouse and Trusheim, *The Case against the SAT*, p. 50.

61. Crouse and Trusheim, *The Case against the SAT*, pp. 43, 51.

62. Crouse and Trusheim, *The Case against the SAT*, p. 51.

63. Crouse and Trusheim, *The Case against the SAT*, p. 55.

64. "Students with Discrepant High School GPA and SAT Scores," College Board Research Summary RS-1, October 1997, p. 1.

65. Crouse and Trusheim, *The Case against the SAT*, p. 769.

66. Christopher Jencks, "Racial Bias in Testing," in Jencks and Phillips, *The Black–White Test Score Gap*, p. 84.

67. Sacks, *Standardized Minds*, p.

68. See notes 15–18 above. The HSGPA of 4.1 at UCLA reflects the high percentage of entering freshmen who took Advanced Placement and honors courses in high school and the fact that grades in these courses are often weighted more heavily than grades in other courses. In other words, where an A usually counts for 4 points, an A in an AP or honors course may count for 5, a B may count for 4, and so on.

69. Sacks, *Standardized Minds*, p. 296 (see also pp. 271, 293).

70. Rebecca Zwick, "Making the Grade: The SAT versus the GPA," *National Crosstalk* 9 (Summer 2001), at www.highereducation.org/crosstalk/ct0701/voices0701-makingthegrade.shtml (accessed November 4, 2003). (National Crosstalk is a forum of the National Center for Public Policy and Higher Education.) See also table 5.3, "High School Grade Point Average and High School Rank Distributions for 1984 College-Bound Seniors," in Crouse and Trusheim, *The Case against the SAT*, p. 94.

71. Crouse and Trusheim, *The Case against the SAT*, p. 8.

72. Crouse and Trusheim, *The Case against the SAT*, p. 103.

73. Crouse and Trusheim, *The Case against the SAT*, pp. 158–59.

74. Crouse and Trusheim, *The Case against the SAT*, p. 160. Crouse and Trusheim suggest that a better model than the SAT II is a battery of achievement exams modeled after the College Board's Advanced Placement program, where specially designed high school courses teach college-level material. Students who get a certain score on the national AP test receive course credit when they get to college, with colleges individually determining what score counts. For AP tests in 2001, in thirty-three subjects, the mean score of whites was 2.99 (out of a possible score of 5), for Asian Americans 3.04, for Chicano/Mexican Americans 2.67, and for African Americans 2.11. (See tables at www.collegeboard.com/prod_downloads/student/testing/ap/sumrpts/2001/pdf/national_2001.pdf [accessed November 4, 2003]). This "better model" obviously won't change the racial/ethnic composition of college entering classes.

75. Crouse and Trusheim, *The Case against the SAT*, p. 50.

CHAPTER 7

1. See www.brown.edu/Administration/Admission/profile.html (accessed November 3, 2003), "Distribution of College Board Scores." See also Gerald W. Bracey, *Thinking about Tests and Testing: A Short Primer in "Assessment Literacy"* (Washington, D.C.: American Youth Policy Forum, 2000), p. 29.

2. See www.brown.edu/Administration/George_Street_Journal/accepts.html

(accessed November 4, 2003) and www.brown.edu/Administration/Admission/faq.-html (accessed November 4, 2003).

3. Or an AI of 2.81 if his high school curriculum was "most difficult."

4. *Johnson v. University of Georgia*, 263 F. 3rd 1234 (2001), at 1242.

5. *Johnson v. University of Georgia* at 1257 (ftnt. 20).

6. An applicant could get an extra point for having combined SAT scores above 1200. *Johnson v. University of Georgia* at 1242.

7. *Johnson v. University of Georgia* at 1257 (including ftnt. 7).

8. *Johnson v. University of Georgia* at 1257 (including ftnt. 7).

9. *Johnson v. University of Georgia* at 1257.

10. 123 S. Ct. 2411 (2003). For extensive discussion, see chapter 10.

11. "Admission Criteria," at www1.admissions.uga.edu/freshman_adm/crit.html (accessed November 4, 2003).

12. Clifford Adelman, "Why Can't We Stop Talking about the SAT?" *The Chronicle of Higher Education*, November 5, 1999, B4.

13. See University of Tennessee, http://admissions.utk.edu/undergraduate/faq.shtml; Lewis and Clark College, www.lclark.edu/dept/admiss/whatwewant.html (accessed May 1, 2002); Santa Clara University, www.scu.edu/ugrad/requirements/freshmen.cfm (accessed November 4, 2003); Johns Hopkins University, http://apply.jhu.edu/apply/apply.html (accessed November 5, 2003); Kenyon College, http://www.kenyon.edu/x1875.xml (accessed November 5, 2003); University of Cincinnati, www.admissions.uc.edu/requirements.pdf (accessed November 5, 2003); Boston University, http://web.bu.edu/admissions/apply/fresh_admission.html (accessed November 4, 2003); University of Nebraska, http://admissions.unl.edu/reqs_after.html#core (accessed November 4, 2003); Smith College, www.smith.edu/admission/firstyear_faq.php (accessed November 5, 2003); Northwestern University, www.ugadm.northwestern.edu/freshman/applying/frosh.htm#prep (accessed November 5, 2003); Arizona State University, www.asu.edu/admissions/requirements/competencyrequirements.html (accessed November 5, 2003); Claremont McKenna College, www.claremontmckenna.edu/admission/apply/freshman.asp (accessed November 4, 2003); Butler University, www.butler.edu/admissions/adm_apply_guide.asp (accessed May 1, 2002); Elon College, www.elon.edu/admissions/about.asp (accessed May 1, 2002); University of Alabama, http://admissions.ua.edu/undergraduate/apply.html (accessed November 4, 2003).

14. James Madison University, see www.jmu.edu/admissions/process.shtml (accessed May 1, 2002).

15. Crouse and Trusheim, *The Case against the SAT*, p. 148.

16. Crouse and Trusheim, *The Case against the SAT*, p. 165.

17. Christopher Jencks, "Racial Bias in Testing," in Christopher Jencks and Meredith Phillips, eds., *The Black–White Test Score Gap* (Washington, D.C.: Brookings Institution Press, 1998), pp. 73–74.

18. Crouse and Trusheim, *The Case against the SAT*, p. 159.

19. Saul Geiser with Roger Studley, "UC and the SAT: Predictive Validity and Differential Impact of the SAT I and SAT II on the University of California" (Office of the President, October 29, 2001), pp. 3–4, at www.ucop.edu, "Rethinking admissions tests."

20. Crouse and Trusheim, *The Case against the SAT*, p. 160.

21. Geiser and Studley, "UC and the SAT," pp. 15, 22.

22. This is the gist of Crouse and Trusheim's brief against the SAT in their chapter on race.

23. For a more sophisticated and rigorous illustration of this result, see Jeryl L. Mumpower et al., "Affirmative Action, Duality of Error, and the Consequences of Mispredicting the Academic Performance of African American College Applicants," *Journal of Policy Analysis and Management* 21 (2002), pp. 63–74, esp. 69–72. See also the discussion of the differential in false negative/false positive decisions in Crouse and Trusheim, *The Case against the SAT*, pp. 106–8.

24. Crouse and Trusheim, *The Case against the SAT*, p. 96; Wayne J. Camara and Gary Echtermacht, "The SAT I and High School Grades: Utility in Predicting Success in College," College Board, Research Note 10 (July 2003), Table I (HSGPA has a correlation with first-year grades of .61 for whites and .46 for blacks), at www.collegeboard.com/repository/rn10_10755.pdf (accessed November 5, 2003); Frederick E. Vars and William Bowen, "Scholastic Aptitude Test Scores, Race, and Academic Performance in Selective Colleges and Universities," in Jencks and Phillips, *The Black–White Test Score Gap*, p. 466.

25. "The College Board Announces a New SAT," at www.collegeboard.com/press/article/0,1443,11147,00.html (accessed November 4, 2003).

26. Christopher Jencks and Meredith Phillips, "Introduction," in Jencks and Phillips, *The Black–White Test Score Gap*, p. 32; L. Scott Miller, *An American Imperative: Accelerating Minority Educational Advancement* (New Haven, Conn.: Yale University Press, 1995), p. 235; Rebecca Zwick, *Fair Game? The Use of Standardized Admissions Tests in Higher Education* (New York: Routledge Falmer, 2002), p. 130.

27. Vars and Bowen, "Scholastic Aptitude Test Scores," p. 460.

28. Lani Guinier and Susan Sturm, *Who's Qualified?* (Boston: Beacon Press, 2001), p. 20 ("Particularly in the education arena, where opportunity lies at the core of the institution's mission, a lottery may be an important advance. Above . . . [a] test-determined floor, applicants could be chosen by several alternatives, including portfolio-based assessment or a more structured and participatory decision-making process.").

29. Lani Guinier, "Colleges Should Take 'Confirmative Action' in Admissions," *Chronicle of Higher Education* 48 (December 14, 2001), B10.

30. Guinier, "Colleges Should Take 'Confirmative Action' in Admissions."

31. Guinier, "Colleges Should Take 'Confirmative Action' in Admissions."

32. Guinier, "Colleges Should Take 'Confirmative Action' in Admissions."

33. See Holyoke Community College, "Guide to Transfer Opportunities," at www.hcc.mass.edu/html/After_HCC/Transfer_Information/Transfer_Information.htm (accessed November 4, 2003).

34. University of Washington, "Direct Transfer Agreement Pathway," at www.washington.edu/students/uga/tr/reqs/dta.htm (accessed November 4, 2003).

35. Pennsylvania Academic Passport Program, at http://pats/sshe.edu/frames.html (click on "Academic Passport") (accessed November 5, 2003).

36. Steve Chatman, "Take the Community College Route to a Selective Public University Degree," presented at the 2001 Annual Forum of the Association for Institutional Research, at www.sariweb.ucdavis.edu/downloads/211TakeCommColl

RouteToSelectivePublicUnivDegree.pdf (accessed November 5, 2003). Also see the discussion in chapter 4 of impediments community college students face in gaining bachelor's degrees.

37. See The Princeton Review at www.review.com/college/testprep.asp? TPRPAGE = 61&TYPE = SAT (accessed November 4, 2003).

38. Kaplan brochure, citing 1995 study conducted by Bruskin-Goldring Research.

39. Donald E. Powers and Wayne J. Camara, "Coaching and the SAT I," College Board Research Notes, RN-06 (April 1999), pp. 8, 7, at www.collegeboard.com/research/html/rn06.pdf (accessed November 4, 2003).

40. Donald E. Powers and Donald A. Rock, "Effects of Coaching on SAT I: Reasoning Test Scores," *Journal of Educational Measurement* 36 (Summer 1999), pp. 93–118.

41. Samuel Messick and Ann Jungeblut, "Time and Method in Coaching for the SAT," *Psychological Bulletin* 89 (March 1981), pp. 191–216.

42. Rebecca DerSimonian and Nan M. Laird, "Evaluating the Effect of Coaching on SAT Scores: A Meta-Analysis," *Harvard Educational Review* 53 (February 1983), pp. 1–15.

43. Betsy Jane Becker, "Coaching for the Scholastic Aptitude Test: Further Syntheses and Appraisal," *Review of Educational Research* 60 (Fall 1990), pp. 373–417.

44. Donald E. Powers, "Coaching for the SAT: Summary of the Summaries and an Update," *Educational Measurement: Issues and Practice* 12 (1993), pp. 24–30.

45. Lloyd Bond, "The Effects of Special Preparation on Measures of Scholastic Ability," in Robert L. Linn, ed., *Educational Measurement*, 3d ed. (Phoenix, Ariz.: Oryx Press, 1993), pp. 429–44.

46. Bond, "The Effects of Special Preparation," p. 438; Messick and Jungblut, "Time and Method in Coaching for the SAT," pp. 193, 201, 202.

47. Messick and Jungeblut, "Time and Method in Coaching for the SAT," p. 191.

48. DerSimonian and Laird, "Effect of Coaching on SAT Scores," p. 13.

49. Bond, "The Effects of Special Preparation," p. 438.

50. Becker, "Coaching for the Scholastic Aptitude Test," pp. 392–93.

51. Messick and Jungeblut, "Time and Method in Coaching for the SAT," provide evidence that coaching gains are not linear. Most gains from coaching come in the early weeks; beyond that point, each additional point gain from coaching requires a geometrically increasing investment of time (p. 215). A further point: a recent study of Israeli students using an instrument very similar to the SAT suggests that coaching gains do not appear to affect the predictive validity of standardized tests. Avi Allalouf and Gershon Ben-Shakhar, "The Effect of Coaching on the Predictive Validity of Scholastic Aptitude Tests," *Journal of Educational Measurement* 35 (Spring 1998), pp. 39–43. See also Bond, "The Effects of Special Preparation," pp. 440–41.

52. Powers and Camara, "Coaching and the SAT I," p. 3.

53. Rebecca Zwick, *Fair Game? The Use of Standardized Admissions Tests in Higher Education* (New York: Routledge Falmer, 2002), p. 172.

54. On Japanese high schools generally, see Thomas P. Rohlen, *Japan's High Schools* (Berkeley: University of California Press, 1983); see also Hiroshi Ono, "Does Examination Hell Pay Off? A Cost-Benefit Analysis of College Education in Japan," at www.nber.org/~confer/99/japan99/ono.pdf (accessed June 3, 2002).

55. "Fear of Dumbing Down Lift Cram School Share Prices," *Asahi Shimbun*, April 11, 2002, at www.asahi.com/english/business/K2002041100357.html (accessed June 3, 2002).

CHAPTER 8

1. Quoted in *Sharif v. New York State Education Department*, 709 F. Supp. 345, at 351. The committee's idea here is not entirely clear; its language implies "an objective merit" different from good performance (the latter being what good family background enables students to achieve).

2. Quoted in *Sharif*, pp. 352-54.

3. Quoted in *Sharif*, p. 355.

4. *Griggs v. Duke Power Company*, 401 U.S. 424 (1971).

5. 42 U.S. Code 2000d.

6. 20 U.S. Code 1681(a).

7. Title VII of the Civil Rights Act (the "Employment Title") prohibited gender discrimination from the very beginning; Title VI, which covered educational institutions receiving federal monies, did not mention gender, an omission remedied by Title IX.

8. 41 Code of Federal Regulations 60-3.5, 60-3.9.

9. See *Larry P. v. Riles*, 793 F.2d 969, 976–77 (1984); *Georgia State Conference v. State of Georgia*, 775 F.2d 1403, 1418–20 (1985); *Guardians Association v. Civil Service Commission*, 463 U.S. 103 (1983).

10. John Chaney, "Losing Proposition," *New York Times*, March 10, 1999, p. 19.

11. "Letter from Black Coaches Association and Fair Test to NCAA" (June 2, 1998), at www.fairtest.org/pr/ncaabca.htm (accessed November 4, 2003).

12. *Cureton v. National Collegiate Athletic Association*, 37 F. Supp. 2d 687 (1999).

13. See *Georgia State Conference v. Georgia*, at 1419, 1421–22.

14. *Cureton v. NCAA*, at 699. The denial rates for 1996 were 26.6 percent and 6.4 percent, respectively.

15. *Cureton*, at 707.

16. *Cureton*, at 710.

17. *Cureton*, at 709–10.

18. *Cureton*, at 709, 710, 711.

19. *Cureton*, at 712–13.

20. *Cureton*, at 714–15.

21. *Cureton v. National Collegiate Athletic Association*, 198 F.3d 107 (1999). The NCAA receives no federal funds directly, although its National Youth Sports Program Fund does.

22. See Gordon S. White, "Should Major Colleges Restore Rule for Freshmen," *New York Times*, November 4, 1980, B12; Craig Neff and Robert Sullivan, "Call for a Fresh Start," *Sports Illustrated*, December 22, 1986, p. 23; Curry Kirkpatrick, "The Class of '92," *Sports Illustrated*, November 16, 1988, p. 6; John A. DiBiaggio, "Don't Let Freshmen Play," *Washington Post*, June 22, 1999, A17.

23. *Alexander v. Sandoval*, 532 U.S. 275 (2001).

24. See Patrick Healy, "Civil Rights Office Questions Legality of Colleges' Use of Standardized Tests," *Chronicle of Higher Education*, May 28, 1999, A28.

25. "Memorandum Regarding Certain Legal Issues Addressed in 'Nondiscrimination in High-Stakes Testing: A Resource Guide,'" at www.collegeboard.org/press/html9899/html/ocr1.html (accessed March 12, 2000).

CHAPTER 9

1. B. Drummond Ayres Jr., "California Board Ends Preferences in College System," *New York Times*, July 21, 1995, A1. Proposition 209, passed by the voters of California in 1996, forbidding use of racial preferences in all state activities meant the board's policy couldn't be reversed under a future governor.

2. "Freshman Trend Table," available at http://osr4.berkeley.edu/newfroshtrend.html (accessed November 4, 2003).

3. "UCLA Ethnic Enrollment—New Entering from High School," one of several tables at www.apb.ucla.edu/apbeth.htm (accessed November 4, 2003). Before 1998, UCLA averaged 17.7 percent Mexican-Americans and other Hispanics in its entering classes; since 1998, the average has fallen to 12.2 percent. Whites (Caucasians) average 32.4 percent of recent entering classes, a dramatic change from 30 years ago when they made up 70 percent. The largest ethnic bloc at UCLA is made up of Asian-Americans/Filipinos, averaging over 40 percent of freshmen the last four years.

4. "University of California Application, Admissions and Enrollment of California Resident Freshmen for Fall 1995 through 2001," at www.ucop.edu/news/facts heets/flowfrc9501.pdf (accessed November 4, 2003).

5. See James Traub, "The Class of Prop. 209," *New York Times Magazine*, May 2, 1999, pp. 44ff.

6. "Press Release, Office of the President," at www.ucop.edu/news/archives/2001/may31art1.htm (accessed November 4, 2003).

7. In the law, "affirmative action" refers to the positive efforts institutions must make to assure their selection procedures are fair and nondiscriminatory. These efforts need not involve the giving of racial preferences. Nevertheless, the term has become so identified with preferences that it has become a virtual synonym for them. We continue this usage in the text.

8. Carl Cohen, "Race Preference in College Admissions," Heritage Foundation Lecture No. 611 (1988), p. 2, at www.heritage.org/research/education/HL611.html (accessed November 5, 2003), quoting Marshall's *Brief of the Legal Defense Fund of the National Association for the Advancement of Colored People in the Case of Brown v. Board of Education.*

9. *DeFunis v. Odegaard*, 416 U.S. 312, 324 (1974). The Court was divided on mootness, with four justices in favor of hearing the case. Justice Douglas wrote a lengthy dissent, notable for its rehearsal of themes soon to be echoed by other members of the Court. According to Douglas, DeFunis "had a constitutional right to have his application considered on its individual merits in a racially neutral manner" (at 337). "The Equal Protection Clause," he went on, "commands the elimination of

racial barriers, not their creation in order to satisfy our theory of how society ought to be organized" (at 342).

10. *Regents of the University of California v. Bakke,* 438 U.S. 265, 269–70, 325 (1978).

11. The affirmative action dominoes began to fall with *Podberesky v. Kirwan,* 38 F.3d 148 (1994).

12. *Grutter v. Bollinger,* 123 S. Ct. 2325 (2003); *Gratz v. Bollinger,* 123 S. Ct. 2411 (2003).

13. 42 U.S. Code 2000d.

14. *Regents v. Bakke,* at 418.

15. Over the last century, the Court has held in a series of cases that the liberty protected by the Fourteenth Amendment (which applies only to the states) includes most of the liberties defined in the first ten Amendments (which apply only to the federal government). In other words, the Fourteenth Amendment "incorporates" the Bill of Rights. The Court has also read the "equal protection" in the Fourteenth Amendment back into the "due process" of the Fifth Amendment. For further discussion, see Laurence H. Tribe, *American Constitutional Law* (Mineola, N.Y.: The Foundation Press, 1978), pp. 567ff.

16. *Regents v. Bakke,* at 352.

17. Section 1, Fourteenth Amendment, U.S. Constitution ("All persons born or naturalized in the United States and subject to the jurisdiction thereof, are citizens of the United States and of the State wherein they reside. No State shall make or enforce any law which shall abridge the privileges or immunities of citizens of the United States; nor shall any State deprive any person of life, liberty, or property, without due process of law; nor deny to any person within its jurisdiction the equal protection of the laws").

18. *Regents v. Bakke,* at 289–90.

19. *Bakke,* at 297.

20. *Bakke,* at 399. On "principles sufficiently absolute," Powell is quoting Archibald Cox, *The Role of the Supreme Court in American Government* (New York: Oxford University Press, 1976), p. 114.

21. *Bakke,* at 306. We examined this standard in chapter 8.

22. *Bakke.* Citations omitted.

23. *Bakke,* at 307.

24. *Bakke,* at 307, 309. Emphasis added.

25. *Bakke,* at 310, 311.

26. *Bakke,* at 311–12 (quoting Justice Felix Frankfurter in *Sweezy v. New Hampshire,* 354 U.S. 234, 263 [1957]).

27. *Bakke,* at 314–15.

28. *Bakke,* at 315.

29. *Bakke,* at 316.

30. *Bakke,* at 318.

31. *DeFunis v. Odegaard,* at 342.

32. For example, only midway through litigation over its Banneker Scholarships, available only to black students, did the University of Maryland see that it needed to link racial preferences to remedying discrimination ("we have never approved prefer-

ential classifications in the absence of . . . violations," Powell had emphasized in *Bakke* [at 303]). Then it hastily produced a brief indicting itself for continuing discrimination even though it was admitting African American students at a rate higher than their proportion in the eligible applicant pool. The Court of Appeals didn't buy the defense, and the university lost the power to reserve the scholarships for black students only. See *Podberesky v. Kirwan*, 38 F.3d 147 (1994).

33. *Regents v. Bakke*, at 328, 369.
34. *Bakke*, at 296, ftnt. 36.
35. *Bakke*, at 359.
36. *Bakke*, at 289–90, 292–93, 299.
37. *Bakke*, at 357–58.
38. *Plessy v. Ferguson*, 163 U.S. 537 (1896).
39. *Plessy v. Ferguson*, at 559. Emphasis added.
40. *Plessy v. Ferguson*, 563.
41. *Plessy v. Ferguson*, at 560.
42. *Regents v. Bakke*, at 375.
43. *Bakke*, at 359.
44. *Bakke*, at 361.
45. *Bakke*, at 295, ftnt. 34.
46. *Plessy v. Ferguson*, at 552.
47. *Regents v. Bakke*, at 310.
48. *Bakke*, at 308.
49. *Lau v. Nichols*, 414 U.S. 563, 569 (1974).
50. *Washington v. Davis*, 426 U.S. 229, 240 (1976).
51. *Washington v. Davis*.
52. *Regents v. Bakke*, at 353.
53. *Guardians Association v. Civil Service Commission of New York City*, 463 U.S. 582, 590–91 (1983).
54. *Guardians Association v. Civil Service Commission of New York City*, 592.
55. *Cureton v. National Collegiate Athletic Association*, 37 F. Supp. 2d 687, 698 (1999).
56. *Regents v. Bakke*, at 380, 387–88.
57. *Cannon v. University of Chicago*, 441 U.S. 677 (1979).
58. *Alexander v. Sandoval*, 532 U.S. 275, 280, 281, 282 (2001).
59. *Alexander v. Sandoval*, at 286.

CHAPTER 10

1. John Stuart Mill, *On Liberty and Other Essays* (Oxford: Oxford University Press, 1991), p. 25.
2. Neil L. Rudenstine, "Why a Diverse Student Body Is So Important," *Chronicle of Higher Education*, April 19, 1996, B1.
3. *Hopwood v. Texas*, 861 F. Supp. 551 (1994).
4. *Hopwood v. Texas*, 78 F.3d 932 (1996).
5. *Hopwood v. Texas*, 861 F. Supp. at 563, 575.

6. *Hopwood v. Texas*, 861 F. Supp. at 561–62.

7. *Hopwood v. Texas*, 861 F. Supp. at 575–76.

8. *Hopwood v. Texas*, 861 F. Supp. at 579.

9. *Hopwood v. Texas*, 78 F.3d at 944, 945.

10. *Smith v. University of Washington Law School*, 2 F. Supp. 2d 1324 (1998); *Smith v. University of Washington Law School*, 233 F.3d 1188 (2000); *Tracy v. University System of Georgia*, 59 F. Supp. 2d 1314 (1999); *Tracy v. University System of Georgia*, 2000 U.S. Dist. LEXIS 11262; *Wooden v. University System of Georgia*, 32 F. Supp. 2d 1370 (1999); *Johnson v. University System of Georgia*, 2000 U.S. Dist. LEXIS 10541; *Johnson v. University System of Georgia*, 263 F.3d 1234 (2001); *Gratz v. Bollinger*, 122 F. Supp. 2d 811 (2000); *Grutter v. Bollinger*, 137 F. Supp. 2d 821 (2001); *Gratz v. Bollinger*, 135 F. Supp. 2d 790 (2001); *Grutter v. Bollinger*, 288 F.3d 732 (2002).

11. *Johnson v. Board of Regents of the University System of Georgia*, 106 F. Supp. 2d 1362, 1369 (2000) ("Justice Powell's opinion regarding the compelling nature of student body diversity in university admissions is not binding precedent"); *Wessmann v. Gittens*, 160 F.3d 790, 796 (1998) (the court is "not prepared" to follow *Hopwood* until the Supreme Court explicitly signals that *Bakke* is dead).

12. Chancellor Charles Young, quoted in Robert K. Fullinwider, "Diversity and Affirmative Action," *Report from the Institute for Philosophy and Public Policy* 20 (Winter/Spring 2000).

13. AAHE Statement on Diversity, at www.aahe.org/diversity.htm (accessed November 5, 2003).

14. Herma Hill Kay, "The Challenge to Diversity in Legal Education," *Indiana Law Review* 34 (2000), p. 63.

15. *Hopwood v. Texas*, 861 F. Supp. at 556; *Hopwood v. Texas*, 78 F.3d at 996.

16. For references, see note 10, above.

17. "Expert Report of Patricia Gurin," *Michigan Journal of Race and Law* 5 (Fall 1999), pp. 365, 387.

18. "Expert Report of Patricia Gurin," pp. 367–68.

19. Richard O. Lempert, David L. Chambers, and Terry K. Adams, " 'From the Trenches and Towers': Law School Affirmative Action: An Empirical Study of Michigan's Minority's Graduates in Practice," *Law and Social Inquiry* 25 (Spring 2000), pp. 416–18.

20. *Grutter v. Bollinger*, Court of Appeals, 6th Circuit, Oral Argument, p. 1.

21. Mitchell Chang et al., eds., *Compelling Interest: Examining the Evidence on Racial Dynamics in Higher Education. A Report of the AERA Panel on Racial Dynamics in Colleges and Universities* (Stanford University, 1999), pp. 6–7, at www.aera.net/reports/dynamics.htm (accessed November 4, 2003). See also "AAU Diversity Statement on the Importance of Diversity in University Admissions," at www.aau.edu/issues/Diversity4.14.97.html (accessed November 4, 2003); *Does Diversity Make a Difference? Three Research Studies on Diversity in College Classrooms* (Washington, D.C.: American Council on Education and American Association of University Professors, 2000), p. 2.

22. *Grutter v. Bollinger*, 123 S. Ct. 2325 (2003) at 2327.

23. *Grutter*, at 2336, 2339. Internal quotation marks and citation omitted.

24. *Gratz v. Bollinger*, 123 S. Ct. 2411 (2003).

25. *Grutter*, at 2339. Emphasis added.

26. *Grutter*, at 2339.

27. *Grutter*, at 2332. Internal citation omitted.

28. *Grutter*, at 2344.

29. *Grutter*, at 2334. Internal citation omitted.

30. *Grutter*, at 2341. Emphasis added. Internal citations omitted.

31. *Grutter*, at 2340.

32. *Grutter*, at 2341.

33. *Grutter*, at 2346. Internal citations and quotation marks omitted.

34. *Grutter*, at 2346–47. Internal citations omitted.

35. *Gratz*, at 2419–21, 2431–32.

36. *Gratz*, at 2432.

37. *Grutter*, at 2343.

38. *Gratz*, Justice Rehnquist Opinion, pp. 26–27; 2003 Lexis 4801, p. 54.

39. Patricia Gurin, Eric L. Dey, Sylvia Hurtado, and Gerald Gurin, "Diversity and Higher Education: Theory and Impact on Educational Outcomes," *Harvard Educational Review* 72 (Fall 2002), p. 330.

40. "Expert Report of Patricia Gurin," p. 365.

41. "Expert Report of Patricia Gurin," pp. 368–71.

42. "Expert Report of Patricia Gurin," pp. 372–73.

43. See, for example, Robert Lerner and Althea K. Nagai, "A Critique of the Expert Report of Patricia Gurin in *Gratz v. Bollinger*" (Washington, D.C.: Center for Equal Opportunity), at www.ceousa.org/pdfs/Gurin1.pdf (accessed September 15, 2003).

44. "Expert Report of Patricia Gurin," pp. 387–98.

45. "Expert Report of Patricia Gurin," p. 367.

46. St. Anselm College, a Benedictine institution in Manchester, New Hampshire, numbers 8 blacks and 17 Hispanics among its nearly 2,000 undergraduates. See Common Data Set at www.anselm.edu/administration/Institutional+Research (accessed September 20, 2003).

47. Located in Wooster, Ohio, the student body's black and Hispanic enrollment totals 5 percent of the total. See www.wooster.edu/oir/cds2002.xls (accessed September 20, 2003).

48. Spelman is a women's college in Atlanta, Georgia, with a 97 percent African American student body. See www.spelman.edu/factbook/factbook0203/2a_spelman_profile_5pgs.pdf (accessed September 20, 2003).

49. Whites and Hispanics make up fewer than 3 percent of the undergraduates enrolled in Florida A&M's College of Arts and Sciences. See www.famu.edu/about/fns/00-01/enroll00.pdf (accessed September 20, 2003).

50. *Gratz v. Bollinger*, 135 F. Supp. 2d at 795.

51. Earl Lewis, "Building an Inclusive Society: The University of Michigan's Place in the Diversity Debates," at www.smsu.edu/mags/building.htm (accessed November 4, 2003). Lewis is vice provost for academic affairs at the university.

52. *Regents v. Bakke*, at 307; *Grutter*, at 2336.

53. James J. Duberstadt, "The Michigan Agenda for Women: Leadership for a

New Century," July 1995, available at http:/milproj.ummu.umich.edu/publications/ womensagenda/index.html (accessed November 4, 2003). Duberstadt was president of the university during the formation and development of the "Michigan Mandate."

54. Lewis, "Building an Inclusive Society," p. 5.

55. The university not only prefers in-state over out-of-state applicants, it also gives a preference to applicants from the forty-five northern Michigan counties that are underrepresented in the student body at Ann Arbor. *Gratz v. Bollinger*, 135 F. Supp. 2d at 801.

56. For a thoroughly developed variation on the integration argument, see Elizabeth Anderson, "Integration, Affirmative Action, and Strict Scrutiny," *New York University Law Review* 77 (November 2002), pp. 1195–1271.

57. *Adarand v. Pena*, 515 U.S. 200 (1995), at 240.

58. *Adarand v. Pena*, at 241.

59. *Grutter*, at 2350ff.

60. William G. Bowen and Derek Bok, *The Shape of the River: Long-Term Consequences of Considering Race in College and University Admissions* (Princeton, N.J.: Princeton University Press, 1998).

61. Carl Cohen, "Race in University of Michigan Admissions," *The University Record*, February 25, 1997.

62. *Grutter*, at 2338.

63. For an excellent discussion of this point, see Jed Rubenfeld, "Affirmative Action," *Yale Law Journal* 107 (1997), pp. 427–71.

64. *Gratz v. Bollinger*, 135 F. Supp. 2d at 792.

65. *Gratz v. Bollinger*, 135 F. Supp. 2d at 799–801. Among the evidence presented by the student-intervenors: "The parents of the [minority] children who present themselves for admissions to Michigan today, did not have the economic and social advantages gained from attending an institution such as Michigan, and thus cannot pass on the full range [of] advantages to their children that many white parents, who are more likely to have attended Michigan, can" (at 800).

66. They are not atypical in this regard. Consider the definition of "institutional racism" offered in one chapter of *Compelling Interest*: "institutional practices or policies [that] systematically create disadvantage for racial minority groups." Shana Levin, "Social Psychological Evidence on Race and Racism," in Chang et al., eds., *Compelling Interest*, chapter 3, p. 4.

67. See Lani Guinier and Susan Sturm, *Who's Qualified* (Boston: Beacon Press, 201), pp. 10–16.

68. See, for example, William Bradford Reynolds, assistant attorney general for civil rights in the Reagan Administration (discrimination, and the elimination of it, are both matters of people's "commitments"), "Questions and Answers," in Robert K. Fullinwider and Claudia Mills, eds., *The Moral Foundations of Civil Rights* (Totowa, N.J.: Rowman & Littlefield, 1986), p. 89; and Senator Orrin Hatch (intent must be an element of discrimination), quoted in Robert K. Fullinwider, "Race and Equality: An Introduction," in Fullinwider and Mills, eds., *The Moral Foundations of Civil Rights*, p. 13, note 5. See also Matt Cavanagh, *Against Equality of Opportunity* (Oxford: Clarendon Press, 2002), p. 199.

69. On the divide between those who think discrimination must be intentional and

those who employ the concept of institutional racism, which depends on the effects of practices and policies, see Judith Lichtenberg, "Racism in the Head, Racism in the World," *Report from the Institute for Philosophy and Public Policy* 12 (1992).

70. Bowen and Bok, *The Shape of the River*, p. 20.

71. Bowen and Bok, *The Shape of the River*, pp. 26, 29. This gap is only partly due to the use of racial preferences. Given that black scores are generally lower than white, even in a completely race-blind selection system a college's student body would exhibit a black-white score gap of some size.

72. Bowen and Bok, *The Shape of the River*, p. 61.

73. Bowen and Bok, *The Shape of the River*, p. 98.

74. Bowen and Bok, *The Shape of the River*, pp. 136–47, 178.

75. Bowen and Bok, *The Shape of the River*, pp. 180–91.

76. Bowen and Bok, *The Shape of the River*, pp. 241–48.

77. Bowen and Bok, *The Shape of the River*, p. 281.

78. David B. Wilkins and G. Mitu Gulati, "Why Are There So Few Black Lawyers in Corporate Law Firms?" *California Law Review* 84 (May 1996), p. 563. Justice O'Connor in her *Grutter* opinion similarly observed that a "handful" of elite law schools "accounts for 25 of the 100 United States Senators, 74 United States Courts of Appeals judges, and nearly 200 of the more than 600 United States District Court judges" (*Grutter*, at 2341).

79. Though graduating from the University of Michigan undoubtedly facilitates entry into Michigan's leadership class, few in that class may be Michigan Law School graduates. In his dissent in *Grutter*, Justice Thomas noted that "less than 16 percent of the Law School's graduating class elects to stay in Michigan after law school" and only "27 percent of the . . . 2002 entering class are from Michigan" (*Grutter*, at 2355). The University of Michigan Law School, of course, considers itself to be a "national" law school, on the level of Harvard, Yale, and Chicago. It is one of the "handful" of law schools whose graduates are prominent in the national political and legal circles Justice O'Connor made note of (see note 78).

80. Bowen and Bok, *The Shape of the River*, pp. 34–36.

81. See Miriam G. Resendez, "The Stigmatizing Effects of Affirmative Action: An Examination of Moderating Variables," *Journal of Applied Social Psychology* 32 (January 2002), pp. 185–206 (studying the effects of affirmative action in employment). Claude Steele's twin brother Shelby Steele, author of *The Content of Our Character: A New Vision of Race in America* (New York: St. Martin's Press, 1990), is better known as the scourge of affirmative action, but Claude Steele's own work on "stereotype threat" might itself contain the seeds of a criticism. Steele was able to induce stereotype threat in his black test subjects not only by telling them they were taking an intelligence test, but also by merely having them write their race at the top of the test sheet. He called this "race-priming." A campus with an aggressive affirmative action program that constantly touts its commitment to "diversity" and advertises a panoply of "diversity" offices and services may inadvertently engage in "race priming," by making blacks students on campus continually aware of their race. See Claude Steele and Joshua Aronson, "Stereotype Threat and Test Performance," in Christopher Jencks and Meredith Phillips, eds., *The Black–White Test-Score Gap* (Washington, D.C.: Brookings Institution Press, 1998), p. 418.

82. See, e.g., Stephen Carter, *Reflections of an Affirmative Action Baby* (New York: Basic Books, 1991).

CHAPTER 11

1. As one black academic has put it, "Affirmative action always was racial justice on the cheap and for the middle class. It didn't mend the inner city or the horrible state of schools there. But it did get the best and brightest black students into elite universities." Quoted in William E. Forbath and Gerald Torres, "Merit and Diversity After Hopwood," *Stanford Law & Policy Review* 10 (Spring 1999), p. 188.

2. See Richard Kahlenberg, *The Remedy: Class, Race, and Affirmative Action* (New York: Basic Books, 1996); and Dinesh D'Souza, *Illiberal Education: The Politics of Race and Sex on Campus* (New York: Free Press, 1991), p. 251.

3. Richard D. Kahlenberg, "Class-Based Affirmative Action," *Boston Globe*, January 19, 1999, A11.

4. Kahlenberg, "Class-Based Affirmative Action," p. 47.

5. Kahlenberg, "Class-Based Affirmative Action," p. 50.

6. Kahlenberg, "Class-Based Affirmative Action," pp. 49, 50.

7. U.S. Department of Education, National Center for Education Statistics, *The Condition of Education 2000*, NCES-2000-062 (Washington, D.C.: U.S. Government Printing Office, 2000), p. 47 (Table: Qualified for College). This table is viewable at http://nces.ed.gov/pubs2000/2000062.pdf (accessed November 5, 2003). A high school graduate is counted as "minimally qualified" if she has at least a 2.7 HSGPA or a combined SAT score of 820 (p. 217).

8. HB 588 (1997), Texas Code Title 3, §51.801—Uniform Admission Policy.

9. When the Court of Appeals for the Fifth Circuit delivered its decision in March 1996, the university had already chosen most of the class for fall admission.

10. *Implementation and Results of the Texas Automatic Admissions Law (HB 588) at the University of Texas at Austin: Report Number 4* (2001), p. 4, at www.u texas.edu/student/research/reports/admissions/HB588-Report4.pdf (accessed November 4, 2003).

11. Danielle Holley and Delia Spencer, "The Texas Ten Percent Plan," *Harvard Civil Rights-Civil Liberties Review* 34 (Winter 1999), pp. 263, 277; see also Forbath and Torres, "Merit and Diversity After Hopwood," p. 187.

12. In 1999, the university enrolled 286 black and 976 Hispanic freshmen. Some of its Top Ten Percent offers of admission did not lead to enrollment, but most did. Consequently, it is clear that very few blacks and Hispanics entered the university outside the Top Ten Percent route. See *Implementation and Results Report Number Four*, p. 4, and *Texas Public Universities' Data and Performance Report* (Austin, Texas: Texas Higher Education Coordinating Board, June 2002), "University Profiles: University of Texas at Austin," at www.thecb.state.tx.us/reports/pdf/0464.pdf (accessed November 4, 2003).

13. David Montejano, "Access to the University of Texas at Austin and the Ten Percent Plan: A Three Year Assessment," at www.utexas.edu/student/research/reports/admissions/Montejanopaper.htm (accessed November 4, 2003).

14. *Implementation and Results Report Number Four*, p. 4.

15. *Implementation and Results Report Number Four*, pp. 5–6.

16. Holley and Spencer, "The Texas Ten Percent Plan," p. 254, note 70.

17. See Education Research Report, "What Do Student Grades Mean? Differences Across Schools," Office of Educational Research and Improvement, U.S. Department of Education, at www.ed.gov/pubs/OR/ResearchRpts/grades.html (accessed November 4, 2003).

18. Jodi Wilgoren, "New Law in Texas Preserves Racial Mix in State's Colleges," *New York Times*, November 24, 1999, A1.

19. "Talented 20: Common Questions and Answers," Florida Department of Education, at www.firn.edu/doe/faq/talented20.htm (accessed November 6, 2003).

20. Holly Stepp, "State Falls Short in Attracting Minority Students to College," *Miami Herald*, September 9, 2001 (see http://members.tripod.com/~ren04governor/index.31html [accessed November 4, 2003].)

21. Carrie Miller, "UF's Minority Report: Officials Aim to Offset Effects of One Florida on Enrollment," *Gainesville Sun*, June 19, 2002.

22. SAT I Verbal and Math, SAT II Writing, SAT II Math, and an SAT II in literature, a foreign language, science, or social studies.

23. The test score total is arrived at by adding the combined SAT I score to the scores of the three SAT II tests multiplied by 2. Thus the combined score for the subject area tests counts twice as much as the combined score for the SAT I Verbal and Math.

24. "University of California Eligibility in the Local Context Program Evaluation Report," May 2002, at www.ucop.edu/news/cr/report02.pdf (accessed November 4, 2003).

25. Carrie Miller and Tim Lockette, "UF Minority Enrollment Rises," *Gainesville Sun*, August 30, 2000; Joe Humphrey, "One Florida Doesn't End Debate," *Florida Times-Union* (Jacksonville), July 29, 2001.

26. See Holley and Spencer, "The Texas Ten Percent Plan," pp. 269–70.

27. See www.utexas.edu/admin/outreach (accessed November 4, 2003).

28. See www.utexas.edu/vp/csr/osr/page10.html (accessed November 4, 2003).

29. See www.avidonline.org, "About Us"—"Frequently Asked Questions."

30. National Commission on Excellence in Education, *A Nation at Risk: The Imperative for Educational Reform* (Washington, D.C.: GPO, 1983).

31. For example, Adelman was among the researchers providing formal input into the National Commission on Excellence in Education's deliberations leading to *A Nation at Risk*.

32. Clifford Adelman, *Answers in the Tool Box: Academic Intensity, Attendance Patterns, and Bachelor's Degree Attainment* (Jessup, Md.: Education Publications Center, U.S. Department of Education, June 1999). See www.ed.gov/pubs/Toolbox/Index.html (accessed November 7, 2003).

33. The test used by Adelman was a twelfth-grade test somewhat like the SAT.

34. Adelman, "Tool Box," Section I: Cultivating ACRES, the Academic Resources Index, p. 3.

35. Adelman, "Tool Box," p. 4.

36. Adelman, "Tool Box."

37. Adelman, "Tool Box," p. 5.

38. Adelman, "Tool Box," p. 5, table 6.

39. College Board, *Equity 2000: A Systematic Education Reform Model, A Summary Report 1990–2000*, at www.collegeboard.com/prod_downloads/about/association/equity/EquityHistorica lReport.pdf (accessed November 5, 2003).

40. College Board, *Equity 2000*, p. 4.

41. See Richard P. Phelps, "Why Testing Experts Hate Testing" (Washington, D.C.: Thomas B. Fordham Foundation, January 1999), p. 18, referring to the College Board study, at www.edexcellence.net/doc/phelps.pdf (accessed November 6, 2003).

42. College Board, *Equity 2000*.

43. American Youth Policy Forum, *Raising Minority Academic Achievement*, at www.aypf.org/rmaa/pdfs/Equity2000.pdf (accessed November 4, 2003).

44. Sandra Ham and Erika Walker, *Getting to the Right Algebra: The Equity 2000 Initiative in Milwaukee Public Schools* (New York: Manpower Demonstration Research Corporation, April 1999), pp. 2, 17–19, at www.mdrc.org/Reports99/Equity2000/Equity2000WrkgPpr.html (accessed November 4, 2003).

45. See www.trioprograms.org (accessed November 4, 2003).

46. Steve Silver, "GEAR UP: A Capstone for Reform," at www.ed.gov/programs/gearup/index.html (accessed November 4, 2003).

47. See College Now, at www.collegenow.cuny.edu/info/faq/index.html#1 (accessed November 4, 2003).

48. See Jennifer Simmons, "New York City Counselor Gets a Leg-Up with GEAR UP," at www.counseling.org/ctonline/news/GearUp1201.htm (accessed March 5, 2002). See also www.lehman.cuny.edu/bronxed/gearup/homeeng.html (accessed November 4, 2003). GEAR UP is willing to counsel families on a wide front, including matters dealing with academics, recreation, health, finances, language, and technology.

49. Ronald Ferguson, "Teachers' Perceptions and Expectations and the Black–White Test Score Gap," in Christopher Jencks and Meredith Phillips, eds., *The Black–White Test Score Gap* (Washington, D.C: Brookings Institution Press, 1998), p. 301.

50. Meredith Phillips, James Crouse, and John Ralph, "Does the Black-White Test Score Gap Widen After Children Enter School?" in Jencks and Phillips, *The Black-White Test Score Gap*, p. 253.

51. Ferguson, "Teachers' Perceptions," p. 313.

52. Ferguson, "Teachers' Perceptions," pp. 278–79. To the extent that there are preconceptions at work, they may arise more out of the class backgrounds than the racial backgrounds of teachers. Scott Miller reports studies showing that the "primary predictor of whether a teacher held positive or negative views of African American students was the teacher's own social class background." Teachers of middle-class origin had more negative views, teachers of lower-class origin more positive views. "This pattern held for both black and white teachers," writes Miller. "In fact, in some respects African American teachers with middle-class origins were less likely to see black students in a positive light than were white teachers with middle-class origins." L. Scott Miller, *An American Imperative: Accelerating Minority Educational Advancement* (New Haven, Conn.: Yale University Press, 1995), p. 241. See also Ferguson, "Teachers' Perceptions," p. 299.

53. Signithia Fordham and John U. Ogbu, "Black Students' Success: Coping with the Burden of 'Acting White,'" *Urban Review* 18 (1986), p. 177.

54. Signithia Fordham, "Racelessness as a Factor in Black Students' Success: Pragmatic Strategy or Pyrrhic Victory?" *Harvard Educational Review* 58 (February 1988), p. 81. See also Signithia Fordham, *Blacked Out: Dilemmas of Race, Identity, and Success at Capitol High* (Chicago: University of Chicago Press, 1996); John Ogbu, "Literacy and Schooling in Subordinate Cultures: The Case of Black Americans," in Kofi Lomotey, ed., *Going to School: The African-American Experience* (Albany: State University of New York Press, 1990), pp. 113–31; John U. Ogbu, "Understanding Cultural Diversity and Learning," in James A. Banks and Cherry A. McGee Banks, eds., *Handbook of Research on Multicultural Education* (New York: Macmillan Publishing, 1995), pp. 582–93; John U. Ogbu, "Beyond Language: Ebonics, Proper English, and Identity in a Black-American Speech Community," *American Educational Research Journal* 36 (Summer 1999), pp. 147–84.

55. Claude M. Steele, "Race and the Schooling of Black Americans," *Atlantic Monthly*, 269 (April 1992), p. 74.

56. Claude M. Steele and Joshua Aronson, "Stereotype Threat and the Test Performance of Academically Successful African Americans," in Jencks and Phillips, eds., *The Black–White Test Score Gap*, p. 407.

57. Jencks and Phillips, *The Black–White Test Score Gap*, p. 413.

58. See Joshua Aronson, Carrie B. Fried, and Catherine Good, "Reducing the Effects of Stereotype Threat on African American College Students by Shaping Theories of Intelligence," *Journal of Experimental Social Psychology* 38 (March 2002), pp. 113–25 (and see citations); Patrick F. McKay et al., "Stereotype Threat Effects on the Raven Advanced Progressive Matrices Scores of African Americans," *Journal of Applied Social Psychology* 32 (April 2002), pp. 767–87; Joshua Aronson et al., "When White Men Can't Do Math: Necessary and Sufficient Factors in Stereotype Threat," *Journal of Experimental Social Psychology* 35 (1999), pp. 29–46; Jeff Stone et al., "Stereotype Threat Effects on Black and White Athletic Performance," *Journal of Personality and Social Psychology* 77 (December 1999), pp. 1213–27. Rebecca Zwick, in *Fair Game? The Use of Standardized Tests in Higher Education* (New York: Routledge Falmer, 2002), describes studies that have been unable to replicate "stereotype threat" (p. 123).

59. See Kenneth D. Hopkins, Julian C. Stanley, and B. R. Hopkins, *Educational and Psychological Measurement and Evaluation*, 7th ed. (Englewood Cliffs, N.J.: Prentice Hall, 1990), p. 148.

60. Ferguson, "Teachers' Perceptions," in Jencks and Phillips, eds., *The Black–White Test Score Gap*, pp. 290–94.

61. Philip J. Cook and Jens Ludwig, "The Burden of 'Acting White': Do Black Adolescents Disparage Academic Achievement?" in Jencks and Phillips, eds., *The Black–White Test Score Gap*, pp. 390–91.

62. Ronald F. Ferguson, "A Diagnostic Analysis of Black–White GPA Disparities in Shaker Heights, Ohio," in Diane Ravitch, ed., *Brookings Papers on Educational Policy 2001* (Washington, D.C.: Brookings Institution Press, 2001), p. 349. John U. Ogbu, in his ethnographic study of Shaker Heights schools, *Black Americans in an Affluent Suburb: A Study of Academic Disengagement* (Mahwah, N.J.: Lawrence Ear-

lbaum, Associates, 2003), describes many black students as doing little or no home-work (pp. 130–31, 239). Whether the impressions generated by his interviews of teachers, students, and parents hold true across the board, and contradict Ferguson's findings, remains unclear.

63. Ferguson, "A Diagnostic Analysis," p. 385 (footnotes omitted and three para-graphs run together).

64. Ferguson, "A Diagnostic Analysis," p. 356.

65. Ferguson, "A Diagnostic Analysis," p. 362.

66. Ferguson, "Teachers' Perceptions," in Jencks and Phillips, eds., *The Black–White Test Score Gap*, p. 291.

67. Here John Ogbu's study of Shaker Heights reinforces Ferguson's contention. Neither the parents nor the students interviewed by Ogbu seemed really to grasp what was required academically to get into college and succeed there (see *Black American Students in an Affluent Suburb*, pp. 29, 54, 254–55, 248). Further support for Ferguson's claim comes from a striking device Scott Miller uses to illustrate the differing quality of educational resources parents from different backgrounds pro-vide their children. Obviously financially well-off and better educated parents have more money to spend on their children and can live in neighborhoods where schools spend more money per pupil. Miller, however, is interested as well in the quality of contact between children and parents that improves the former's academic skills and aspirations. He estimates that "parents will have spent, on average, a total of 7,665 hours personally investing education-relevant resources in their youngsters by the time the children are eighteen." To measure the quality of this resource investment for well-educated versus less well-educated families, Miller assigns a dollar value to these hours using the market value for the human capital possessed by the adults in each of five hypothetical families who range over a spectrum from highly to poorly educated. The educational resource investment of the best educated family is $169,626 (in 1990 dollars), four and a half times the investment of the lowest educated family. Miller then adds in the dollar values of the per-child incomes these five fami-lies command and of the per-pupil expenditures by the schools to which these fami-lies are likely to send their children. In sum, the best educated family invests $579,626 per child over the eighteen-year period from birth to high school graduation, the least educated $173,794. Although the assignment of dollar figures to the first item—parent–child interaction of an educational nature—rests on necessarily crude assumptions, nevertheless the huge difference in the figures might serve as a graphic proxy for the differences in efficiency by which different families translate their interest in education into their children's academic performance. Miller, *An American Imperative*, pp. 311, 326, and 335.

68. Information provided by Peggy Caldwell, Director of Communications, Shaker Heights Schools (personal communication).

69. Meredith Phillips et al., "Family Background, Parenting Practices, and the Black–White Test Score Gap," in Jencks and Phillips, eds., *The Black–White Test Score Gap*, p. 131.

70. Miller, *An American Imperative*, p. 273.

71. *Tools for Schools: School Reform Models Supported by the National Institute on the Education of At-Risk Students*, U.S. Department of Education, April 1998, sec-

tion 1, at www.ed.gov/pubs/ToolsforSchools/index.html (accessed November 6, 2003).

72. Ronald Ferguson, "Can Schools Narrow the Black–White Test Score Gap?" in Jencks and Phillips, eds., *The Black–White Test Score Gap*, p. 344.

73. Ferguson, "Can Schools Narrow the Black–White Test Score Gap?" p. 346.

74. Robert E. Slavin and Nancy A. Madden, "Research on Achievement Outcomes of Success for All: A Summary and Response to Critics," *Phi Delta Kappan* 82 (September 2000), p. 40.

75. Jeanne Weiler, "Success for All: A Summary of Evaluations," EDO-UD-98-9 (ERIC Clearinghouse on Urban Education), p. 4, available at http://eric-web.tc.columbia.edu/digest/dig139.asp (accessed November 6, 2003). There are some questions about Success for All's overall success. Two major school systems, Memphis and Miami–Dade County, have abandoned it after extensive trials. For some of the controversy surrounding Success for All, see the April and September 2000 issues of *Phi Delta Kappan* for articles by Stanley Pogrow and a response by Slavin and Madden.

CHAPTER 12

1. See Immanuel Kant, "On the Common Saying: 'This May Be True in Theory, But It Does Not Apply in Practice'" in Hans Reiss, ed., *Kant's Political Writings* (London: Cambridge University Press, 1970).

2. See Judith Lichtenberg, "Racism in the Head, Racism in the World," *Report from the Institute for Philosophy and Public Policy* 12 (1992).

3. See chapter 10, section titled "Do Not Discriminate."

4. See chapter 8, section titled "A First Attack: The SAT and the Regents Scholarships," and *Griggs v. Duke Power Company*, 401 U.S. 424 (1971).

5. See www.umich.edu/~provost/slfstudy/ir/criteria (accessed November 4, 2003).

6. Williams College website, www.williams.edu/admin_depts/registrar/geninfo/mission.html (accessed November 5, 2003).

7. For a discussion of the costs and benefits of affirmative action see chapter 10. To some readers our forward-looking, consequentialist defense of affirmative action will seem insufficient. Deborah Malamud, for example, insists that an adequate defense of affirmative action must show that the "*entitlement* of affirmative action beneficiaries to be present in . . . institutions [is] rooted at least in part in their own moral worthiness." Deborah C. Malamud, "Values, Symbols, and Facts in the Affirmative Action Debate," *Michigan Law Review* 95 (May 1997), p. 1710 (emphasis added). See also Charles R. Lawrence III and Mari J. Matsuda, *We Won't Go Back: Making the Case for Affirmative Action* (Boston: Houghton Mifflin, 1997), where affirmative action is tied to the *deservingness* of its beneficiaries.

8. See Lani Guinier and Susan Sturm, *Who's Qualified?* (Boston: Beacon Press, 2001); and Lani Guinier, "Colleges Should Take 'Confirmative Action' in Admissions," *Chronicle of Higher Education* 48 (December 14, 2001); and the discussion in chapter 7.

9. Karen W. Arenson, "Public College Tuition Increases Prompt Concern, Anguish, and Legislation," *New York Times*, August 30, 2003, A8.

10. Greg Winter, "Change in Aid Rule Means Larger Bills for College Students," *New York Times*, June 13, 2003, A1.

11. See chapter 5, section titled "Money."

12. We single out binding early decision rather than early admissions policies in general—which include nonbinding early action—because it is the former that most clearly works to the disadvantage of the student in need of financial aid. See chapter 5, sections titled "The Legacy of Legacy" and "Early Decision."

13. See chapter 2, section titled "Sports: A Case Study," and James L. Shulman and William G. Bowen, *The Game of Life: College Sports and Educational Values* (Princeton, N.J.: Princeton University Press, 2001).

Index

259

About the Authors

Robert K. Fullinwider is senior research scholar at the Institute for Philosophy and Public Policy at the University of Maryland, College Park, where he works on issues about civic and moral learning. He is the author of *The Reverse Discrimination Controversy: A Moral and Legal Analysis* (1980).

Judith Lichtenberg is senior research scholar at the Institute for Philosophy and Public Policy and associate professor in the Department of Philosophy at the University of Maryland, College Park. She writes and teaches in the areas of ethics and political philosophy, with special interests in higher education, international ethics, and the mass media.